The Full Stack Developer

Your Essential Guide to the Everyday
Skills Expected of a Modern Full
Stack Web Developer

Chris Northwood

Apress®

The Full Stack Developer: Your Essential Guide to the Everyday Skills Expected of a Modern Full Stack Web Developer

Chris Northwood
Manchester, UK

ISBN-13 (pbk): 978-1-4842-4151-6   ISBN-13 (electronic): 978-1-4842-4152-3
https://doi.org/10.1007/978-1-4842-4152-3

Library of Congress Control Number: 2018964579

Managing Director, Apress Media LLC: Welmoed Spahr
Acquisitions Editor: Louise Corrigan
Development Editor: James Markham
Coordinating Editor: Nancy Chen

Cover designed by eStudioCalamar

Cover image designed by Freepik (www.freepik.com)

Distributed to the book trade worldwide by Springer Science+Business Media New York, 233 Spring Street, 6th Floor, New York, NY 10013. Phone 1-800-SPRINGER, fax (201) 348-4505, e-mail orders-ny@springer-sbm.com, or visit www.springeronline.com. Apress Media, LLC is a California LLC and the sole member (owner) is Springer Science + Business Media Finance Inc (SSBM Finance Inc). SSBM Finance Inc is a **Delaware** corporation.

For information on translations, please e-mail rights@apress.com, or visit http://www.apress.com/rights-permissions.

Apress titles may be purchased in bulk for academic, corporate, or promotional use. eBook versions and licenses are also available for most titles. For more information, reference our Print and eBook Bulk Sales web page at http://www.apress.com/bulk-sales.

Any source code or other supplementary material referenced by the author in this book is available to readers on GitHub via the book's product page, located at www.apress.com/9781484241516. For more detailed information, please visit http://www.apress.com/source-code.

Printed on acid-free paper

To everyone who makes those contributions to society that add up to a better world.

Table of Contents

About the Author

Chris Northwood is a senior engineer working for BBC Research & Development, the research arm of the world's largest public service broadcaster. Chris' career began with computer science degrees from the University of York (BEng) and the University of Sheffield (MSc), and he has worked for major organizations including ThoughtWorks and the University of Oxford, as well as many freelance clients. He wrote this book distilling the information he learned over his career—it's the book he wishes he'd had when he started.

About the Technical Reviewer

Brandon Scott is a software architect with a passion for improving experiences for both end users and engineers alike. Over his career, Brandon has built his experience across many industries, including finance, entertainment, and education. His primary focuses have been creating distributed systems, developing coaching strategies for engineers, and leading experience design workstreams. Recently he has partnered with Razer Inc., focusing on the design of their SDK products and open source libraries. Brandon has also previously worked with Microsoft on exploring their Microsoft Store capabilities in the education sector.

Acknowledgments

Most of this book was born in Manchester Central Library's reading room, but it was the team at Apress—Nancy Chen, Louise Corrigan, and James Markham—who've transformed it from a long-running side project into something that shipped. I'd also like to thank Brandon Scott for acting as technical reviewer, for his suggestions, and for sense-checking me!

The skills and knowledge I've gained that have qualified me to write this book have come, to differing extents, from everyone I've ever worked with professionally. Every article I've read, tweeter I've followed, and conference speaker I've watched, combined with those whom I've paired with, mentored, or had my code reviewed by has contributed to the sum of knowledge that's gone into this book. I want to specifically call out the BBC Knowledge & Learning team, where I grew from a graduate to a senior developer, and the TRIP project team at ThoughtWorks, who gave me the space to grow my technical ability.

There are a number of people I wish to call out who've shaped my worldview into what it is today, which I express through my work. My Auntie Jayne, who as godmother steered my ethical development; Rosie Campbell, who introduced me to intersectionalism; Rebecca Forbes, who kept me sane at the chaotic start of this whole project; Alina Apine, who continues to encourage my radicalism; and, most importantly, my Mum and Dad, without whom I would be nowhere.

CHAPTER 1

The Modern Web

The electronic computer, the Internet, and the World Wide Web are the greatest inventions of our time, and we are lucky to be working on the crest of the wave that the impact of these inventions is having on society.

Developers have typically worked in technology companies, or inside technology departments of other organizations, but as the earliest developers are now retiring, the latest generation is finding employment in many different areas. The term "digital industry" is often used to describe more traditional businesses that are waking up to the potential that technologists have paved the way for. For these organizations, technology is not just a cost center and a utility, but a core part of whatever business they're in, even if the services or products they provide are not technological in nature.

It's with the rise of these digital businesses that the nature of development has changed. If the products and services you provide aren't technological, it no longer makes sense to align your development teams around technologies, but to instead have your development and delivery teams working alongside non-techies in these digital businesses. To some, "digital" may just be a buzzword, but for those who use it, the change it suggests is very real.

For developers working on these digital teams, deep technical knowledge is less important than knowledge of the business and organization, and speed of delivery becomes key. Getting something out there three weeks early can give a digital organization an edge over its competitors, and with communication being one of the greatest overheads in development, it becomes advantageous for a development team to be able to implement all parts of a new feature, or to fix a bug that impacts multiple components, without having to negotiate with another team to do so. The developers working on these teams are sometimes referred to as T-shaped, because their breadth of knowledge is just as important as any depth of technical specialty they may have. Similarly, when software fails, having a team operating the software that is separate from the team that builds it increases the communication overhead. Digital teams eliminate those communication overheads by adopting ways of working and a culture known as DevOps, which blends the lines between development and operational responsibility.

1

© Chris Northwood 2018
C. Northwood, *The Full Stack Developer*, https://doi.org/10.1007/978-1-4842-4152-3_1

All of these factors have given rise to the "full stack" developer.

For some, the term full stack is a misnomer. It's rare to see a developer who's as comfortable writing x86 assembler as they are slinging Sass, but for the organizations these developers work for, the stack they care about is the one that gives them value. Everything below this—from the programming language to the OS to the physical hardware—is a utility. A development team in this kind of organization should be able to each part of the stack that matters. For some organizations, the stack does extend much further, but it's only because at their scale, there is value over using off-the-shelf solutions for those lower levels, or it exists for legacy reasons. Many organizations still run their own data centers, for example, as the investment has already been made, or they have particular requirements (legal regulations, heightened security, or very large storage), but for many others, running that part of the stack themselves offers no value over buying it as a utility.

For these digital organizations, development teams are no longer full of programmers. The output that matters to these teams is not code; it is solutions to problems. Many of these problems tend to involve interaction with users, which has led to the rise of User Experience as a discipline, or may simply be process issues, where a dedicated business analyst can add value. The traditional roles of developer, QA, and project manager are all still there, but we now have a bunch of other people to help us.

The breadth of modern web development is staggering, and it'd be hard for all developers in a team to be equally good at all parts of it. In reality, there is no such thing as a full stack developer, but instead the full stack development team. You can make a full stack development team from individual specialists, but it will never be as effective of ones filled with "specializing generalists". Work comes in peaks and troughs, and is never evenly distributed over all parts of the stack. The full stack development team should therefore be greater than the sum of its parts, and share traits with the concept of the High-Performing Team in management theory.

Teams of specialists are also less adaptable to change. LAMP is no longer as cool as it was, MEAN is the new thing, and new languages on the JVM are reviving the popularity of the Java stack, but specialized generalists who work on the principles and foundations rather than the details can adapt to these changes more easily than those who have deep knowledge of one thing.

The stack is dead; long live the stack.

The modern digital business sees tech stacks as a tactical, rather than strategic, decision. They want to be able to leverage the best utilities to help them fulfil that goal, rather than to build and double down on a technical platform that can be hard to change. New languages and techniques are appearing all the time, and a good full stack team should be empowered to choose the best tool for the job, and should be able to adopt new tools as they mature.

So, who is this book for? It's for junior developers and graduates who want to understand modern web development in a digital business. It's for engineers in traditionally structured organizations who are transitioning into this new digital world. It's for leaders of development teams who want to understand more about the work that they lead. It's for developers already on these full stack teams who want to refine their skills. It's not for people who don't know how to code, or who are starting out in their web development journey.

This book assumes a basic understand of web development techniques (i.e., you've probably built at least a web page, or an API), but won't go into details of implementation. The beauty of full stack development is that you get to choose your own parts of the stack, based on the best tool for the job, and in a rapidly changing environment, any concrete recommendations are likely to quickly date. What it does aim to teach you is the techniques that apply to modern development, and the pitfalls to avoid when building an application on today's web.

Rise of the Web

Interest in the Web has never been higher. New frameworks, better tooling, and the evolution of standards are emerging from everywhere, and it's hard to keep up.

The modern Web is constantly growing, more devices than ever can access it and interact with it, and techniques are constantly growing to address this. The addition of media queries to CSS allowed web page styling to target screens with specific characteristics, rather than have the page look the same on every device. This small adjustment fundamentally changed how sites were designed, giving birth to a brand-new set of techniques for building websites known as Responsive Web Design, in which the design of a single web page should respond to the capabilities of the device it is being rendered on. However, CSS is still missing some of the features needed to make responsive web design a success—the only information we can reliably use is the screen size and pixel density, whereas there are many other characteristics that would influence design if they were available, such as interaction methods (mouse, touch-screen, speech, five-point remote control, etc.) So the Web is still a constrained format. Regardless of these constraints, the Web's distribution method has seen the replacement of the traditional desktop app in many cases.

In the early days of computing, users interacted with applications on servers via terminals, or thin clients. This was powerful, as it meant the application was only running in one place, and everyone was using the same one. The rise of personal computing and more power on individual desktops enabled a move to fat clients, where more and more of the business logic ran in programs distributed to the end users' desktops. This caused problems with distributing those applications to all the people that needed them as well as maintaining different versions on individual devices. It was a slow way of doing things. There were many benefits to computers becoming smaller and more portable, allowing them to appear in people's homes and not just in large connected facilities, but an always-connected world was still a long way away.

With the rise of the Web, we can now benefit from both worlds: servers distribute software to clients at the point of request, rather than the software being preloaded onto machines. At first, we lost the ability to use an app without a connection to a server, but the rise in mobile connectivity made this less of a problem, usually by considering an internet connection as the primary state, then using various controlled modes of failure or degradation to handle being disconnected (such as error messages, or being temporarily offline). More recently, the Web has adopted better support for working offline, using features such as service workers that allow apps to continue working while disconnected.

For a long time, the standards of the Web and the performance of browsers were far behind that of a native application. Microsoft and others introduced tools such as ActiveX, Java applets, and Flash to work around this, but each of these approaches had its own challenges. It was Microsoft that kick-started the rise of what would eventually allow web standards to be used to produce applications that would replace those desktop ones, with the introduction of the XMLHttpRequest API (XHR) to JavaScript. Now, web standards have matured to the point of meeting many needs of rich applications, and development of the Web is happening at such a pace that any missing functionality will quickly appear. The Web has become a tool for distributing these applications, and web technologies are even replacing parts of native apps, with web apps packaged for native distribution mechanisms.

Mobile Web

Just as web applications are replacing many desktop applications, native apps on mobile platforms have gone the other way. Most major mobile platforms now have a built-in app distribution mechanism. Desktop Linux distributions had this for years as well, but Linux on the desktop has never had the breakthrough that many enthusiasts hoped for. Apple and Microsoft, on the other hand, now bring app stores to their desktop OS's as an extension of their mobile stores.

This "app store" distribution mechanism has two key advantages over the Web that desktop applications never had: an effective market with a mechanism for charging a fee to obtain the app, and the ability to live on the launcher for that device to gain headspace for the user. The mechanism of charging fees is also one of the weaknesses of the distribution model, as the owner of the store can include unfair terms or limit certain apps from the store, which has led some app publishers to bypass the store. Websites and web applications can be added to launchers too, but this process is often clunky by comparison and rarely used. Of course, mobile applications, like desktop apps before them, still have some run-time performance gains, as well a higher level of access to the device and its hardware. But the mobile market is more fragmented than the desktop market, and in order to maximize reach, "cross-platform" toolkits are often used to build native apps to target multiple devices. Many recent examples of these are actually just wrappers for web technologies. For many organizations, web remains the default distribution mechanism, unless there are specific requirements that only native apps and app marketplaces can fulfill, or the perceived mindshare that a native app seems to have over a web app is too tempting to ignore.

The State of HTML

HTML is the language of the Web. To build a web site, at some point HTML will be involved. The HTML standard doesn't just cover the tags you write on a page (the markup), but also specifies the Document Object Model (how you manipulate web pages from JavaScript) and CSS too.

And HTML is a little bit complicated right now. The World Wide Web Consortium (W3C) originally specified the HTML standard, and were happy with the HTML4 standards. Focus then moved to XHTML, a subtly different form of HTML based on the XML standard. XML, the Extensible Markup Language, offered a large degree of power—for example, other XML documents could be embedded inside an HTML document, but as XHTML was famously never supported by Internet Explorer, this power was never realized. There were other issues with XHTML too: a standards-compliant XML parser refuses to render anything if there's an issue with the XML, which hindered migration from the much laxer HTML4 standards.

Browser makers, most famously Opera and Mozilla, disagreed with this move to XML, and were frustrated by the slow approach of a standards body, so they took matters into their own hand and put together the WHATWG (Web Hypertext Application Technology Working Group) which developed it's own variation of the HTML standard. They proposed this standard —HTML5—to the W3C, and it was adopted, but the W3C and WHATWG definitions of HTML5 have drifted. The WHATWG defines HTML5 as a living standard, which means there will never be a definitive specification of HTML5 to implement.

Sounds like a nightmare, right? Fortunately, most browser makers have now reacted to this living standard and moved to a much more frequent release model, and users have followed, so the time between a new feature in HTML being accepted and it becoming available in browsers is getting shorter all the time. The biggest exception is Apple, which still links versions of Safari and Mobile Safari to OS X and iOS releases (this is particularly bad on iOS, where users are restricted from installing alternate runtimes), and some Android vendors who bundle their own browser instead of Google's Chrome.

Fortunately, there is a lot of tooling to help you here. More often than not, you can write HTML, CSS, or JavaScript using the latest techniques, and there are tools in the front end that will transform your code in a backwards compatible version that can handle the old browsers for you. Fortunately, with HTML markup, most browsers will treat unrecognized tags as generic `<div>` tags, and they can be still be styled as such (although some older browsers require a polyfill, such as the famous `html5shiv.js`). Additionally, there are many JavaScript libraries, known as "polyfills," that exist to provide a pure JavaScript version of any new features of the JavaScript language, allowing them to be used on older browsers. These are covered in detail in the Front End chapter.

With two differing standards, it can also be hard to know which documentation to turn to. In reality, what really matters is what the browsers actually do. Fortunately, the days of the browser wars—where different vendors would implement the same idea in different ways—are over, and there is much more collaboration between browser developers in order to make the standards work. Browsers also indicate a non-standard feature with a "vendor prefix," where the JavaScript API or CSS attribute is prefixed with the name of the browser maker to indicate that it is a browser-specific feature (such features should be used with caution as part of a progressive enhancement approach, or avoided entirely). The Mozilla Developer Network is a fantastically thorough resource, and the brilliant website caniuse.com will tell you how well supported a particular feature is, and any quirks it may have.

Many sites being built today will have to run on a vast number of browsers, all with different versions and different levels of support, but there are also many that don't have to. If you're building an internal app for a company, and that organization uses Internet Explorer on Windows, it's very tempting to build and test only in that browser, but things could suddenly change— for example, the sudden introduction of tablets to an organization. Targeting a known runtime can make your life easier, since you'll have less to test, and you won't have to support very old/broken devices, but don't lull yourself into a false sense of security—write to the standards, and verify this by testing it in a different browser. Doing this upfront can save you and your organization a lot of pain down the line.

Sometimes, you'll find a feature you want to use that isn't supported by every browser you want to target. In cases like this, a technique known as progressive enhancement is very useful. Progressive enhancement is a technique where you deliver a basic version of some functionality to a device, and then test if the device can support a more advanced alternative, then enable the enhanced alternative if the test is successful. Progressive enhancement is a useful technique to solve many different problems, and is covered in much more detail in the Front End chapter.

Applications vs. Web Sites

With the rise of the Web being used as a delivery platform for what once would have been a desktop application, the line between what once would have been called a "web site" and what is now called a "web app" has blurred. Web sites were generally content-based sites—they existed to communicate information, often with some interactivity involved, but at their heart, they were about information. Many frameworks have risen to help build web apps, and these frameworks are often used to build web sites too, even though that's not what they're best suited for. Angular and Backbone are examples of these types of frameworks, and are optimized for when data needs to be modified by the users of these apps by providing abstractions for these operations. These abstractions are often not helpful for content-based websites. Before embarking on a project, you have to decide whether you're making a web site or a web app. Many projects are likely to include both—for example, a catalogue a user browses works best as a site, but inventory management tools work best as an application.

You could consider a website as a subset of the functionality of a fully-fledged web application, but by identifying it as purely a website, it becomes easier to use a set of more constrained tools that will often give you a better result, as well as let you reach that result in less time. Web app toolkits and frameworks may appear powerful, but often break an important fundamental of the Web - that the Web is made up of a series of linked pages. If content on your site needs to be linked to directly from a URL, either through sharing the URL on social media, or from a search engine, then considering it a website, and avoiding web app toolkits will allow you to benefit from many fundamental features of the Web (such as shareable URLs, as well as caching and archiving).

Keeping Up

By the time this book is published, I'm sure some of the specific examples used will already be out of date, but the techniques discussed are, for the most part, not new, and will remain applicable to systems for years to come. What will be constantly changing is the ways in which these techniques will be applied, and the exact tools, languages, and frameworks used to apply them.

When a new framework or tool comes along, it's important to evaluate it in the context of what you already know. Most of them will be implementing an existing technique in a new (potentially better) way, and if you can draw parallels to concepts you're already familiar with, it will be easier to see how a new tool is useful (or not).

Many new tools are not useful! Often, a mature, familiar toolkit will be much more productive than a shiny new one. However, it's important to be aware of those shiny new things, because suddenly one will appear that has significant adoption and maturity, and that you will want to implement. As always, it's important to strike a balance, and only you and your team can make the decision. A development team in a digital organization has to react quickly in order to keep up with the pace of change, and it only makes sense to adopt new tools if they offer significant benefits over existing methods to help you achieve your goals. It's also important to check that those benefits aren't immediately lost in the time and energy involved in making the switch in the first place. Keeping things small can make adopting these new techniques easier, as you can iterate quickly on a change to see if it works out, and potentially even decide against a change without having committed too much—this is known as failing fast. These concepts are discussed in depth in the Designing Systems chapter.

Attend conferences, read blogs and aggregators, buy books, follow people you respect on social media, go to local user groups or meet-ups, and collaborate with an open mind. Like most skilled professions, this isn't a nine-to-five job. That doesn't mean it's okay for you to continually work overtime just to build a product; just that you need to invest your own time into your career too, and this "continuing professional development" is an important part of that. If your employer doesn't give you time or space to do this, you may be working in a toxic environment.

Summary

The rise of the full stack developer hasn't happened in a vacuum. Organizations are moving towards digital, where the technology is fully embedded in the rest of the organization, rather than living in an IT department, and full stack developers are needed to give these organizations the agility and skill sets they need. The full stack developer must therefore be a specializing generalist who can take on a number of different tasks, and work with skills from other disciplines.

The Web has become a natural place to develop applications. From its humble beginnings as a way of reading documents, through an explosion in tools and browser technology that shows no signs of slowing down, the Web allows you to deliver increasingly complex apps to many different devices. It's important to understand the history of the Web to allow you to pick the right tools for complex and rich applications known as web apps, which may not be the same for content-driven web sites, which follow different interaction patterns.

CHAPTER 2

Planning Your Work

Developers who are just starting out often believe that their job is to build what they're told to build by their managers or clients. The more experienced a developer becomes, the more they realize that building the right thing is more important than building the thing right. A quick hack that does what the user needs it to do is much better than a beautifully crafted codebase that doesn't solve the user's problem, although a working but hacked-together system will quickly stifle progress.

Having an effective way to develop plans for the work you're going to do is the best way to ensure that you approach the work so that it actually meet the needs of the user. It's a commonly held misconception that developers exist to write code, but a development team without an effective planning process will often spend time writing the wrong code, or getting stuck and being unable to move forward with the code they do write, stumbling over obstacles and falling victim to risks they've failed to mitigate. An effective planning process, including the whole team, can minimize or avoid these problems altogether. A competing concern with the planning process is that it is often also used to develop estimates and communicate to external stakeholders how well the team is performing. This concern can often make a planning process toxic, and give planning as a whole a bad reputation. However, it is possible to implement a planning process that avoids these pitfalls while keeping those people outside of your team happy.

One key difference between a digital organization and a traditional one is the relationship between the development team and the business. In a traditional organization, developers live in their own team, and so don't necessarily have the domain knowledge around the area of the business that they're developing software for. Communicating that domain knowledge to developers is hard, so the people who actually had the knowledge to define the organization's software needs were tasked with communicating this information to the development team via documents with names like "specification document" or "functional requirements document." As building software can be expensive, it was believed that getting the specifications right from the beginning would minimize the cost

© Chris Northwood 2018
C. Northwood, *The Full Stack Developer*, https://doi.org/10.1007/978-1-4842-4152-3_2

of any potentially expensive re-work, so a significant amount of effort went into preparing these documents. The problem is that these documents became a replacement for team members communicating with each other. Furthermore, as the overhead of preparing these documents, and getting sign offs, was quite large, it made more sense to have fewer, larger projects. The documents were as comprehensive and precise as the code that was written to implement it, but had the downsides of being written using the imprecision of human language, and processes made them difficult to change.

One term I've not used so far in this book is "agile," but the eagle-eyed reader will have noticed the essence of the agile movement creeping into the previous chapter. The agile movement has had one of the biggest effects on the growth of digital businesses and the changing structure of development teams. The process described above is often called the "waterfall" model, characterized as the opposite of agile. In reality, no organization really works in a strictly waterfall way. And even the best agile teams will have some sort of mini-waterfall, although a mini-waterfall can feed into itself; you can't test a thing until it's built, and you can't build it until it's defined, but you can define those tests before it's built, and building a part of a system can inform another part.

At the core of the agile movement is a manifesto that defines agile as bringing people back into the process of building software, breaking down communication barriers, and embracing change.

We are uncovering better ways of developing software by doing it and help-ing others do it. Through this work we have come to value:

- *Individuals and interactions over processes and tools*

- *Working software over comprehensive documentation*

- *Customer collaboration over contract negotiation*

- *Responding to change over following a plan*

That is, while there is value in the items on the right, we value the items on the left more.

—The Agile Manifesto: http://agilemanifesto.org/

When you read the agile manifesto, it's important to understand what it really means. "Individuals and interactions over processes and tools" doesn't mean "don't use Jira." It means don't *only* use Jira, or let Jira get in the way of communicating.

The third paragraph of the agile manifesto is often forgotten; it's not a binary choice between the left- and right-hand concepts, but a preference for those on the right. So, have some processes, and use tools, but don't let those get in the way of individuals and interactions. Documentation can help with communication, so use that, but don't document every part of what you're building before you build it. Contracts are important—they're how you get paid—but building something that the customer doesn't want just because the contract says to is a waste of everyone's time. And having a plan makes getting started very easy to do, but you should make sure the plan can change.

Digital organizations (as opposed to traditional ones) are agile because they have broken down barriers to communication by mixing business teams with development teams. Without arbitrary barriers, lighter processes for defining what needs to be done can emerge. Better ideas emerge as well, as communication can now flow freely between the people with domain knowledge and the technical knowledge, and these silos break down. With a lighter process with a lower overhead, each change can be smaller, which minimizes the time between defining a project and it actually getting done. Minimizing this time means that big changes halfway through a build—to respond to some external change or new discovery—are no longer needed, as there is less time for things to change in the first place. When a change does occur, the impact itself is then minimized, as it either requires replanning of upcoming work, or by altering the work currently in progress. Work in progress should be scoped to be small, so the impact of such a change is not huge.

Agile is not a set of processes, nor is it a series of "rituals" like a daily standup, user stories, or retrospectives. Agile is a way of thinking, and must expand beyond the development team and into the rest of the organization. An "agile" team in a traditional organization may, at best, have an effective delivery approach and satisfy internal stakeholders, but unless the whole business can operate in an agile way by applying the above principles, you'll be limited in how quickly you can get software into people's hands, rather than actually making a whole organization respond to changes, which is what a modern business needs to do. At worst, an agile team in a traditional organization will be at constant loggerheads with the rest of the organization. For example, the organization may want long-term stability and visibility of their IT systems that agile simply can't provide; the very nature of being quick to respond to change means you can't pin down a six-month roadmap, unless you agree not to change it, which is no longer agile. In traditional organizations, if the development team can't iterate with the business, then they can't respond to the change that the rest of the business is responding to. Worse, if the whole organization is locked into this long-term planning and stability process, then the organization can't respond to changes from outside the organization, making it harder for everyone to achieve their goals.

Applying agile techniques in a traditional environment like this is doable, but if the team is asked to build big things all at once, the project becomes like a "waterfall" project, where large chunks are defined up front, and the smallest chunk the business is willing to launch is the whole product. Development and QA happens in sprints against this backlog, but the backlog itself can't change in response to external circumstances. The agile process should start with the initial idea for a project or feature, not just at the point developers pick it up.

Identifying Requirements

The role of a developer in identifying requirements can vary a lot between teams. At the simplest level, identifying the requirements of the thing to be built is often a matter of asking the rest of your organization to give them to you, and although this can work well in mature organizations, or where there's a supplier/client relationship, you can't always assume that the organization knows what they want. What they ask for is not necessarily the same as what they actually want.

Many teams, especially larger teams, designate an individual who is largely responsible for this. This is sometimes called a business analyst, but even if you have no one with that job title, the role will exist somewhere in your team—perhaps in a product owner, or a project manager, or even a tech lead. One-person freelancers typically occupy this role too.

It's better to fill that role in your team rather than outside it, but it's also important that the individual does not become a one-person silo or bridge. It's important for developers to work with them to truly understand what they are making, and to also feed back into the process. If you understand what the organization is trying to achieve, you will reduce your feedback cycle time, allowing you to complete work more quickly. If you have a question, rather than having to wait for an answer, you can make an educated guess and continue work. In cases where the question is more fundamental to what is being built, then stopping and asking is still important, but by better understanding the requirements, you know which questions are truly important, and which aren't.

This is especially important for senior developers and leads, or those who want to grow into those roles. Senior developers are often expected to attend meetings with a wider group of stakeholders to help define a product and gain an understanding of what the stakeholders want. At first it may seem that time away from code is not as productive as time spent coding, but for a full stack developer, extending beyond the code actually allows them to produce a better end product, and help those around them work better. The days of requirements being thrown over a wall to developers, and the downsides that entails, are over.

Workshops are one of the most common ways of eliciting requirements. Workshops involve getting a bunch of people together and running activities, with the hope of getting some useful information out of them. The people from outside your team who attend a workshop are often referred to as stakeholders; these are the people who have an interest in what you're building. For a news web site, this might include people like the editors, or for an online store, it might include the marketing team and buyers. It can also include people from outside your organization; in an e-commerce example, the backend systems might include the suppliers you work with. It also probably includes your end-users.

The format of these workshops varies depending on who the stakeholders are and what phase of the project you're in. Early on, it is common to initiate a discovery phase to understand the problem you're trying to solve, rather than jumping straight to a solution. Some may think this is anti-agile, but it's important to do just enough to avoid starting your journey in the wrong direction. You do not need to fully understand the problem space and fully define your solution before starting to build.

Workshops in the discovery phase might involve a large group of stakeholders, getting everyone together in a room to define the problem that needs solving. The stakeholders might not agree on what the problem is, but by eliciting all of their thoughts you should be able to pull out some common themes that will allow the delivery team to identify the challenge, and define a set of steps to hopefully overcome it.

This is referred to as the double-diamond model, which can be seen in Figure 2-1.

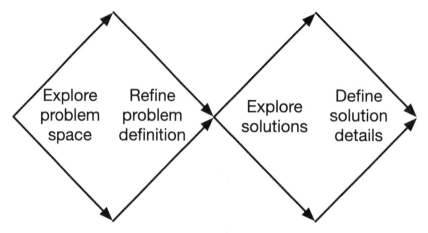

Figure 2-1. *The double-diamond model, which shows how to diverge to generate breadth of ideas, and then converge to generate depth on both the problem and the solution*

In this form of double-diamond model, you get everyone together to explore the entire problem, and then the team that is responsible for devising a solution refines it into the actual work that needs to be done to solve the problem at a high level. First, you identify the general shape of the problem space by first exploring the breadth of it, and then drilling down into any detail and unanswered questions. Then, the second converge-diverge diamond is followed, with first identifying possible solutions, and then eliminating inappropriate ones and defining the actual specifications and details for each part of the solution. Remember that your job is to actually come up with the solution; stakeholders might understand their problems best, but not necessarily the best way technology can help them. This is where the double-diamond model can help, as it involves stakeholders to get the relevant information from them to design an appropriate solution, but a core group (often just the most senior members of the team) then refines that into what actually gets built. This prevents the dreaded design-by-committee outcome, and also the situation most famously described by Henry Ford: "If I had asked people what they wanted, they would have said faster horses."

There are many other techniques that make use of the double-diamond model, and many other models and ways of running workshops to gather requirements, but this is one example.

The field of User Experience (UX) has grown out of a mixture of the academic field of human-computer interaction with the traditional role of visual and interaction design, and many UX teams follow a user-centered design approach, which puts the user at the heart of the requirements-gathering process. A user experience practitioner is a very powerful ally during a requirements elicitation process. Many of the most successful organizations out there put user needs first and have teams with engineering and UX practitioners working side by side. Often the lines of those roles blur, and some UX practitioners contribute to the engineering, or developers take part in the UX processes, increasing team effectiveness through reducing communication overheads.

These forms of requirement gathering are known as qualitative research—that is, they focus on abstract facts and information and how humans feel. Another way of eliciting requirements comes from a method called quantitative research, where raw data is analyzed to discover information. Quantitative data gathering is most effective when your product is in front of a user, and can give stakeholders a great deal of comfort as compared to qualitative research, which can often be driven by "gut feelings" or other subjective information. On the flip side, humans are not rational beings, and many will trust their gut over statistics!

There is a definite science behind the analysis of quantitative data, and it's important not to underestimate it. Statistics is a complicated subject, and it is easy to apply an inappropriate form of data analysis, or misinterpret the results, leading to bad decisions.

When working with users, quantitative data is much easier to gather than qualitative, so quantitative data can become more helpful later on in the development of a product when there are many real world users of your application. Continuous delivery is a technique that encourages releasing early and often, and for teams that practice continuous delivery, the use of quantitative data can become much more effective as it allows for collecting data whilst parts of a new feature are beng developed. This is discussed further in later chapters.

The most common form of quantitative data comes from using analytics systems, which report on how users interact with your product, but it can also come from elsewhere in your organization. For example, if building a tool to be used in a call center, looking at the data such as the average wait time can prove enlightening when it comes to discovering what requirements you might need to consider in your product.

Defining the Work

Once what a product needs to do has been discovered, it's important to define that work. This definition works as both a method of communicating to the wider team what needs to be done and a way of ensuring that the problem is truly understood to the point where a solution can be expressed in code.

Within many teams, the user story has become almost synonymous with agile, although there are many other ways of documenting a requirement, and user stories can be used in non-agile settings too.

User stories frame a new feature from the point of view of a user, and are commonly expressed in the form:

As *someone*

I want to *do something*

So that I can *achieve something.*

Other popular techniques include hypothesis-driven development, the famous functional requirement document, or even more ad-hoc approaches such as free text on the back of an index card.

It's very easy to write bad user stories. Take for example:

As a user

I want to register for an account

So that I can check out quicker next time.

This type of requirement will often come from someone inside the business, not a user, and is then retrofitted onto a user. Do users really care about checking out quicker? Maybe for a site they use a lot, but not for those that are accessed infrequently. Be wary of requirements that have been retrofitted onto a user; they are often not actually plausible, and can result in wasted effort. Framing user stories correctly can change your approach, and help better meet the desired goals. The above user story may be more reasonably expressed as:

As the business

I want users to register for accounts

So that I can gain more insight into my customers, and research shows that customers with accounts are more likely to return to the site.

Retrofitting often happens when it is hard to write the "so that" part of a user story. If it's hard to write that line, the value may not be obvious and needs more definition. The second user story here can be more easily challenged, and be subjected to wider discussion with the rest of the organization. For example, does the value added here outweigh the cost of adding more friction to the checkout process? Also, the definition of what data to capture is different between the two stories.

Another sign of a poorly defined user story is one that simply says, "As a user." Most users have different needs, and in the first story above, the statement doesn't apply to all users—only users that are likely to return to the site. When building for users, it's important to have good understanding of who your users are and the differences between them. Very few systems have only one type of user. It is common practice to develop "personas" that represent typical users and to give them identities to make it easier to understand their behavior.

Sometimes a user story is hard to define because it covers a wide range of related technology and user journeys. These types of user stories can often be converted into "epics," which are user stories that have been broken down into (or are being broken down into) a number of smaller, more granular user stories. Epics often appear very early on, when an idea first comes around. For example, if you're building a brand new e-commerce web site, an epic might exist in this form:

As a customer,

I want to purchase an item from the web site,

So that I can have that item delivered to me and I can enjoy it.

This can then be broken down into smaller user stories based on the different mechanisms of purchasing something. For example, user stories might emerge around searching the catalogue to find an item to purchase, or different ways of paying for an item. These individual user stories can be much easier to reason through and prioritize. For example, if you potentially have users outside your country, you will often need to build in an address finder, or have shipping cost calculators for those countries, but such functionality can be deprioritized to focus on the local market first and then picked up at a later date. Trying to tackle a user story that is too large can cause problems, as it is harder to see what has been missed, and can cause unnecessary work as it brings unnecessary features along with it.

Bill Wake proposed the mnemonic INVEST to remember the important characteristics of a good user story.

- Independent

- Negotiable

- Valuable

- Estimatable

- Small

- Testable

An independent user story is one that is achievable without any other user stories being done first. This means that you can reprioritize your stories at any point, by moving them up or down your backlog in response to any changes in your organization.

Negotiability means that a story can be changed, rewritten, or discarded at any point until work starts on it. For example, if a story is proposed that has significant technical implications, it should be possible for developers to challenge that story and determine if there's a simpler way of implementing it that still satisfies the business needs.

A user story must be valuable for it to make any sense. Stories that call for busywork, or fun technical items (for example, trying out a shiny new technology) but actually deliver no value to the organization have no worth as stories, so should not be on the backlog. Some teams go further than simply requiring a story to be valuable and assign "value points" to an item, which are an abstract concept similar to story points that can help with prioritizing items. High value/low cost items tend to be the highest priority, whereas low value/high cost items can be discarded. This is why user stories must also be estimatable. If a user story isn't estimatable, it is difficult to prioritize. It is also indicative of an underlying issue with the story. If something isn't estimatable, it may be because a story is not clear or defined enough. This also usually means it's not clear or defined enough for a team to be able to implement it.

Small is another important characteristic of a user story. Many teams will define a rule of thumb for how large a story can be. Teams running in sprints will often declare a story must be small enough to complete in a single sprint, and others will use a different rule of thumb based on what they feel comfortable with. When a story is large, it is easier to miss subtle details within it, which can lead to wasted effort, and it also becomes harder to realize parts of that story that might have value sooner, as instead the whole story must be defined. Anecdotally, large stories cause the biggest issues in delivery teams.

The final requirement of INVEST is that a user story must be testable. If a story is not testable, it means there's no way of figuring out if what the team has implemented is correct, or if it has the right impact. Testability here often refers to the work done by a QA or automated tests within a team, but is becoming more widely used to refer to a way of measuring the impact of delivering that feature on an organization (and therefore checking that the story did have value). When a requirement isn't testable, it's often due to a lack of clarity on what it is supposed to do and how it is supposed to behave. A lack of testability can also mean that the value isn't well-defined.

These requirements can sometimes be in conflict with each other. Often, to make a user story independent, you must make it quite large. This is especially true when you start building the foundation of a system. The first item you build might require you to set up build tooling, or have dependencies on other systems—for example, a login system. Some teams choose to address this by communicating that there will be a "first story overhead" to the first item they build, or by having a "foundation sprint" to get things ready. There are challenges beyond this initial foundation stage, too. For example, if a group of related but independent stories presents itself, it is common for the first in this group to require a larger set of technical tasks, which then makes implementing the later stories easier. This can challenge the estimatability of stories, as the order in which they are done will change those estimates.

Another example occurs when the build of a minimum viable product (MVP) is underway. The MVP is the bare minimum a product must do to be useful or valuable, so by its very definition, the product does not have value until the MVP phase is written. All stories in the MVP therefore become dependent on each other, and an item by itself may not be seen as valuable (for example, why have the ability to browse a catalogue until you have a way of checking out?).

In these early stages, taking the mnemonic literally is difficult, although as a product continues beyond MVP into continuing or BAU (business as usual) development, it becomes much easier to stick to the principles, and doing so becomes a key enabler for continuous delivery.

When new stories are proposed, they do not always meet the requirements of INVEST immediately. A new story is often a placeholder to indicate more work is needed to identify the value, or discover enough information to make it estimatable. It is common to have an "ideas" or "discovery" phase of your planning process where these stories are refined before moving on to being a full-fledged part of your backlog.

Once the high-level definition of a requirement is complete and it appears on the backlog, it then becomes necessary to define the rest of the work needed to make it ready for the team to implement. The kind of definition required will vary between teams. Relatively immature teams will require more definition before moving to the next phase, whereas more mature ones can work with less detail. Getting the level of detail just right is tricky! Too much and you've wasted time and effort in over-specifying; too little and you risk re-work or the wrong feature being built.

As work progresses from the idea phase into production, it requires differing levels of detail. As a developer, you may have certain expectations about what you are given, meaning there are also often stages before the development stage (such as visual design) that must be completed. Since this definition happens inside your team, it's necessary to have good communication and clear expectations about what happens during each phase. Senior or lead developers may be brought in early to help other team members (such as UX practitioners) understand any technical restrictions to that process, as well as identify alternative ways of solving a problem.

As a developer, the most common level of definition required is a set of acceptance criteria, and often some wireframes or visual assets if there is a UI component involved. It is unhelpful, though, for these to appear suddenly in a perfectly polished form; it's useful for the development team to have visibility on work that is coming their way, before it is fully defined.

The method of communicating this definition to the development team is important too, and depends heavily on the way the team likes to work. One effective method of doing this is called behavior-driven development, which relies on a mixture of conversation and written record to establish these acceptance criteria. Behavior-driven development is discussed in more detail in the Testing chapter.

Verbal communication is a much richer method for humans to communicate than written communication, and although definitions often come to developers from other roles on the team, that is not the only direction communication can flow. Asking questions—and, for other roles on the team, being available to answer those questions— is as crucially important as producing a good definition in the first place! There are many effective teams that use verbal communication over a written record, and although this often causes problems with scale, it can work very well. Remember the agile manifesto: "People over processes."

Tracking the Work

Even a one-person team will often find that they need to track the work being done. Tracking work is often a minefield, with many different people wanting the work to be tracked for different reasons. The team might want work to be tracked so they can have better visibility on what everyone is doing; external managers might want to track the effectiveness of one team relative to another; stakeholders might want to know when a feature they care about is completed; and project managers might want to know how long people are spending on each feature so they can charge customers appropriately.

However, producing reports and alternative views to satisfy all of these differing needs can be a considerable overhead for a team, so many use tools to automate as much of this work as possible. Despite many claims, there is no "one true tool" for tracking work. A team that uses Jira may find Trello completely unsuitable for what they want to achieve, and one that uses a physical wall with index cards will probably never be able to apply their process into a team that embraces remote work.

Regardless of which tool you use, you're unlikely to find something that's perfect for everyone, and you may have to make some compromises to get the best fit for all. The method used to track work should be revisited to make sure it's working for everyone, and not causing unnecessary work.

In addition to the visual tools you may use to manage your work, there are other tools that can be used to manage the flow of work to your team. Sometimes called methodologies, there are many to choose from—one popular option within agile communities is Scrum. Some other broader methodologies or frameworks, such as PRINCE2, cover a whole range of other techniques (such as requirements gathering and testing), in addition to the process of running a project.

Scrum

Scrum has become very visible in the field of software development, to the point where Scrum is synonymous with agile in some communities.

However, Scrum is not a silver bullet, and it is not perfect.

The agile movement in general, and Scrum in particular, grew out of the Extreme Programming (XP) world, and one criticism of Scrum is that by discarding the technical aspects of XP, it has resulted in a weaker process. Another is that a focus on "rituals" within Scrum (such as the fixed-duration sprint, daily standup, planning, and retrospective) has given rise to a cargo cult movement, where organizations "adopt" Scrum by taking on these rituals, but it still sits within a larger waterfall movement. This is amplified by the proliferation of Scrum trainers and certifications that teach you the rituals and principles of Scrum, but not how to apply it in the context of your organization. This can lead to the worst of both worlds and a disillusionment with agile in general. When implementing Scrum, it is important to remember that you can adjust the framework for your circumstances, and you do not need to follow a textbook definition of Scrum.

At the core of Scrum are several key artifacts, roles, and rituals. The single most important thing is the backlog, which is a prioritized list of things to work on. In Scrum, the development team works in fixed-length sprints (often between one and four weeks, but they do not vary, and the length of the sprint is agreed upon up front), and agrees at the start of the sprint how many items to accept from the backlog into the sprint. By the end of every sprint, the development team should have produced a "potentially shippable increment" of the product, so value is being added on a regular basis.

A Scrum team consists of a product owner, who should be empowered to make decisions around the product being built and is responsible for building the backlog, and should be accessible to the development team; a Scrum Master, who is responsible for facilitating Scrum within the team and working with the product owner and stakeholders to produce a backlog, and who can facilitate removing impediments or "blockers" that stop work in the sprint; and the development team itself. A development team should be cross-functional and capable of doing all the work to deliver a backlog item within a sprint.

A sprint starts off with a planning session. In the first half of the sprint planning session, the product owner and the development team negotiate which backlog items should be accepted into the sprint—the idea is that the team only accepts items it thinks it can complete in the sprint. A "definition of done"—an agreement on what an item being completed actually means—is determined by the Scrum team. Commonly, a "definition of ready" also exists, defining what it means for a backlog item to have sufficient definition for a team to accept it.

An example definition of ready

For a feature to be considered ready for development, the following things must be complete:

- The product owner has prioritized it.

- UX, product, and dev have developed and agreed upon acceptance criteria for it.

- The development team has estimated it (or re-estimated, if the scope of the item has changed).

- The technical lead is happy with the proposed approach, if it impacts the technical architecture.

- If the feature involves any changes to administrator workflow, the administrators have been consulted.

- If the feature requires any changes to the data schema, the data architect has reviewed it.

- Any dependencies on external APIs have been identified.

- If any new UI assets are needed, they have been identified.

An example definition of done

For a feature to be considered done, the following must be complete:

- The code should conform to the coding style guide.

- All new code should have unit tests written against it, and all unit tests must pass.

- The tech lead must have reviewed the impact on the cross-functional requirements of the product.

- The code should have been written by a pair, or reviewed by a peer.

- The UX designer and product owner should have seen the feature in the QA environment.

- The tester should have exercised the functionality and smoke tested the product in the QA environment.

- Browser-based automation tests should have passed in all supported browsers.

- Any bug tickets identified by the manual QA should have been resolved.

Estimation techniques known as "story pointing" and "velocity tracking" are used to help determine how much work a team can accept into a sprint—these are discussed in more detail in the Prioritization section.

In the second half of the sprint planning session, developers break down the individual stories into tasks that make sense for that team. For a truly cross-functional team, these tasks can often be things like "create acceptance criteria," "produce wireframe," or "add new API endpoint to backend." One of the weaknesses of Scrum is that it expects the entire team to be able to work on these tasks, but in reality, there are specialties within a team, so the wireframe tasks may require a designer to work on them before a developer can pick them up.

While the sprint is in progress, each day should start with a daily standup, where the product owner, Scrum Master, and development team get together around the task board and discuss what they did the previous day, what they plan to do that day, and whether there is anything stopping them (blockers). Each person should be limited to one minute, and only one person should talk at a time. An alternative approach is to "walk the board," so instead of individuals giving updates, the discussion focuses on the progression of individual tasks or backlog items. The standup is referred to as such because standing (for those that can), as opposed to sitting, keeps the meeting short. The standup is not intended to serve as an update for management, and only those who are part of the core team should talk, although others are allowed to observe.

> *There was once a pig and a chicken. The chicken turns to the pig and says "We should open a restaurant. We could call it 'Ham & Eggs.'" The pig disagrees, saying "You'd be involved, but I'd be fully committed."*
>
> —Old fable

Sometimes members of the core Scrum team at a standup are called pigs, and the observers and stakeholders are called chickens. Only the pigs should speak.

If any blockers are identified in the daily standup, they should not be solved in the meeting unless absolutely necessary. Instead, the Scrum Master should make a note of them and mark the corresponding item as blocked. After the standup, team members can discuss as a smaller group any actions that may be needed and allocate those appropriately in order to unblock the task.

At the end of the sprint, the sprint review occurs. As with sprint planning, this occurs in two parts. The first part is the demo, which is a chance for the team to show the completed work and the shippable increment to any stakeholders, and the second is the sprint retrospective. The sprint retrospective is a chance for the team to look back at how the sprint went, and to identify any ways their processes can be improved to make the next sprint more successful. The retrospective must be as open and honest as possible, and is attended only by team members—other stakeholders are rarely invited. The Continuous Improvement section further on in this chapter discusses retrospectives in more detail.

Within a sprint, it is common to have a burn-up (or burn-down) chart, which tracks the progress of the team within the sprint, and to indicate whether or not it's likely that all the backlog items will be completed. The backlog as a whole can be tracked in this way, across sprints, to track progress towards any larger goals, or to help make estimates.

One example of a burn-up chart is shown in Figure 2-2. The chart shows the total number of story points committed to in the sprint (you can see a mid-sprint increase in scope), as well as how many have been completed. This can be used to predict whether or not the items in the sprint will be completed on time.

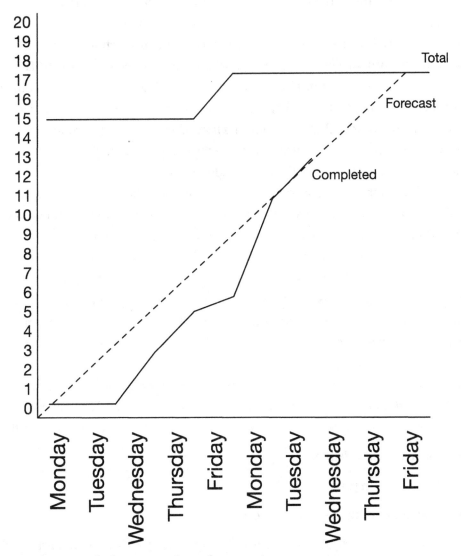

Figure 2-2. *A sample burn-up chart for a sprint*

There is extensive literature available on this form of project management, and the many styles of tracking and potential extensions to it (especially if you're considering having multiple inter-connected teams working on it), although this summary should be enough for a developer to have a basic understanding of the concept.

Kanban

An alternative to Scrum within agile teams is Kanban. Kanban grew out of the lean manufacturing movement, and draws analogies between that movement, which revolutionized car manufacturing, and software engineering. Kanban is often used as part of a set of processes known as "lean" software development.

In the late 1940s, Toyota started analyzing its supply and production chain and comparing it to the way supermarkets managed their inventory to keep enough of every item in stock that is sold, but to minimise storage overhead and shelf-time when food could rot. By the 1990s, this had evolved into a more generalized movement called "lean manufacturing," which was based on the idea that smoothing the flow of work can make production more efficient. If a station on a production line is producing components too quickly, it causes waste due to the chance of spoil or introducing additional storage requirements; but if one station is too slow for the next stage in its process, this causes a bottleneck. Placing minimum and maximum limits on the size of queues between stations in a production line allows you to identify where issues may arise and maximize the efficiency of your plant.

Although on a surface level these concepts seem fairly disconnected, the underlying principles work surprisingly well when applied to software. Instead of a physical production line, we have ideas, which progress through a system at increasing levels of definition until they reach the highest level of definition, which is an expression in code. Although there are clearly differences in the details of those steps, managing the way work flows between the steps is very similar.

Kanban is more a general set of principles than the more rigidly defined practice of Scrum. There is no Certified Kanban Master qualification to pay for. The principles of Kanban are fairly straightforward (although there are many different variations on them):

- Make all work visible.

- Limit work in progress.

- Practice continual self-improvement.

As Kanban is more flexible, it can seem harder to adopt. However, by starting with these principles, and examining some of the common scenarios in which Kanban is used, you should be able to identify a version that is appropriate for your organization.

A team inside a modern digital organization should be empowered to organize their work however they see fit, according to what works best for their team. Although it is sometimes difficult to convince skeptics, if your team is not empowered to manage work the way you'd like, then those constraints can limit your output.

For teams who are new to an agile way of working, Scrum can be a comforting first step, with rules and procedures similar to the waterfall method or change control processes. If Scrum does not work for you, it is not necessarily because you are "doing Scrum wrong"; perhaps Scrum is not a good fit for your team. Drop the limitations that are holding you back and don't add value, and alter the process until it works for you.

Teams that use Kanban from the outset can look similar to ones that use Scrum. The daily standup often features as a regular event, and there's still a task board, which will look familiar to those coming from a Scrum background. Figure 2-3 gives an example layout, but upon closer inspection, you will see there are differences between a Kanban board and a Scrum board.

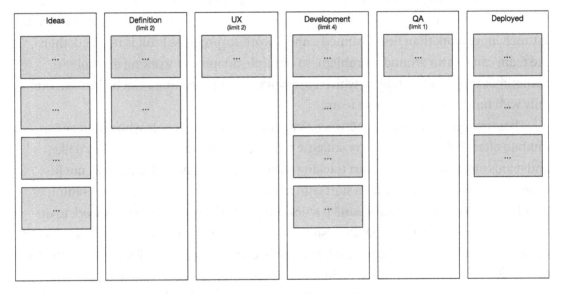

Figure 2-3. *A Kanban board with items in each column*

One important difference is that Kanban does not work in sprints. Instead, once the status of a task changes, you pull it from one column into the next one. Additionally, "work in progress" limits are applied before something is pulled into a stage of development. Teams work on one item at a time until completion, rather than having multiple tasks in flight at once. When an item is completed, work can then move to the next priority. This encourages a regular flow through a team, instead of Scrum's focus on only having a potentially shippable increment every two weeks. It can also allow for fast responses to changes—instead of having to wait for a new sprint to take on a new task, or having to change the scope of a sprint halfway through, a high-priority item can be moved to the top of the backlog and picked up like normal work.

Work-in-progress limits can feel like a constraint on a team, but they are designed to keep the team efficient. A work-in-progress limit is a limit on the number of items that are in a particular column at any one time. For example, a team with three developers may choose a work-in-progress limit of three. Working on more than one ticket at once is discouraged, as context-switching can lead to lower productivity. n+1 is also a common work-in-progress limit (e.g., four items for three developers). This allows for the fact that sometimes external blockers can occur, which means a ticket has to be paused for a while until that external blocker has resolved itself. Ideally, these blockers should be identified ahead of starting development, as the longer code sits without being deployed, the more likely the requirements for that code will change, as well as adding overhead if the way that code integrates into the system changes, yet the code brings no value at that point, just overhead. If many blockers are identified at once (for example, if a ticket is much more work than first assumed), and a work-in-progress limit is reached, then the team can swarm around a problem, so multiple people are working to resolve it. Sometimes this isn't feasible, in which case work-in-progress limits can be broken, but only with buy-in from the whole team.

There are other differences between Scrum and Kanban. People who embrace Kanban often feel empowered to configure the columns on their board as they'd like, and teams are encouraged to start tracking work all the way through the cycle, not just development tasks. Many boards start with a first column of "idea" and a last column of "ready to deploy" or "in production." If a ticket is on the board, then there is work to do on it. Simply being "ready to deploy" isn't enough, as there's still a step to deploy the work before the benefit of it can be realized. For teams that are running A/B tests or embracing hypothesis-driven development, an item "in production" is not complete until any useful information has been identified or until the experiment has finished running.

These columns will often have entry/exit criteria against them, which behave like "definition of ready" and "definition of done" in Scrum, but instead of determining whether or not a story is accepted into a sprint, it determines transitions between columns. These criteria serve as checklists to make sure a story, an item, or work is truly ready, especially between columns that are handled by different people within a team.

Although Kanban doesn't use sprints, it is common for teams (especially teams that have moved to Kanban from Scrum) to have regular meetings that occur at the same frequency as in a sprint. For example, getting a team together to plan does not necessarily have to result in the formal outcomes of Scrum, but can be a useful way to estimate work and make sure the whole team is aware of any upcoming pieces of work, and allow them to make contributions in that planning or design phase (for example, pointing out technical dependencies). Similarly, retrospectives often run at a regular pace, following a similar format to Scrum, as a way of satisfying the Kanban principle of continuous self-improvement.

Other teams do not feel a need to do this (especially small teams where people are working cross-functionally). For example, items of work might be discussed ad-hoc as they arise, negating the need for a formal planning session, or retrospectives might be run as the need arises. Some teams have a "retrospective area" on the board, where any team member can add a sticky note or index card with an issue on it, and these are discussed and resolved after stand-up. The flexibility of Kanban allows you to find what works for you.

A technique known as Scrumban also exists, of which there are many variants. One Scrumban variant combines the time-boxed iterations of sprints in Scrum with the flow of Kanban. In this method, Kanban is used to manage all the pre-sprint and post-sprint activity—for example, requirements gathering, UX work, or post-deployment analysis of a KPI—but a core development team works in the meantime by taking a batch of tickets and working on them in a sprint. This balances the stability of upcoming work for the development team while giving more structure to the activity around the work of developers. This form of Scrumban is often implemented as a precursor to the elimination of sprints and full Kanban.

An alternative option is one where time boxes are not used, but bundles of items are sprinted on as a group. Many organizations have developed their own variant too, as a way to mix existing Scrum practices with the benefits of Kanban, or to transition to full Kanban. "Scrumban" is a very loose term.

While in Scrum you use burn-up/burn-down charts to track the progress of work within a sprint towards a goal, Kanban also offers tools that can be used to check the team. The most-used tool is that of a continuous flow diagram (CFD). In a CFD, you create a line chart showing how many items are in each column in a system at a particular point in time. In an ideal system, the lines should remain flat, with the exception of "done," which should increase. When Kanban is being used against a fixed project backlog, the "to-do" line will decrease, although for many sustaining products (where Kanban works best), work should come in at about the same rate as it gets completed. Figure 2-4 shows a typical CFD where there is mostly a smooth flow through the system. This example does show a small bottleneck about half-way through, where there is a bulge in QA, but this was remedied by refocusing dev effort into QA (so the dev line goes to zero and touches the QA line).

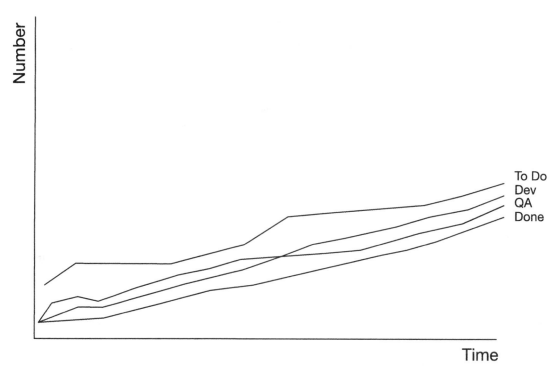

Figure 2-4. *A Kanban continuous flow diagram showing mostly smooth flow*

If any of those lines are not flat, as is the case in Figure 2-4, there is a bottleneck in your system that needs resolving to avoid losing continuous flow and people being spread too thin. Figure 2-5 shows a team that is being asked to do far too much work; to-do is growing much quicker than done, and there is a bottleneck in dev.

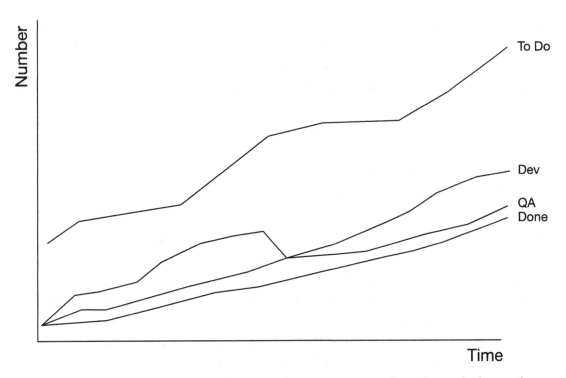

Figure 2-5. *A continuous flow diagram showing uneven flow through dev and a growing backlog*

Continuous Improvement

The way your team goes about planning and tracking work should not be static. It should constantly evolve in response to how your team grows and changes. In Scrum, the end-of-sprint retrospective (or "retro") was introduced as a way for the team to reflect on their work and how they improved. Other methodologies, like Kanban, don't explicitly call for a meeting like this, but it is common for teams to engage in retrospectives on a regular basis.

There are many formats for running retrospectives, but the most common ones look back to identify what went wrong, and then come up with actions to address those deficiencies. There are many books and blogs written on the subject of retrospectives, and this is just one way of running them.

Regardless of how you run a retrospective, there are a few principles to take into account. One is known as the "prime directive" of retrospectives: regardless of what we discover, we understand and truly believe that everyone did the best job they could, given what they knew at the time, their skills and abilities, the resources available, and the situation at hand. The other key piece is that the team should feel that the retrospective is a safe place for them to engage in constructive discussion and suggest improvements. The substance of the discussion should also be available to stakeholders who are not in the room, so any potential improvements can be shared, and wider feedback acknowledged. Keep in mind that these last two components can be in conflict with each other, in which case the principles can be put to one side while those issues are dealt with. For example, if adding transparency means people no longer feel they can talk freely, that's an issue to be addressed directly with coaching so that veil can be slowly lifted, rather than sacrificing the team's ability to talk openly.

Another important practice is to keep the retrospective focused on things that are under the team's control. If a sprint went badly due to external factors (for example, company-wide redundancies, or a DDoS on the web site), although it can be cathartic to indulge in a complaint session, it's not especially productive to do so.

One possible format for a retrospective might be to start off by reflecting on any planned actions from the last meeting, seeing if any were completed, and determining which ones should be carried forward, if any. It's then often useful to make a simple observation on how team members think the last sprint went, and see if there's consensus and whether or not the feedback was positive.

This can flag issues to talk about immediately; if not, it's then a good idea to reflect back on individual factors from the previous sprint that influence what went well and what went badly. Once these specific events are identified, you can cluster them around themes and discuss what caused them to happen, before moving on and identifying ways to either make sure they continue (if they were good things), or avoid them happening again (if they were bad). Throughout the whole process, it's key to make sure you're reflecting on the good things that are worth celebrating and continuing, as well as the things to be improved.

The Retromat[1] is a tool that can generate activities within this framework, though you should make sure you adapt them for your team's particular situation.

Retrospectives are an important part of your team's work, but it's important that they aren't the only time you reflect and practice self-improvement. Some teams have an area of their task board for sticky notes based on observations as they happen, and if some major event occurs, it's okay to deal with it then and there rather than defer it to a retrospective. However you decide to do self-reflection and continual improvement on processes, you should make sure it works for your team.

---

[1]http://plans-for-retrospectives.com

The retrospective is one method of self-improvement, but it's not the only one. Tackling technical debt is another way, and a key concern for any team. It's often tempting to place technical debt on your backlog as a thing to be solved, but it often never is, as it's hard to explain its business value to your stakeholders, and it makes it hard to prioritize. There are two ways around this. The first is to ensure you express any technical items in the same form as any other user story. For example, if your tests take a long time to run, and you wanted to experiment with parallelization, it might be tempting to add a backlog item that says, "enable parallel test running." Instead, you could say:

As a developer,

I want my tests to complete in under 60 seconds, So that I can make deployments quicker.

This is clearly stated in language other stakeholders can understand, and can hopefully be prioritized by your product owner like any other work.

Another approach to tackling technical debt is to apply the Boy Scout rule: always leave the campsite cleaner than you found it. This time, our campsite is our codebase. Every time you work on a new feature, if you come across some technical debt, tackle it immediately rather than deferring it to later. Alternatively, if you know there is technical debt that needs solving, and there's an upcoming feature that would benefit from that debt being solved, then simply build it into the estimate of that feature, as the two are linked.

Some teams also have "tool time." If there are common tools used by multiple teams, but your organization isn't big enough for a dedicated platform team, then it is common to dedicate one dev per week for general maintenance tasks, like upgrading Jenkins, or other minor improvements. If there are different teams in an organization, this can be cross-team work, so all teams benefit. The flipside is that it can then be hard for an individual team to prioritize, in which case each team donates one person for a set period to make improvements everyone can benefit from.

Prioritization & Estimation

Regardless of how you choose to manage your work, there's one question you'll find yourself asking whenever you finish something. "What should I work on next?"

Sometimes it doesn't take much thought. If the system is down and the servers are on fire, it probably means you should be fixing the critical bug that's starting fires. Other times, there's less pressure, and there's nothing that's obviously critical. Even worse are times when there are a number of tight deadlines coming up, and a whole bunch of work needed to be done in preparation.

A backlog is essentially a big, ordered to-do list. The concept of the backlog started in Scrum, but at its simplest, a backlog is ordered such that the most important thing is on the top, and you automatically pick that most important thing off. You can then either continue working on it until it's done, then start the next one, or if something more important comes along, you stop and work on the new most important thing. The latter scenario can cause lots of half-finished work to build up, which can increase wastage, but the former can mean important work is delayed until it's too late. Minimizing the size of each story or item on your backlog reduces the chance of you either being interrupted mid-work or a new, more important thing being delayed too long.

There are many different ways to prioritize your backlog, but often in a team it's useful to have a single person be responsible for it, as there often will be as many different ideas on what is highest priority as there are people on the team. The simplest way to mitigate this is to ask stakeholders what they think the most important action is, but with a diverse set of stakeholders you will often get a very different sense of priority from each of them. This can be useful for identifying which items impact a lot of people, though. Another option is to weigh the cost of implementing a particular idea against the impact its execution will have.

It is also acceptable to say "no" and prune the backlog. If an idea is low value and high cost, then it may never be worth doing it. Alternatively, if it has been on the backlog a long time, then it is worth asking whether the idea is even valid anymore; perhaps the original need has gone away or changed so much that it's no longer useful.

When it comes to determining the cost of an idea, this is often done using a process called estimation. Estimation is often one of the hardest parts of tracking work, as it's seldom accurate, despite how badly people want it to be.

It's rare for a development team to be working on something that's exactly the same as it's done before, and if it is, it tends to be a small task to do, so estimation will always include an element of uncertainty. Early methods for estimation revolved around predicting the actual time a task would take. This yielded concrete figures that could be communicated to stakeholders, but the confidence level around those figures was often not clear, and deadlines were often missed, leading to a lack of trust on the development team.

Commonly used with Scrum is the concept of story points. Story points are a useful tool for detaching hard dates from the estimates, but have the downside of making it harder to communicate what they actually mean to stakeholders. A story point is a unitless number that is supposed to indicate the size of a story, relative to other stories on the same backlog. There is no absolute guideline as to what the numbers mean, and even within a single organization, the numbers are not directly comparable between teams. Each item on the backlog is assigned a story point value, and then you can add these up to determine how big the backlog is. The velocity is then the number of story points that are completed in an average sprint (often computed by taking the mean of the total story points that were completed in the last three or four sprints), and with the velocity, you can estimate how many sprints it will take for you to either complete the backlog or reach a particular item on it.

The possible values for story points are usually not linear, to recognize that larger tasks are often harder to estimate than smaller ones. Instead, the Fibonacci sequence, or a variant, is used. A story can be 1, 2, 3, 5, 8, 13, or 21 points (sometimes larger, but often when a story is too large it is good to break it down into smaller stories). A good rule of thumb is to imagine the simplest thing for a team to complete—for a web app, this might be something like a small re-design of a button—and then designate that as "1." You can then estimate the relative complexity and size of an item compared to that. And this is where it becomes clear that story points are not directly comparable between teams. A team with a relatively greenfield project that has good development tools and an effective automated test suite might be able to complete a "1" much more easily than one with a legacy codebase with few tests. It could also be that a team simply has a different idea of what the simplest things to complete are.

Story points can be used in methodologies other than Scrum too. For example, in Kanban, instead of using sprints as the time frame to determine velocity, you can instead choose a fixed period of time and calculate using that instead.

As you start to use story points and velocity to predict projects that are further out, it is important to recognize that the way velocity is computed (usually as a mean) can hide underlying complexity. This is sometimes known as the cone of uncertainty—things that are close can be predicted with a higher degree of confidence than those that are further out. Figure 2-6 shows an example of this cone of uncertainty. The cone of uncertainty can be used to plot the likelihood of a story's true value in points being between two extremes, depending on how far the story is from completion.

Story points can be an effective internal tool, but are often dangerous to communicate outside of the team. Stakeholders who are not fully versed in story points may misinterpret them, especially if there are other teams using them. One common mistake is for management to see them and then assign a team a performance target to increase their velocity. Velocity is a measure used to help planning, rather than a measure of a team's speed or performance. The easiest way to increase velocity is to start estimating higher numbers, which can be fine as long as the numbers stay relative to each other, but as older stories were not subject to this point inflation, it means historial sprints can no longer be used to determine velocity. A more useful technique is to give stakeholders dates. Dividing the velocity by the number of story points that are ahead of a particular item on a backlog can give an estimate as to when something will be completed, but this doesn't take the cone of uncertainty into account. Instead, you can apply statistical techniques, such as taking a standard deviation of the velocity calculation in order to determine a "high" and "low" estimate of how many sprints are needed until a particular item is finished, and therefore translated into a date range. This can still infuriate stakeholders, as they tend to like concreteness. In this scenario, the worst-case estimate of the two should be used, and then there's a reasonable chance of delivering early, which will make them happy.

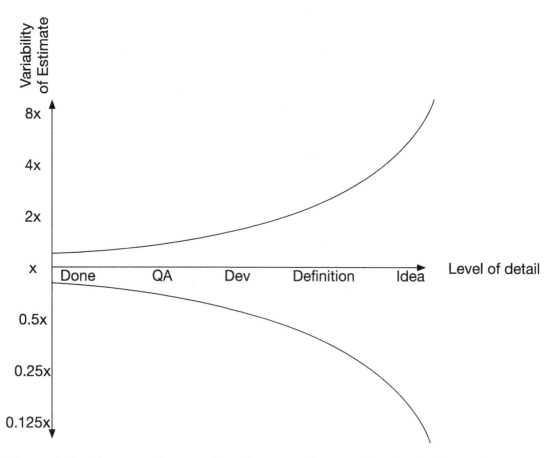

Figure 2-6. *The cone of uncertainty diagram, showing that the further a thing is from being done, the more uncertainty there is in the value of the estimate*

When story points are used, it is important to re-estimate as tasks move through the pipeline. As a story is better understood, what first seems very complicated can become simpler, and what first seemed simple can develop many hidden complexities. Some teams go a step further and use "t-shirt sizing" for their least defined stories. With t-shirt sizing, stories are rated small, medium, large, or extra-large, which correspond to story points for estimation purposes.

Some teams have embraced a movement known as "no estimates," and, beyond that, "no backlog." No-estimates teams make no guarantees to stakeholders and promise to work as quickly as possible, simply picking up whatever is the highest priority at any given time. This works well when the backlog is short. No-backlog teams go a step further; the team does not accept work unless it is immediately ready to address it (this is sometimes implemented as a WiP limit on the backlog). This approach is rare, as it can lead to important tasks being missed due to them arising at an inconvenient time, and can make stakeholder management difficult.

In order to determine these story point estimates, a powerful technique known as Planning Poker is used. In a Planning Poker session, everyone is given playing cards (or an app) with the sequence of story points on them. For each item, each individual on the team chooses a card that reflects the story points they would assign that item, sometimes after some discussion of the exact scope and purpose of a story. The cards are then revealed simultaneously—this is done to reduce influence between team members, so a truly representative sample of the entire team is taken. If there is consensus, then that value is used as the story point value. Otherwise, the team can discuss why they may disagree on any values (perhaps someone forgot some technical challenges that needed to be implemented, or they over-complicated the task in their head) and then further rounds of voting occur until a consensus is reached.

Whereas Scrum uses the story points process with a velocity, Kanban uses time as a measure of work through your system. It is therefore helpful to use Kanban with INVEST to try and make all items in your process a similar "size" in terms of work that needs to be done, and any variances get averaged out. To use estimation with Kanban, you must measure how long an item takes between it being created, work starting on it, and then it being completed. The difference between creation and completion is called the lead time, and the difference between work starting on that item and its completion is the cycle time.

Cycle time is the absolute minimum time that a ticket can be delivered in, if work starts on it immediately, and can often be minimized by the team through process improvements. However, the lead time is what external stakeholders care about, as that's how long it takes for their ideas to be delivered, aside from just the time the work actually takes to do, but also includes any waiting times for the work to be picked up. If a team has a long backlog, then it can mean that lead times are long, which indicates that the team has too much work to do. If the lead time is increasing, that's also showing that the stakeholders are asking too much of the team (the cumulative flow diagram should show this too).

Managing Bugs

Bugs (sometimes known as defects) are a result of unfinished work, and while there are always likely to be undiscovered bugs in your system, having too many discovered bugs can become crippling to a team.

Many teams track bugs alongside other work that needs to be completed, and this works well for them. Others have separate bug trackers, which can cause issues when teams have to look in multiple places to find bugs.

Like any other pieces of work to be completed, bugs need to be defined. Often this is done by an analyst or tester, with a tried and tested format of:

1.   steps to reproduce

2.   expected behavior

3.   actual behavior

When you're in a time crunch, it can be very tempting to ignore bugs in favor of hitting a feature deadline, but doing so increases the amount of work in progress. Bugs represent something that's been missed (either by a developer, or at an earlier stage in the definition process) in a piece of work, and it's not fair to call that piece of work completed if it is buggy.

Regression bugs are even worse, because they're taking something away from the user that they have come to rely on, and rather than just stopping us from completing a piece of work we thought we had finished, they add an additional piece of work back into the project that's currently in progress.

For a full stack web developer, many bugs occur as a result of browser incompatibilities or are device dependent. These are the most annoying bugs to fix, as technically the bug is not in your code (if you've written your code according to standard). Since adding a workaround to fix this bug incurs a cost, it is often effective to have a bug triage, where bugs are discussed and prioritized.

Some bugs that surface are simply not bugs at all. Rather than being issues that we decide not to fix, they are things that have been identified as bugs due to a difference in understanding between the person doing the testing and the person who implemented it. These types of bugs can also be discussed in a bug triage session, where the intention can be clarified.

A bug triage should not be a formal meeting, but rather a casual get-together for people on the team to discuss bugs. Scheduling a triage can often delay a fix (for example, having to wait a whole day to implement a 30-minute fix), but for some teams it's necessary to book time with stakeholders—such as a product owner—to make those decisions. For other teams, a bug triage can be as simple as tagging someone in a comment, or sending an IM.

An obvious bug occurs when a tester identifies something that they believe a developer has missed, and the developer agrees that they have indeed missed something. When everyone is in agreement, there's no need to go through a formal triage session for this; the developer can fix it and the tester can verify it fairly quickly. A triage should not become a replacement for ad-hoc communication channels within a team.

The main danger with bugs is when they sit languishing for a long time somewhere on a backlog, so this should be avoided. Remember that minimizing work in progress is important, and leaving work open causes cognitive overhead and can also impact the quality of our product. A very effective technique for managing bugs is to either fix them immediately (so bugs always go to the top of the backlog), or decide that it's not worth ever fixing. The latter can be uncomfortable for some teams, but if a bug is not important enough to fix now, then why would that ever change? Perhaps you can envision a future where there is no high-priority project work, in which case these bugs could be picked up, but if a bug can be left, then it's often because it only causes a very small or insignificant impact, and in reality, it's unlikely that new feature developments will ever have a lower impact than that. It's better to kill off these bugs than let them sit on your backlog. If a bug is important enough to be fixed, then you should do so now, rather than defer it. It's causing issues on your web site or app right now, and it's clearly worth fixing.

Continuous Delivery

As touched upon above, qualitative data can be a very effective method of discovering information about the product you're building. However, it's very hard to gather qualitative data without a product being out there in the real world. Continuous delivery (CD) is one of many ways to approach the delivery of an idea all the way into production, and is organized around the idea of minimizing the time it takes to get an project into production.

Continuous delivery works like a pipeline. One end of the pipeline is an idea or problem, and the other end is running software. It is an imperfect metaphor, as you will often want to then use the released software to generate insights into your users and the performance of that feature to inform new features. One key difference from other approaches is that software always moves forward through the pipeline. Instead of rolling back, with continuous delivery you "roll forward," so if a release is bad, a version with the fix or with the faulty code reverted is pushed forward, rather than an old version of the same code.

At its core, continuous delivery is about minimizing the time and friction required to make a change to an application. A team practicing continuous delivery should formally define the pipeline of product delivery from idea to delivery, and articulate how something moves from one phase to the next. A pipeline might consist of several phases, such as:

- Discovery, where research is done on an idea to get a high-level understanding of the problem space and what solutions might be necessary;

- Definition, where formal acceptance criteria and design work yields the necessary information for development work to proceed;

- Development, where the product is built and functionally tested;

- Acceptance, where high-level acceptance testing is done and any required stakeholder signoffs are obtained;

- Deployment, where the change is put into production;

- Verification, where any analytics are investigated to make sure that the change is having its intended impact.

A checklist at each phase defines what is needed for a change to move forward. Sometimes these high-level phases are broken down even further—for example, the development phase may have additional technical architecture, build, and code review phases. This kind of flow might seem similar to a waterfall process, but individual items should flow through this pipeline, rather than large batches of multiple items where the definition of the whole batch is done up front. Different stages of this pipeline can involve multiple people with varying skills, so different tasks can be worked on in parallel at different stages, but each task being independent and worked on by different people.

By allowing individual tasks to flow through this pipeline, team members are encouraged to engage in appropriate activities more frequently, based on the idea that doing something more often means you get better at it. Any rote tasks, such as some kinds of regression testing, or deployment ability, or data analysis, are then encouraged to be automated to increase the efficiency of the pipeline. Applying the techniques discussed earlier in this chapter, like INVEST, can also give you items in a suitable form to take through a CD pipeline.

In my experience, continuous delivery works well for teams that organize themselves using Kanban. Although Scrum does not necessarily limit you to only releasing at the end of a sprint, this often seems a natural place to do so. With Kanban, by limiting work in progress, and working on an item until it is complete, then moving to the next one, teams break free of an arbitrary cycle mandated by Scrum, and into a more regular flow of ideas into production.

If your backlog consists of user stories that satisfy the INVEST mnemonic, you will likely see success with continuous delivery. By making each user story small and independent, you can deploy it to production the moment it's finished, having tested it to ensure that it satisfies the requirement. Making lots of small changes reduces the risk of each individual change and minimizes the time between the work being done and being able to capitalize on that work.

It's often surprising to realize that there's a strong link between how you plan and go about your work and how you manage your source code in a repository like Git. There are two dominant approaches to managing source code in the world of software engineering. One is often referred to as feature-branching, and the other as continuous integration (CI), or trunk-based development. Continuous integration is often confused with the set of tools that support the practice, but these tools can also help in feature branch–based development approaches, so it's important to focus on the principles of CI, not just the use of CI tools.

In a world without CI, every time a new feature is developed, a new branch is created in the source control system and all of the work for a feature done in that branch, without having to worry about accidentally destabilizing the mainline or having half-complete work deployed to live. Sometimes there is a branch for each developer. Once the work has been done, or a release is due, which could be several days or even weeks later, the branch is then merged into the mainline. There are downsides to this approach, as it can mean a large number of changes happen at once, and if there are many feature branches, then yours may have deviated from the mainline enough that automated merges cannot happen until you to do some rework. This is sometimes called "merge hell." If a feature is large, there may be incremental benefits during the development of that feature to the end-users that is not revealed until after the merge, increasing the time between doing the work and the value being realized.

CI was created as an alternative method to address these downsides. Every developer commits to the master branch frequently, usually at least once daily. In a pure application of continuous integration, developers always commit directly to master, but it has become common to use a variant where short-lived feature branches are used as a mechanism for code review. This enables code review before pushing into master, but each branch is very short-lived (often only a few hours) to still enable most of the benefits of continuous integration. One advantage of feature branching before the widespread adoption of CI was that the mainline was always stable and complete, as features were not merged until they were done and tested.

Continuous integration tools, like Cruise and Jenkins, were created to run automated tests on every commit to mainline, to bring that same level of confidence around stability to teams that were using continuous integration. However, feature branch teams also saw the value of these tools, and still set them up to run after every merge, or even on every branch in isolation. Be wary of confusing the concept of continuous integration with the use of continuous integration tools!

Teams that do continuous integration often run into an issue where they want to commit code that is stable but does not necessarily represent a complete feature. It's common for these teams to commit code that is either "dead" (i.e., only uses tests that exercise whether it works or not, but is not enabled in the actual application), or behind a "feature flag." A feature flag (sometimes called a feature toggle) is a config setting of the application that indicates whether or not a particular feature is available to the user. In a web app, this might enable/disable various URL routes on the backend, or hide UI widgets that mean code can never be triggered. This allows you to develop in pre-production environments, but not enable it in a production environment until the entire feature is complete. This means that the code is being enabled gradually, rather than all at once, which can be an effective way of managing risk, albeit with the additional overhead of managing it.

For larger refactors, for example, if you're replacing one feature with another brand new one, it's common to have both versions of the code in place, and then a feature toggle that switches between the two. Doing things in this way makes it easy for you to do other tests with your code, such as only enabling it for a certain percentage of your user base to test it whilst rolling it out, or to perform A/B testing, where you have two versions live at once and see which performs better by looking at statistics. This is covered in the Constant Learning chapter.

Another concept that is related to continuous delivery is continuous deployment. Continuous deployment takes continuous delivery to the next level. In continuous deployment, every commit (that passes the tests) is actually deployed to the production environment, whereas in continuous delivery, every commit is capable of being deployed to the production environment, but the actual deployment still happens when the team defines it as possible. Continuous deployment requires a complete level of automation from commit to production, as there is no scope to stop for a manual QA phase. Teams that practice continuous deployment often still do manual QA, but often in the production environment itself, rather than beforehand in a QA environment. Continuous deployment is covered in more depth in the Deployment chapter.

Summary

Effectively planning your work before you do it increases your effectiveness, as it ensures you properly understand the problem you're trying to solve. Historically, this planning was done formally with a large amount of definition up front, but in many situations that has been replaced by agile methodologies.

Agile methodologies focus on only planning what is actually needed right now, leaving you free to plan or re-plan other parts of your project in a way that reacts to change.

Planning starts with defining a backlog—a prioritized list of what the team will be building—and these items should be structured so that they are not purely technical to allow for them to be prioritized in line with the organization's goals. Items of work then move through a workflow where additional detail can be added, perhaps by stakeholders in other disciplines such as UX, adding elements such as visual design, until finally it is deployed to your end users. Two major agile techniques are Scrum and Kanban, which take different approaches to tracking and managing work. Both Scrum and Kanban encourage teams to reflect on their workflows and update them often to ensure they meet the unique needs of that team. Where they differ is in how they allow prediction of when future work may be delivered, with Scrum using story points to determine a velocity, and Kanban using the average time of previous feature delivery.

In addition to planning new work, you must also manage bugs that occur during development, perhaps as a feature is being developed, or potentially hidden until later. These bugs can still be treated as backlog items, but capture their requirements in a different way.

Continuous delivery and continuous integration are two distinct but related approaches to managing the engineering work to enable the process of delivering a feature. Continuous delivery applies automation to make it easy for a backlog item to transition through the different stages—from idea to realized and deployed system— and continuous integration is how developers coordinate changes onto one shared codebase.

CHAPTER 3

User Experience

One characteristic of software development in a modern digital organization is that it puts the needs of the user at the core of the purpose of the team, rather than just focusing on more detached engineering goals. The discipline of user experience (UX) works hand-in-hand with this new style of development to help build software that truly meets the user's needs.

There is no clear definition of UX; the discipline is relatively young, and rapidly evolving. UX has evolved from a number of separate, but related, fields, into one that brings them all together. It merges the more academic discipline of human-computer interaction (HCI) with the traditional "designer" roles of visual design, interaction design, and product design, but it also covers designing processes and services, which may previously have been done by a business analyst.

Before UX, many digital designers came from a traditional print background. For many marketing or content-driven web sites, these were designed in the same way as a newsletter or poster campaign might have been. This often left a big gap in skills between designers and the developers; Photoshop files were thrown over a wall and expected to be implemented in pixel-perfect fashion. The rise of responsive design made this increasingly challenging, as the initial reaction was to make a design that fit perfectly on an iPhone, but failed to adapt to the rapidly changing sizes of screens that evolved from other manufacturers. This forced designers and developers to work closely with each other, as these designs could no longer be specified perfectly in Photoshop, but instead had to be specified in a more abstract way that conformed to the intent of the designer. The developers then had to understand the design intent to express that in code, rather than just creating a facsimile of the design.

For other types of applications, especially process-driven ones, many early digital projects were taking existing paper-driven processes and implementing them electronically. Traditionally, these types of forms were designed by business analysts, who developed processes that satisfied the needs of the business, and when it came time

© Chris Northwood 2018
C. Northwood, *The Full Stack Developer*, https://doi.org/10.1007/978-1-4842-4152-3_3

to implement these forms electronically, a business analyst would often specify these interactions in the same form as the paper-based system. Sometimes a designer would take those designs and style them to be aesthetically pleasing, but this missed any wider scope of seeing how the process as a whole met the user's needs, not just the business's.

The study of human-computer interaction arose as a field within academic computer science in the 1970s, but as web design grew out of the world of print design, these two arenas were disjointed until the spread of a process known as user-centered design. This new approach evolved from the traditional design of processes and interactions by taking the scientific approach that HCI researchers used. This was to test prototype user interfaces out on real users when they were in an early draft stage, then use the observations from these experiments to iterate and evolve the design.

Combining this process design with UI design and applying a scientific approach to bring users to the center of the process amounts to what is now known as the field of UX.

The UX of a product is more than just its UI; it is also the principles behind it and how it works as a whole system. There are many sub-fields within UX, although only the biggest organizations are fortunate enough to be able to employ specialists for every field. Instead, most UX practitioners do a bit of everything.

Like in software engineering, job titles and roles are not universal. Some people within UX use "designer" as a catch-all term, while others use it to refer to someone who focuses more on visual design, but there are three main types of roles you might come across. UX designers are similar to a traditional visual designer, who can produce high-quality designs and assets for a developer to implement, and sometimes have some front-end development skills themselves. Researchers, or user testers, are typically focused on designing and running studies with potential users to test the suitability of particular designs and proposed experiences. Finally, a UX architect (or information architect) thinks about how the system is structured as a whole and where the information is presented to users based on their needs. Something an information architect might produce for a traditional web site is a site map showing how the user might navigate through the pages, but ultimately the goal is for a user to find the information they want to find where they expect to find it, and make sure that information is at the level of detail they expect—not too detailed, but also not so general that the user doesn't end up satisfying their original need.

There are overlaps between these roles. A content-heavy web site may have a role that combines the architect role with that of a copywriter. The output here isn't the visual design, but instead both the content that will fit into the website and the architecture that holds that content. The content is written in direct response to user need, and the same UX discovery and design processes still apply to develop this output. It's increasingly common for UX designers to also have front-end development skills, so that they can implement their designs directly in code, as well as skills related to the process of understanding and testing user requirements. Conversely, full stack developers will often learn skills that were previously in the domain of a UX specialist, further realizing the benefits of full stack development.

User experience has become so prevalent that if an organization doesn't embrace it, they will quickly be outclassed by competitors who do. Sometimes the smallest teams have no one dedicated to these UX activities, but it's important for the whole team to stay focused on meeting the needs of customers who use the product. Any user interface will have some design to it. Even if that design hasn't been fully developed by a designer, it will emerge from the implemented code. As a developer, fully understanding the UX of what you're building from the point of view of those who are building it will help you make a better product, and you'll likely work with UX practitioners on this endeavor.

Information Architecture

If the end goal of a UX designer is an aesthetically pleasing look and feel that makes each feature easy and obvious to use, then the ultimate goal of an information architect is making sure each individual component on a page is where a user expects to find it, with minimal ambiguity. This goes beyond a single page, though, and applies to the structure of a whole site, ensuring that a user can navigate a site or app to find the information they want.

On a team where there is a silo between UX and developers, UX designers might often hand over visual specifications for components, and UX architects hand over the site map and wireframes showing how a page displays its components. In the world of a full stack team, these teams work hand in hand. In fact, aesthetics are actually the least important concern of a UX team. If your users can't find the information they're looking for, then it doesn't matter how good it looks. Similarly, once they get to the right place, the information they're looking for or the feature they're trying to use must have "affordance," meaning it should behave in an obvious and unsurprising way. Together, these concepts are thought of as usability, and the main goal of a UX team is to produce a usable web site, and then apply branding and aesthetics on top of that as a "cherry on top." A classic example of design versus aesthetics is Craigslist. The visual design of Craigslist is very basic, but the site offers a strong user experience. Information is structured in a logical way, and it is obvious how to use each feature of the site.

Affordance is an important concept in HCI, and therefore in user experience. It applies to design in general, not just digital design. The affordances of an object are said to be the way its form indicates how it can be used—for example, a handle on a teapot, or a handle on one side of a door versus a push panel on the other. Computer user interfaces will usually have non-physical affordances. It is typical to make use of common patterns to indicate a way of interacting with something (for example, a button on a web page may have padding and be surrounded with a box, and have some hover state), or to suggest affordances by using skeuomorphism—borrowing design from a real-world object.

The concept of perceived affordances puts any affordances an object may have into context. For example, the affordance of a toilet door lock is often that it will be green to indicate it is available and red if not, but this affordance is not a perceived affordance for color-blind people. Similarly, in UX design, the reasons people might come to a web site or use a web app will often put them in a certain mental state or give them expectations about how a thing should work. Designers need to take these perceived affordances into account.

Affordances by themselves are often not enough, especially when the user is undertaking an action that is especially complex. In these cases, it is important to make sure the user is aware of the logical model underlying the operation they are trying to achieve and guiding them through the action. Designers must also try to pre-empt and restrict any actions that may be taken due to a faulty understanding of the underlying model. However, this should not be used as an excuse for bad design. The "guided tour" pattern that many web apps use now is often executed inappropriately and used when the underlying model is overly complex. Although users can navigate bad design (especially when given no choice to do so, such as with internal tools), it should still be avoided, and fixing it is the ethical thing to do as it will reduce stress, increase efficiency, and reduce mistakes for an organization. Given a choice though, many users will eschew a badly designed site completely.

It is common to see job openings for "content designers," especially in the financial services sector, and there is often some overlap between the role of an information architect and that of a content designer.

A content designer goes one step beyond that of a copywriter (although many content designers end up creating the content too), in that they help determine the content that needs to be conveyed. They can help determine the high-level structure of this content within the context of an entire site, as well as the structure of a piece of content itself, and the links between them.

One area of overlap between an information architect and a content designer is the process of naming things. As the old joke goes, naming things (alongside cache invalidation and off-by-one errors) is one of the two most difficult tasks in computer science, but consistent and clear naming can make it much easier for users to find what they are looking for. Names should be chosen from the point of view of the user, rather than that of the business. For example, a rail operator may announce that they have a "vehicle failure due to a pantograph issue," but this can come across as meaningless jargon to many members of the public. Instead, announcing that "the train is cancelled due to a fault with the overhead lines" is clearer and still conveys the same information.

One important responsibility of an information architect is to make sure the structure of the site reflects what users actually want. In organizations without information architects, it is common for different parts of a site, or different sites for the same organization, to be run by different internal teams, and as a result the structure of a web site then reflects the management hierarchy of the organization, meaning that some information might not be where a user expects it to be. This is an example of "Conway's Law," which states that anything designed by an organization is destined to mirror the internal corporate structure of that organization. When an organization takes information architecture seriously, its information architects must break down these siloed walls. An information architect might belong on one team but have to work with other teams (or work with other information architects across an organization) in order to produce something that works holistically from the perspective of a user outside the organization.

One final note on information architects: there is another similar-sounding job title of data architect. Data architects are responsible for defining structures and relationships, but as the name suggests, they work with the raw data underlying an organization. Data architects also usually focus on the needs of the business, rather than that of the users, often addressing on concerns such as removing duplication, security, and accuracy of the data. Ultimately, this data is used to convey information on a web site, so information architecture has an impact on data architecture, but the skills are quite different.

Getting the User Experience Right

On a project where user experience and development teams are separated, it may be the case that a designer would build a design based on their own experience and the requirements of that particular feature and hand that over for a developer to implement. Often, aesthetics are one of the driving forces of the design.

Following the principles of UX, when a designer builds a design, or an architect comes up with a structure, they think about the assumptions they've made. If different assumptions can be reasonably made and it is unclear which ones are correct, then different designs are built that each focus on different assumptions. These designs are then tested with real users to check whether those assumptions are correct, and ensure there are no hidden issues in the design and that it behaves as a user expects it to.

One of the biggest indicators that a team is working in a modern way is how often they do user testing, and how they do it. A team that user tests constantly might be new to it and trying to find the balance between this new way of working and the old, whereas teams that never user test may be stuck in a traditional mindset.

User testing at its core seems deceptively simple. You simply invite users to interact with your web site and give them tasks to complete, watching them as they do so. It's important to not only watch what they are doing and saying, but also their body language, as this can suggest frustration or other problems that might not be obvious from what they're saying or doing. However, correctly designing your test (the tasks you ask the users to perform) and selecting the right users to test with can be quite tricky, which is where the role of dedicated researchers come in. Often having a psychology background, these researchers can use their formal training and experience to help develop tasks that focus on the nature of the system being tested, avoid any leading questions, and ask appropriately probing questions to get a good level of insight.

In terms of the number of users you want to test with, one school of thought promoted by Jakob Nielsen is to run many tests, where each test focuses only on one thing, and has five participants. An alternate school of thought is to use larger groups (perhaps a dozen participants), but look at many parts of an application at once.

The final thing to consider is what to test. Of course, you're not actually testing the user, but rather your application (or a part of it) to see if it's usable (in terms of perceived affordances of the UI components and the discoverability of a goal within an information architecture). In some cases, it may be acceptable to test a finished product— perhaps if it's a current legacy site you're trying to improve—but often waiting until the end of development before user testing can be expensive if it turns out there are significant issues that need to be resolved. As a result, user testing is most often done on some level of prototype.

At the other end of the spectrum to testing with the final product is testing with a paper mockup. Although some details will get lost, this type of prototyping is often quick to make and useful for checking any high-level concepts that underpin the entire site, and is especially useful if you're making any assumptions about the mental model a user may have about the actions they are about to undertake.

In between these two extremes is where good collaboration between developers and designers can be effective. Prototypes can be built in actual web technology that are suitable for user testing, often without the full level of robustness that would go into production code. Depending on exactly what is being tested, concerns such as responsiveness, cross-browser compatibility, accessibility, and error handling can be disregarded. It is common for a prototype front-end component to be developed in isolation, using canned responses and without being connected to any back ends. These prototypes are then thrown away, even if the design was successful, as retrofitting the concerns of accessibility, responsiveness, etc., is usually more effort than re-building it from scratch and considering these qualities from the start. Speed, rather than quality, is more important here.

You may be tempted to ask a user directly what they want it to do, but this often does not work as well as you may hope. It's not easy for a user to realistically visualize the way they want a thing to work, and they often don't come up with the best ideas in practice. Performing these more formal user tests allows you to check against the "gut" feeling of a user. However, some UXers will undertake "co-design" workshops, where stakeholders (including users) will get together and design something collaboratively, rather than just being presented with a finished design at a user testing session, and this can be a valuable way of working to generate designs too.

There is a downside to running formal user testing sessions and experiments however, which is the cost. If a new feature on a site is not especially groundbreaking in terms of requirements or interactivity, or is largely similar to another one elsewhere, it can be effective to simply apply a known pattern to that feature instead of testing everything, and then sense-checking that by using analytics after it has been fully built, if there's a low risk of getting that design wrong.

This trade-off can be dangerous, where common web patterns that seem effective have been shown to actually not achieve their goals very well after further scrutiny. This includes patterns such as the "hamburger menu," icons without a label next to them, and carousels, which have seen widespread adoption.

It's important to remember that user testing does not need to be very formal. There are low-cost ways to execute user testing without having to hire a specialist or rent a facility with one-way glass or recording devices. Although these don't give you as detailed or accurate insight as a more formal session, they can help you identify the most obvious issues with your app. These low-cost sessions are referred to as "guerrilla" user testing. A common guerrilla testing session might take place in a coffee shop, where (with permission from the owner) you could offer to buy someone a coffee in exchange for 10 minutes of their time, where you observe them using your site or carrying out some common tasks. If you are developing internal tools, then this becomes even easier; you just need to ask potential users whether you can observe them using your designs in situ, and many will be more than happy to do so.

As we will discuss in the Ethics chapter, user testing is a form of experimentation on humans. In this regard, we must behave ethically. Fortunately, there is much we can learn from other disciplines (especially social sciences), as they have honed a good understanding of how to undertake these kinds of experiments ethically. The general rule of thumb is informed consent: the user must be aware of what they're being asked to do and agree to take part, with the ability to withdraw from the agreement at any time. The user tests shouldn't aim to mislead or trick a user, and should treat them with respect. The results should also be suitably anonymized.

Although user testing has become the poster child of the UX process, it is not the only technique you can use to check the usability of your site. A web app or site with good analytics should allow you to interpret the data to answer certain questions about how your site performs in production.

Halfway between user testing in person and purely focusing on analytics after the fact is a type of testing known as A/B testing. A/B testing involves presenting a number of variants (often two) to a user along with a "control" case of the current site with no changes. A subset of users on your site are randomly selected to take part in the trial and then given one of each variant. Analytics are then used to determine how many users completed an activity using each variant and the control, and this number determines which was the most successful (or not; it is not assumed that both variants will perform better than the control) by applying a statistical test to the collected data.

Despite what many companies might try to sell, A/B testing is not always an appropriate tool to use. A naive approach to A/B testing might be to directly compare the number of people who were able to complete the action you were testing. However, the theory of statistics tells us that these numbers are actually slightly fuzzy underneath.

The statistical significance of the result needs to be determined in order to evaluate whether the relevance of these numbers. This concept comes from the idea of "sampling." In this case, a sample is a subset of your user base that undertakes the experiment. It's impossible to pick a perfectly representative subset, so a level of fuzziness is applied to the results to determine if differing results are a result of the different subsets just behaving in subtly different ways, or if there is actually a real change there. When analysis finds that two numbers legitimately represent a difference in the performance of two versions, this is said to be "statistically significant." With few participants, the fuzziness of the numbers is more intense, so it is harder to determine if one number is accurate or not, so a large number of participants is needed to determine if a difference is actually significant. A/B testing is therefore inappropriate on low-traffic areas of a web site, although by running tests for a long period of time (perhaps as long as several weeks) you can increase the number of participants and hence get more accurate results. On very busy parts of a web site, it might seem that you only need to run a test for a short period of time, but this can be biased too. For example, running a test for an hour on a Friday afternoon will only give you data for that period of time, and users may behave different in the morning versus the evening. Running your test for at least a whole day, and often a week, is recommended.

A/B testing also becomes complicated if you want to run multiple tests at once. These tests can interfere with one another and invalidate each other's results. Although it is possible to run multiple tests on the same site, they should test distinct activities a user might want to undertake. Similarly, when you A/B test something, the changes made should be fairly small. For example, if you're experimenting with changes to your checkout process, if you redesign the flow of the forms as well as the visual elements, it will be hard to determine if user changes are due to the improved flow or the visual elements. With A/B testing, you also need to implement the full version of all the variants being tested; a prototype isn't good enough.

The ethics of A/B testing are still under debate. It is not feasible to get informed consent in some cases, while in others, having users opt in to a "beta" mode might be sufficient. Much of the discussion around A/B testing has focused on whether or not the results of the test could cause harm. A famous example was an A/B test Facebook undertook that involved showing posts with positive and negative sentiment in users' feeds, and then seeing if that impacted the sentiment of the posts that user then made. Many decried this as bringing harm by making people sadder. Another common type of A/B testing (especially in startups) is by experimenting with different pricing structures.

If a user signs up at a higher price, which they are still happy to pay, despite the fact they were randomly disallowed from knowing there was a lower price, has this caused them harm? Some organizations work around this by always giving the lower price at the end of the process regardless of which flow the user chose, but the answer to this question is not clear.

A downside of using analytics and these kinds of "quantitative" methods is that they often lack depth. It can be easy to miss the "why" of people behaving the way they do, which the "qualitative" methods like user testing do pick up. For example, Google used A/B testing early in their existence to compare two user experiences, and then later found that one performed poorly because it had a larger load time for technical reasons, rather than usability ones. Conversely, the "qualitative" methods are often expensive to run at scale, and it can be difficult to generate large enough directly comparable data sets. The most powerful teams will use both, with user testing giving depth and analytics further validating those assumptions at scale, or suggesting where further work needs to be done.

Polishing the User Experience

As patterns and frameworks are useful for developers as they implement code, patterns are useful when designing user experiences. Even when designing more complex or novel experiences that are being user tested, having a set of patterns to draw from can speed up this process. The "principle of least surprise" comes into play in user experience; a feature should work the way the user expects it to work, and consistency across your app, and the Web as a whole, is an effective way to help achieve this.

There are non-functional requirements that go into a user experience too. Things like use of images and colors, and the voice of the text, can set an atmosphere for users. For organizations that also have a physical presence, such as brick-and-mortar retailers, it can be important to make the web site feel like part of that same chain of physical stores, as this can reinforce any marketing messages that are being transmitted and set expectations for the experience based on that atmosphere.

A brand book is often the foundation for what a UX team delivers. It doesn't change often and provides a set of fundamentals for implementing a design: colors, typography, logos, and rules about how the brand should be projected. For example, a financial services company may be trying to project an image of being reliable and trustworthy with money. Writing error messages in an overly friendly format, or illustrating features with pictures of cartoon cats, may not be compatible with this goal, and these kinds of rules should be expressed in the brand book. These simple primitives, like colors and typography rules, are very effective in establishing consistency. Especially in large web sites or digital presences where there are different microservices for different parts of your frontends, any inconsistencies between these primitives can reveal the underlying seams of your application, which can be jarring for users who perceive you as a single site regardless of the underlying application structure.

When it comes to implementing new features, or entire new pages or screens on a web site, you can use different levels of fidelity to give these to a developer. The lowest level might simply be a wireframe, such as in Figure 3-1, which is a loose sketch showing how the page fits together and the high-level information architecture of that page.

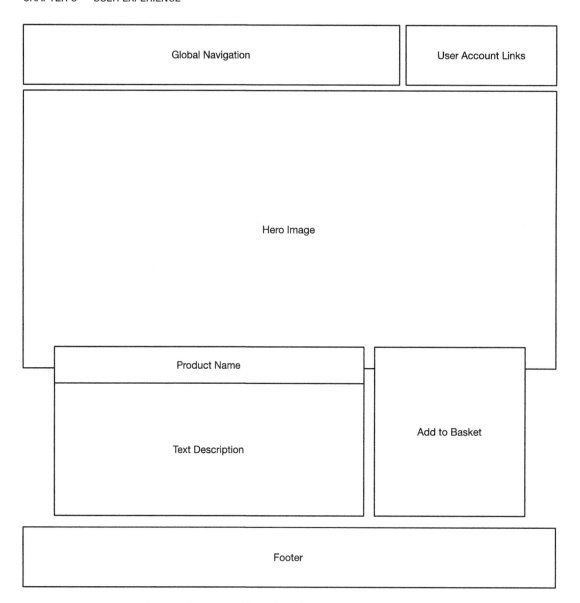

Figure 3-1. *A wireframe for a product landing page*

At the other end of the spectrum might be a fully detailed and annotated design specification representing every element on the page in pixels, such as in Figure 3-2.

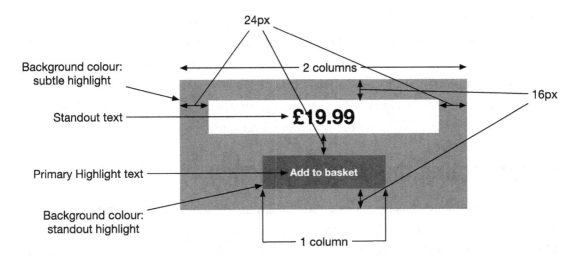

Figure 3-2. *An annotated design specification*

But as mentioned earlier, a new page will often make use of patterns that have existed before, and if a page reuses a pattern, there's often not a need to re-specify these details.

Sometimes these patterns are just re-using fundamentals, such as referring to colors that are referenced in the brand (e.g., instead of expressing a hex code in the design, reference to colors such as "primary color," which are defined in the brand book). Specifying these kinds of details can make it much easier for us to implement as developers, as it makes the underlying intention clear so we can optimize and reuse an implementation, rather than potentially re-implement the same code as it's not obvious that it's a reuse of a design pattern. Specifying typography in terms of common primitives is very powerful too.

When it comes to specifying layout, alignment of items on the page can have a pleasing aesthetic effect. This is sometimes referred to as a rhythm, and pages that do not have a rhythm can look messy and jarring. Attributes like even vertical spacing and alignment of items horizontally contribute to the aesthetic and feeling of a rhythm. A common tool to help enforce a rhythm on a page is to apply a "grid" to the page. Grids are made up columns, and they define column widths and gutters (white space to give elements room to breathe). All elements on the page then line up with column boundaries, and when it comes to dictating a page layout, a designer can simply specify the number of columns an item should take up. Grids can also help in designing variable width and responsive web sites, such as on mobile phones, as these columns can be defined as a percentage of available screen width, but still maintain the desirable property of "rhythm."

Many designers, especially for more complex applications, go a step further, and develop a library of components that can be reused. In this case, a wireframe can simply refer to components that may already exist in such a library (this is sometimes called a style guide, component library, or pattern library). If a new component is involved, then this is often first specified as a standalone item rather than in the context of the page where it is used, easing the ability to implement it reusably.

Implementing the User Experience

Once a user experience has been designed, it must be implemented. This is another area where collaboration between UX practitioners and software engineers can be invaluable. Most UX designers will work with an underlying set of rules, especially around alignment and rhythm of the placement of elements on a page, and an awareness of what these rules are will make it easier to create robust implementations of the designs a UX team has developed.

Many developers who have worked with CSS frameworks like Bootstrap will be familiar with the concept of a grid, in which elements are aligned vertically and horizontally across a page. Figure 3-3 shows a 12-column grid overlaid onto a web site design. Each column has a gutter separating it, allowing items in columns to have breathing room, but also for individual items to spread multiple columns.

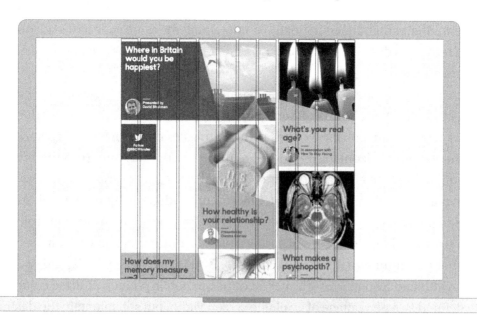

Figure 3-3. *A 12-column grid laid out over a landing page*

UX designers will often produce designs that align with their own concept of a grid, so it is important to make sure that whatever grid you use in your CSS is configured the same way as your designer's grid. Also common is the use of padding and margins in a design to give elements a consistent rhythm (through even spacing of elements). Understanding how a UX designer employs this concept means you can also start using variables to define these kinds of elements, as well as other elements that end up being reused, such as a color palette.

You do need to be careful when coordinating with a designer, in that sometimes the same words may not necessarily mean the same thing to both of you. For example, the way a designer uses the words "padding" and "margin" might not be exactly the same as the way a CSS box model defines them; a designer might specify a 12px padding between the text and the border of a box it's in. You might think a simple `padding: 12px` would suffice here, but if there is a `line-height` attribute applied to the text that makes the height of the line taller than the text within, then that could affect what a designer sees as the padding (they might define it as the top of the text to the edge of the border), in which case you might need to reduce the top and bottom padding described in CSS in order to match the padding the designer expects. Learning about the differences between the domains of design and implementation, through learning or just open communication, can help clarify the intent and avoid these kinds of misunderstandings. This works both ways, not only for a developer to understand the language of design, but for designers to understand the language of implementation, as both can grow to blur boundaries and work more closely together.

The CSS box model is an important concept to understand, including the way it differs from the way designers might express margins, paddings, and sizes. Figure 3-4 shows how the sizes of the different parts of the box compose together into the overall size. The CSS box model is used to define how the sizing specifications of a component are interpreted when it is presented on a page. The original box model was first defined in 1996 by the W3C as taking the width as specified in CSS and then adding on the padding, border and margin to determine the width of the whole element. However, until Internet Explorer 6, Microsoft implemented its own interpretation of the box model, where the width defined everything up to the border, and only the margin was added on.

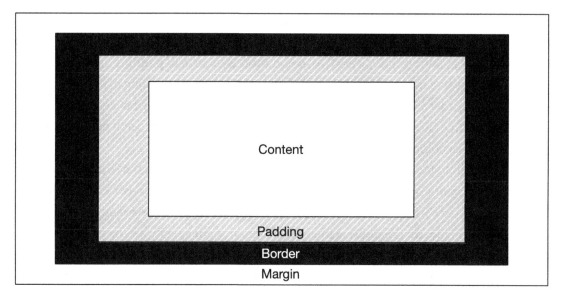

Figure 3-4. *The CSS box model*

Microsoft eventually replaced its implementation with the standardized one, but many felt that the Microsoft definition was more useful, and in CSS3, the option to change the CSS box model was introduced with the `box-sizing` directive. The default W3C style is known as `content-box,` and the Internet Explorer alternative is defined as `border-box`.

In order to generate a consistent look and feel across a site, designers will often reuse components. There are various common patterns used to do this, but they all derive from the same principles of having a hierarchy of components that are arranged to make an end result.

A popular system for doing this was defined by Brad Frost and known as atomic design. In atomic design, there are several levels of hierarchy:

- Atoms

- Molecules

- Organisms

- Templates

- Pages

An atom is the smallest unit of design, and often has one-to-one mapping with a HTML element—for example, a generic button or text field. This will often include all the possible states—for example, a button in a disabled or hover state, or text fields where validation is failing. Atoms are combined into molecules, which are a more useful component because they represent some distinct functionality. A molecule might be an address finder or a search box, something that represents a distinct part of user functionality but not so much that it becomes a stage of the journey in its own right.

The layer above molecules is known as organisms. Organisms are distinctive elements of a page that may be reusable in theory, but are often only used once. The ubiquitous header and footer of a web page may be an organism that is reused, but a "confirm shipment" organism, which consists of atoms and molecules to build forms and capture other bits of information, will only be used once in a checkout process.

Templates put organisms into a structure (without content) that is essentially a whole view for the user. Pages are templates that have been populated with content, either dynamically, if it's a product information page or similar, or statically, if it's something more like an "About Us" page.

The good thing about this kind of structure is that it maps well into the ways of implementing design specifications using HTML and CSS. Atoms can be implemented as CSS classes, which are applied to plain HTML elements. Molecules and organisms are often implemented either as template partials or as components in virtual DOM libraries like React, then get composed together into templates that are populated with real data to make a page.

The other most important aspect to translate from a design into an implementation is the typography—the look and feel of the text on the page. Typography is one of the most studied parts of design, since as far back as movable type in East Asia at the start of the second millennium. Many typography purists decry the lack of control that web technology gives designers and developers over the rendering of text, but many have overcome the challenge, and with proper control, good typography can be achieved.

As with individual page components in atomic design, it's a good idea to design a series of typography atoms that are then included in the individual components, rather than constantly reimplementing typography rules per component. This can give you a high level of consistency in the look and feel of text across your application.

It can be tempting to simply apply typography rules to headings and paragraph tags directly, but this can reduce flexibility. For example, if the visual structure of your page means it makes sense to skip a heading level, then doing so introduces accessibility issues into your application. Additionally, you might want to style elements such as form labels at different levels depending on their context, so having a series of CSS classes or SCSS mix-ins is a more flexible approach.

A popular school of thought dictates giving your typography atoms generic names that do not link them to specific page elements, which can give designers and developers more freedom to use the right classes, rather than having a jarring feeling of applying a class called "heading" to a `<p>` tag if that's the right thing to do. The BBC's Global Experience Language, for example, uses names such as "Primer," "Canon," and "Trafalgar" as typography identifiers.

It is no surprise that the transition of digital design from being analogous to print design to embracing the UX-focused methods we see today has happened hand in hand with the need for and rise in responsive design. Responsive design is all about making your site or app work on all sizes of screen. For many designers, this was a significant shift in mindset, as previously "pixel-perfect" designs were produced and expected to be implemented. In responsive design, the concept of a breakpoint is introduced. A breakpoint is usually based on device width (but could be based on attributes such as device height or aspect ratio, too), and designers will often design each component or page with a mode for either side of a layout, perhaps changing attributes of the typography, spacing, or layout. It is common to produce design specifications that are representative of each break point, but it is impossible to cover every case, especially for smaller screens where variable width is most common.

Implementing a responsive design once again shows that a close working relationship between a designer and a developer is important. The developer must understand the designer's intention, as it is no longer a simple case of just replicating a design pixel-for-pixel, as there are gaps between any representative breakpoint structure a designer may have designed for. Similarly, a developer may find gaps in a design— certain screen widths where assumptions (commonly about how much text can fit into a particular area) fail, in which case a designer must rethink and correct.

Another difference between the worlds of a visual designer and a developer is in the definition of a pixel. You might think that a pixel is an individual bit of light on a computer monitor, but in CSS, this is not true. The underlying pixel implementation is called a "display pixel," but CSS pixels are known as "reference pixels." A reference pixel is defined as a single pixel on a 96dpi screen that is at arm's length from the viewer. This might seem complicated, but it allows you to design a site that will appear roughly the same size regardless of the pixel density of a screen and the viewer's distance from it.

Mobile phones often have a smaller physical pixel size, but as mobile phones are held closer to the eyes, the ratio is maintained, and devices with "retina" or high-DPI screens will map a single CSS pixel onto multiple device pixels. It is important for designers to understand this, as this means if a designer is working on a responsive design with a specific screen size in mind, it is the CSS pixels that matter, not the display pixels. For example, when the iPhone 4 (the first "retina" iPhone) came out, you still specified dimensions as if the width of the device was 320px, despite the actual screen being 640 physical pixels across.

You can take advantage of the fact that there are multiple device pixels underlying a CSS pixel, as text and vector graphics will render at the higher resolution with the upscaling being handled by the underlying browser renderer. Similarly, you can load bitmap graphics that may appear to be scaled down when their size is expressed in CSS pixels, but will render at their native resolution if the device pixels allow it.

The final thing to consider is that there may be cases where the skills of a dedicated designer aren't available to you. This is often the case for views like admin panels or other development tools. Fortunately, by working with designers on other components, and through designers using systems like atomic design, you should have enough knowledge to proceed regardless. By picking and choosing components from a component library, and using color palettes defined in a brand book, as well as using components that have some proven usability, you should be able to implement a design that feels consistent with the look and feel of the rest of the product. There's no harm in doing ad-hoc guerrilla testing yourself (especially if the users are your peers, in the case of development tools) to help refine the front end too.

Information architecture is important too when it comes to implementing a design. Understanding the underlying information hierarchy can help you avoid mistakes in choosing HTML elements such as heading elements or `<aside>` tags. Although it may be tempting to be satisfied with the hierarchy being expressed visually, using the correct semantics for the underlying HTML is important for users of accessible technology to understand your design too.

Summary

User experience is a relatively modern discipline that's arisen from several interconnected fields, and is most often associated with the principles of user-centered design, where the needs of the user are placed first and foremost, with any aesthetic design considerations being secondary.

The lines of UX become blurred between business analyst and front-end developer, and as a full stack developer, you'll be expected to understand those UX principles too, even if you have dedicated UX specialists on your team.

Information architecture is one aspect of UX that deals with how content is organized on a web site or app, specifically to be in a place where the user wants to see it. Another aspect of UX is that of testing, where any assumptions in the design of a feature or a site can be tested to validate that they are correct and increase the usability of a site. This user testing can range from small-scale observations to generate deep insights (qualitative data) to using analytics to generate shallow but broad insights on performance with your entire user base (quantitative data).

Designing and implementing a user experience needs to happen hand in hand and use a common language to minimize friction. Using techniques to break down designs into components is one way of doing this, and also allows for reusability of implemented code and increases usability of the site by implementing common patterns. Documenting the fundamentals of a design also helps with consistency.

CHAPTER 4

Designing Systems

It's rare for a web application nowadays to be built in isolation. As a full stack developer, you're likely to have to work on entire systems, not just a single component within a system, and doing this effectively means being able to think at a different level of abstraction when problem solving.

In a modern organization, the system will be constantly growing and changing, although individual components may remain stable. Your job is to design those components in a way that maximizes agility—that is, when something changes in the future, it shouldn't be painful to transition. These components can exist at any level of abstraction, from very high levels of an organization's architecture to individual classes and modules in a codebase, and these principles can be applied at any level as well.

The type of systems a full stack developer will come across in their career will range from the simple (such as a brochureware site) to the massively complex (e.g., an account management site for a utility, which has many functions and has to integrate with the central billing and CRM components of a huge enterprise architecture), and it's important to know how to work within all these types of environments. Even what might at first seem like a simple, standalone component can quickly become entangled in other systems without careful thought, or can become a silo that could duplicate functionality or isolate data that already exists inside the organization.

A well-designed system can quickly become greater than the sum of its parts through the network effect. Some organizations have an "architect" role (or several) that is solely responsible for designing these systems and the interactions between them, usually at an application level. Even when there is a dedicated architect, it is important to ensure that you're thinking about the system as a whole too, and not just the single components within it.

© Chris Northwood 2018
C. Northwood, *The Full Stack Developer*, https://doi.org/10.1007/978-1-4842-4152-3_4

System Architectures

Two common types of system architectures you may come across are "monolithic" and "microservices," but in reality, most systems will lie somewhere on the spectrum between those two extremes. These generally refer to organizing individual applications within the system, and how they interact, rather than at a smaller level. Both styles have their pros and cons: monoliths can be easier to build initially, but have the downside of becoming large and difficult to change if multiple teams work on the same codebase. Microservices require a strong platform to grow from, but can be easier to adapt and change in the future.

WHAT IS A MICROSERVICE?

A microservice is a small service that takes responsibility for one part of a system. It can be deployed and scaled independently of any other part of the system, and communicates through well-defined APIs. Microservices can be thought of as applications of the single responsibility principle from SOLID (discussed in more detail later in this chapter) at a system rather than class level. A microservice architecture is therefore composed of a number of these microservices that are deployed and orchestrated as a larger system of individual components.

By contrast, a monolith is a single codebase with a single application that performs all the functions of that system. It may be scalable, but the scale is achieved by duplicating the whole system on other machines, rather than individual components of it. Although it may expose an API for external systems to integrate with it, internal components of the system communicate via method or function calls.

Figure 4-1 shows the contrast between these two architectures. Although the microservices system seems more complex, this is only because it forces you to make interactions between services explicit, rather than the potentially complex hidden interaction model within a single app.

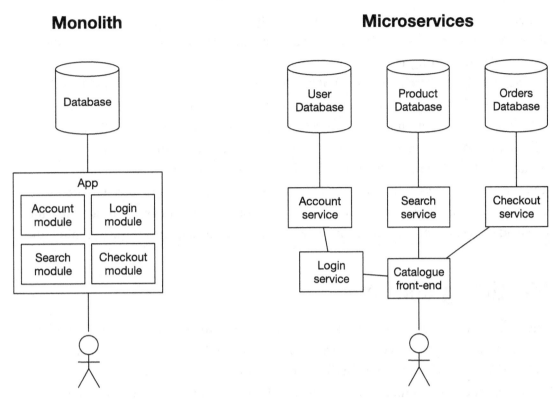

Figure 4-1. *A monolith systems diagram versus a microservice equivalent*

When working with large systems, a well-designed microservice architecture will allow you to limit those changes and growths to individual parts of the system, meaning it can be quicker to move since there are fewer moving parts involved. But this can be hard to design. For small systems, the overhead of managing microservices can be too big to be worth it, and can slow down initial development. Microservices are slow to get started, but often allow you to maintain a good pace of development that can be tricky with a monolithic design.

Even when designing systems with growth in mind, it can be especially helpful to start with a single application and codebase, and then break that out into microservices when that single application starts to become too big.

The trick to designing a system at the application level is to make each component as small as it needs to be, but no smaller. This is easier said than done, and there is no hard-and-fast science or rules to apply. System design can be more of an art, and very context dependent, so it's useful for a team to design collaboratively. Following patterns for software architectures that might already exist inside your organization is a good start, as it can make integrating against dependencies easier.

What a software architecture is *not* is a list of a technologies that are used to build your system. At the point the architecture is designed, you should only care about capturing the concepts and their interactions, and then determine where they sit within the system. Once you have identified these, you can use your non-functional requirements to determine the properties each component in your system must have, and then find the best technology fit for each one of those. Trying to force technology choices into an architecture before the concepts, interactions, and systems are identified can lead to decisions that compromise the goals of making a good software architecture.

Identifying Concepts

The tiered application hierarchy is a common approach to designing systems, whether it's the ubiquitous Model-View-Controller architecture (shown in Figure 4-2) of most web applications (or a variation on this, such as Model-View-View Model) or the three-tier model of an enterprise architecture. In order to fit your system into these models, you first need to identify two things: the domain concepts that you care about (for example, this could be customers, stock inventory, or news articles), and the ways the users interact with them.

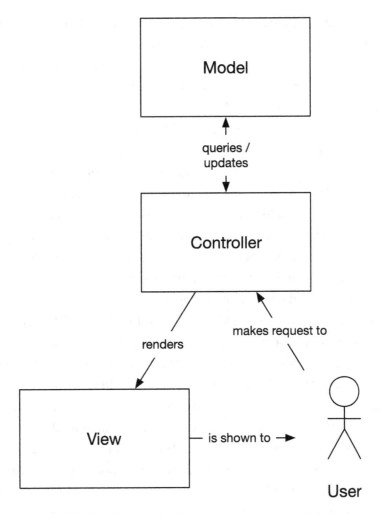

Figure 4-2. *Model-View-Controller architecture*

The domain concepts will form your model layer in a Model-View-Controller (MVC) app, or your persistence/business logic components in a three-tier architecture. The interaction methods will form the view and controller (or view model) of an MVC app, or the presentation layer in a three-tier architecture.

In MVC, the view deals with actually presenting the detail to a user (in a web framework, this is often HTML templates), whereas the controller deals with getting all the data and values that are needed to create a template, and performing any actions that a request may have asked for.

It can be tempting to add logic relating to models into a controller in an MVC app (for example, building a model up), but a controller is too heavily coupled to a particular view, and most logic actually belongs to a concept itself, making the model a more appropriate place for it. The "fat model, thin controller" approach can make refactoring an architecture much easier at a later date, as it can allow you to extract concepts into their own APIs, which are shared across multiple components.

In an object-oriented world, the downside of the fat model approach is that it can bloat your classes significantly. Rather than adding lots of methods to a class, you can instead implement other useful classes that help you manipulate models. If you're using a language that mixes different paradigms, such as JavaScript or Python, then implementing these as functions can also be helpful, leaving the only state in the model. There are many different types of helpers you can separate from a model. For example, builders are useful to help build a model (out of a form, for instance), and validation logic could also be extracted when it makes sense to do so.

The Model-View-View Model (MVVM) pattern differs from MVC in that the controller disappears and a View Model is bound specifically to a view. In a typical MVC controller, you may have a controller with a method for dealing with a GET and one for dealing with a POST. For the GET case, the controller would fetch an appropriate model and render the view by passing through values. In the POST case, the controller would read the request, perform any appropriate validation, and then apply those changes to a model. In MVVM, a view model is instead "bound" to a view, so that when the view is rendered, getters on the view model make the values available in the template appropriately. To deal with the POST case, setters are used to make the changes back.

Beyond variations on MVC like MVVM, MVC has evolved beyond its initial function. Although many server-side web frameworks, such as PHP's Laravel, Ruby's Rails or Python's Django use MVC (although Django confusingly uses the terms Model, View, and Template for the Model, Controller, and View, respectively), it is not uncommon to see slight adaptations to the MVC architecture, especially when it comes to things like kicking off long-running actions.

The lines of MVC tend to become blurred in client-side code. As JavaScript has become more common on the server too, it's not uncommon to find NodeJS applications that do not strictly subscribe to MVC patterns. This is often because of the tendency of JS applications to be made by composing libraries together, rather than choosing frameworks. However, many apps (sometimes by design, other times through a natural tendency, as it is an effective way of organizing concerns) using NodeJS will have an MVC-like structure, even if not explicitly.

In the popular React+Redux combination, it is common to structure your app such that the Redux store is your model, and then have the React components as the view. The Redux connect() function then maps the state in the store and dispatchable actions to properties, and this mapping provides the role of the controller. However, views can also nest other components, which themselves might be wrapped in a connect(), so a view can include another controller. This hierarchical method might look like MVC close up, but from further away it becomes clear it is not, though the separation of concerns remains useful.

MVC often falls down when there is rich UI interaction. For example, when manipulating the UI, not every action necessarily needs to persist in the model, but there is some temporary state that is stored somewhere. If you wanted to implement a drag-and-drop interface, then in pure MVC, you would have to persist every movement to the store going through a controller. Instead, it is common for the "View" to instead store its own state, only going through the controller when the item is dropped, so that the model is correctly updated. MVC is a good starting point, but you should not artificially constrain yourself strictly to the pattern-it has limitations when it's okay to break the pattern too.

Similar to the way a React+Redux app is composed of many layers of things that are loosely analogous to layers of views and controllers, you will often find yourself doing the same in your application too. Your server-side code will often be structured in MVC, along with any rich UI code, although the two may not necessarily be linked. Although some models may be shared, it's likely your server-side and client-side code will differ somewhat, and the concerns of the controllers will be different. The server-side code is often more concerned with validation and security, while the client-side code may be less concerned with these factors.

When identifying the concepts that make up your models, it's also important to understand the context in which you're making those identifications. Domain-driven design (DDD) is a methodology in software engineering that helps manage these problems. At the core of DDD is the concept of the domain: the things that your organization knows and does that are relevant to a project. The domain is based in the reality of your organization, and it is through reality that we can identify the models. By starting at the level of what people in your organization currently do and how they refer to things, and using this as a basis for building your models, it becomes easier to build software that matches the actions people actually want to do.

Sometimes, this collection of models is known as an ontology—that is, the structure that defines your domain. It is usually helpful to use consistent terminology throughout a system. For example, an e-commerce store might refer to "items of stock" in the logistics area, but "products" in the front end, but these may mean the same thing, so using a single term throughout your system can simplify things.

Although it can be very tempting to rely on a single model definition that can be used throughout a system, it is also important to recognize that those models are also used in different contexts. As I touched on before, the context of an item in client-side code may be different to that of the data store, so using an appropriate variation of the model in that context makes sense. These models may be different implementations of the same concepts, but they need to translate to the same concept in another context. For example, moving from a client-side to server-side context can involve POSTing a form to a server, and it can be tempting to just re-use the POST data directly. However, what you should instead do is translate between the two contexts, using a method that accepts the form data of that model, and returns a new object that makes sense in the context of the server-side code. This translation can often be fairly simple, but is also a good place to do things like authorization checks or validation. Performing this translation as things move between your contexts can reduce bugs, as each context comes with its own set of assumptions, and moving data between contexts without translating it appropriately can mean different assumptions on that data that are no longer true.

A common pitfall here is to conflate similar concepts in your domain, or work at a level of abstraction that's too high. One example may be in a large enterprise system, which has to deal with the concepts of customers and employees. It can be tempting to try to unify these into some sort of "people" concept, but in most systems, the concepts of employees and customers are different enough to benefit from remaining separate, and any concerns about "duplicating" data (for example, if an employee also appears in the customer database) are never realized.

Many of the identified core concepts will have state that needs to be managed, which means that there needs to be a data store and the business logic for querying and manipulating the store. The exception here is where components and concepts for user interaction are used, which either have no persistence, or only persistence relating to temporary or session data, rather than core concepts. When the architecture is realized, this persistence and business logic can be split into separate components—one for your database, and then an API that interacts with that database and implements your business logic. When modelling your system architecture, it's useful to think of them as one concept that's bound together.

When it comes to realizing the architecture, it's important to choose the right data store for these concepts to enable persistence. NoSQL datastores are popular, but there's still a place for relational data, especially when integrity is very important, or the model is very well-defined and stable. This is discussed further in the Storing Data chapter.

Dealing with the business logic of the core domain concept with the datastore as a single high-level component provides a good level of abstraction for the other components to deal with those concepts. All manipulation of these concepts in your persistence layer then becomes an implementation detail of an API, rather than the persistence layer becoming an integration point itself. Multiple applications accessing the same database directly can cause problems for data integrity and deployments, especially if any schema changes are involved, so the API that implements the business logic wraps the database and becomes the single point of interaction for other components. Remember that the goal here is for each component to be able to grow and move independently of each other, and this encapsulation enables that.

Identifying User Interactions

User journeys and stories (or epics) can help identify user interactions. Once you identify which journeys a user wants to take, they can come together into a single front-end component. It's very tempting to group your user interactions by concept, but this will often result in a lot of unrelated code in the same component, and ideally you want each set of related things to move at its own speed. Separating by user can often go far. For example, on an e-catalog site, staff may be responsible for updating and maintaining the catalog that users then browse, but the user journeys for browsing the catalog are very distinct from maintaining it, so these should be different components.

For those who have worked with a framework that's good at making CRUD (Create-Read-Update-Delete) apps, this may at first seem counterintuitive—it's typical in these frameworks to designate one controller per concept, with actions for things that occur on those controllers. Often, the code you need to execute this is auto-generated for you! However, one of the key goals we want to achieve is the ability to grow each part of the system independently, without introducing risks to other parts of the system, so we can maintain our pace of change. The user stories and interactions in a management system will often grow in a very different direction to one relating to the browsing component, and by linking the two together, you may find yourself being dragged down by having to change more than if you'd kept them separate.

Handling Commonalities

Once you have identified the individual components in your system, you are then likely to have a good understanding of the boundaries of those components, but it's also likely you have identified some common dependencies in your system (these are likely to be core elements of your organization, such as content, customers, or inventory). If these common dependencies are domain concepts, they can be abstracted together behind an API, and if they're interactions, a shared library or component between your front-end applications is the best place for it.

Working with Legacy and External Dependencies

In many organizations, there are likely to be systems outside the scope of what you're responsible for. This could be an off-the-shelf or SaaS system bought by your organization or a project managed by another team. You need to capture these dependencies so you know how your system interacts with them. It's important to remember that although you're likely to have less influence over these external dependencies, they are not set in stone, and you can request that the people that own these make changes. If you're having to ask for lots of changes, perhaps this component should actually belong to your team, in order to reduce the risk of introducing blockers. If these systems are legacy, or are a dependency for a number of components within your system, it can be helpful to insert a facade or an abstraction layer between it and you. Especially if a system is legacy, introducing a new interface can assist in decommissioning it, as this interface can be changed to abstract away a replacement service without having to update all the clients that depend on the legacy component. This is known as the strangler pattern.

When designing your system, it's important to understand any non-digital components that might exist in it, and how any interactions they have—for example, printing out dispatch labels, or shipping a physical product. You may not be responsible for building these, but it's important to ensure that the design of any physical processes fits in with your architecture in order to avoid painful integrations later. Ultimately, you should be able to trace every interaction with a user, data, and response to an action that is generated through the entire system, including its real-world components. Treating these non-digital dependencies like external dependencies will often help.

Component Interactions

It's important to understand the relationships between these components, and the way they need to communicate. The way to do this is to reflect on the different scenarios through which a user may come to use the system, and the paths and workflows a user takes to accomplish their goals. These are called user journeys, and it's useful to identify which front-end component each journey belongs to, consider which concepts it needs to interact with, and determine the nature of that interaction.

In a typical web architecture, there are three ways for components to interact: asking for data; taking an action synchronously, such as when the result of the action, or knowing when it was completed, matters; or taking an action asynchronously, when either the result doesn't matter, or the time taken to perform this action is so long that it makes no sense to wait for it to finish before showing the user. The latter case includes actions that are completely digital and take a long time, like video transcoding, or involve activity in the real world, such as sending out a membership card or shipping a product. For these types of asynchronous actions, all the user needs to know is whether or not the request to take the action has succeeded, so the asynchronicity can be hidden behind a synchronous service.

There are two common communication types between components in a system: requests using HTTP and message queues. For requesting data or making synchronous changes, HTTP is a natural fit, and a particular type of HTTP interaction known as REST is a popular choice—I will cover this later. HTTP GET can be used for requesting data, and HTTP POST or PUT should be used for making changes. For asynchronous actions, where it doesn't matter to the user whether it succeeds or not (this could be something like recording analytics), message queues are a good fit. However, if the code is front-end code, it is often easy to make a fire-and-forget XHR call (XMLHttpRequest, a browser API for making HTTP requests, and an important part of the asynchronous JavaScript and XML-AJAX technique). With this kind of fire-and-forget call, the result of processing may not need to be surfaced to the user— they simply need to know that the request has been made—although for others, tracking progress may be needed, where RESTful queries can be used to interact with jobs on a message queue.

With all of these things identified, it's then important to reassess the boundaries of these components, and also at what level these components live. If there are two components that seem to communicate with each other a lot, this could indicate that they actually belong in the same component. On the other hand, if there's a central component that everything seems to talk to, this may suggest that this component does too much, and there could be smaller elements that should be extracted, or that perhaps it's capturing a concept at too high a level of abstraction.

When defining the interactions above, we also determine the actions that a concept needs to be able to perform. Some of these actions, especially if they're large or asynchronous, may belong in their own components. With this in mind, it's important to identify these new components and their communication style. When multiple events are triggered by a single action, or when an event happens in response to multiple actions, it can be helpful to introduce topic-based message queues. In this approach, the thing that causes an event does not necessarily need to know all the actions that event will cause. It simply sends a message to a topic queue, and everything that listens to that queue will perform appropriately.

An enterprise service bus (ESB) is a popular tool that, on the surface, appears similar to a message queue, but offers a much deeper set of features. In an ESB, you place a message onto the bus, and then the ESB distributes that message to all the components that need it. The ESB becomes a single point of integration for all components, as shown in Figure 4-3, which is both its major selling point and its biggest weakness. It is often the ESB that controls how messages are routed (rather than an application determining which topics to subscribe to), and ESBs can perform additional actions on messages in flight, such as changing the transport mechanism or transforming the message itself, as well as auditing and security. They essentially become a single point of failure and a single integration point at which to scale. The most common use case for ESBs is integrating many distinct components together, as the ESB can hide the complexity of integration, but you should instead consider having well-defined APIs on these services, as this can allow for more independent scaling of systems.

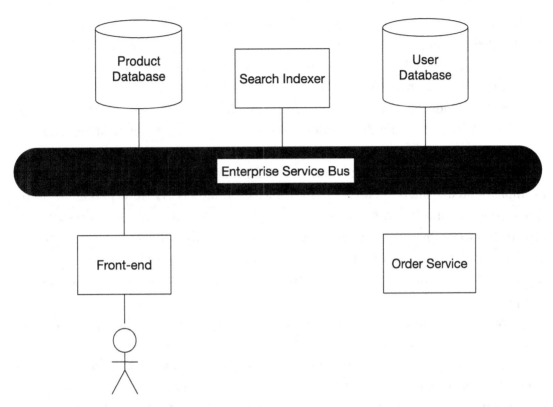

Figure 4-3. *Modules connected to an enterprise service bus*

It can be very tempting to introduce an ESB to handle the interactions between backend components, especially if you're moving from a legacy system that uses an ESB already. But you should be aware that many ESBs are designed to be plugged into existing components (often sold by the same vendor as the ESB) and serve as a place to configure those components. This is where the need for many of the features of an ESB come from. By making use of these features, you run the risk of subtle logic ending up in your ESB, so changes will be spread across multiple applications, and managing changes to this single shared component become tightly controlled to avoid risk. A microservice approach where each components maintains a higher degree of independence aims to avoid this.

Using standard approaches for communications (like message queues and REST) will generally give you more flexibility than an ESB can, and usually at a much lower cost. Avoiding this kind of vendor lock-in can give your organization more agility too; there's no need to get locked in to expensive contracts.

One of the primary reasons to use an ESB is that it offers abstraction towards many different legacy components. To get around this, a common pattern known as the facade pattern can be used. Where a component has an odd API, or an action is actually spread across many different backend services, a facade can be implemented. An application that uses the facade pattern doesn't actually do much by itself; it simply exists to present a common API on top of another service and translate between that new API and the original one.

Though there are desirable features to an ESB, such as logging, these benefits can be implemented in alternate ways. For example, a common HTTP library could be used across your organization with defaults for logging, or tools such as API gateways can provide these (but beware, as many API gateways provide the same kind of functionality as ESBs, and should be avoided). Otherwise, providing easy-to-use libraries or other functionalities to teams means they can be integrated in a way that makes sense for that component.

A warning for using message queues: make sure you understand the characteristics of the message queue you use. For example, guarantees about delivery vary between implementations. You should also keep the actual communication logic of the message queue at the edge of the application, in case you need to move to a different message queue implementation (for example, if you move from AWS cloud to another one). This mitigates the risk of vendor lock-in, where some technologies may no longer make business sense for an organization to use, but technology coupling prevents the organization from making that choice.

Applications vs. Modules

Some of these components could just be modules inside a larger application, or they could be applications by themselves. A good rule of thumb to follow is the "single responsibility principle," in which each application only does one thing, but does it well. This is sometimes known as "the UNIX way," after a design principle used to build the original UNIX command line tools.

However, the real world involves many more trade-offs, and for whichever platform you're using to deploy, there will always be an overhead for each application, and it's important to balance the overhead for each application with the benefits of keeping each component small. An ideal platform would make that overhead as small as possible: being self-service, with high levels of automation, while providing common functions. This is discussed further in the Deployment chapter. There is also often a cost implication of having multiple applications. It's very common in the cloud to deploy one application per (virtual) machine, so more applications require more machines, although a technique known as containerization can address this at the risk of introducing additional complexity and a lower level of isolation to your platform.

Cross-Functional Requirements

The cross-functional requirements of your system will also have an effect on the architecture, and how you decide whether or not different components belong as distinct applications or just as modules inside a larger service. Cross-functional requirements (often called non-functional requirements) are those that cross every feature of your system, rather than a feature built once in isolation. The most important cross-functional requirements are those that specify the desired performance and scale of a system, as well as attributes such as security.

Satisfying performance requirements can be hard in a distributed system. Generally, the more connections exist between your components in order to complete a single journey, the slower they will run unless you optimize (caching is one common way to do so).

Making a RESTful call across an HTTP interface will always be much slower than calling a function in another module in the same application. Instead of introducing caching, you may be tempted to make a shared library that is distributed with each application in your system, but this can be an anti-pattern. If your business logic changes, you now need to update that library in every component that uses it (which means you have to keep track of everywhere it's used) and redeploy that component. If it's a big change, different parts of your system might have different versions of the business logic as all these deployments happen. It's much better to have one place where your business logic is specified, that can be managed without having an impact on a large number of systems when it changes. Be wary of even small shared libraries, if having different versions of that library in production will cause problems.

One example of a successful case of using a shared library was an HTTP library. This library wrapped an HTTP request library, but added additional logging to help diagnose issues and transparently handled our HTTP authorization scheme. Having multiple copies in production caused no issues—for example, fixing a bug didn't call for a new version of that library to be immediately rolled out, as the bug only affected one service that used a particular feature. The shared library was decoupled from the logic of the backends it communicated with to enable this.

In terms of security concerns, you can identify which actions in your system are "trusted" and which are not to ensure that the endpoints are appropriately protected. It can be very effective to separate applications along security lines. For example, a component that can register a user (an action anyone can perform) may want to live in a separate application from the one that can search the user database (an action that may be limited to call center staff). This allows "security-in-depth," assuming your platform and API calls have a good security system, allowing you to put the searching application behind platform-level security rather than relying on application-level security. Platform-level security is usually more heavily audited and reviewed, and this reduces the risk of an application-level bug.

Regardless of the architecture you decide on, it's often very effective to build each application to be stateless; for example, not storing sessions server-side, or in a database that lives outside your application. This allows you to make deployments by replacing an application at the level of the machine and scale horizontally with multiple boxes behind a load balancer, which can go a long way to addressing scale. More detailed techniques for achieving this are discussed later on in the book.

Caching

When considering performance or load requirements, one powerful aspect of HTTP is its native support for caching. It can be tempting to put caches everywhere, especially around your HTTP GET calls, but this has an effect on the user experience of your application, as the information the user is seeing may be out of date. This is especially problematic when the user has updated something themselves (such as saving a new address and then still seeing the old one). Caches are also cumulative, so if there are multiple layers of caching between the user, it can take an unintentionally long time for the caches to expire.

Caches are also effectively an additional data-store, as they keep multiple copies of the data, and this can become out of date with the truth. In some contexts, this does not present a problem; for example, a new product not appearing in search results for five minutes may not be problematic, but a news site publishing breaking news that has to wait 30 minutes for a front-page index to update is. It's important to understand the effects of these delays on your user experience. When caches are used, it can be useful to combine them with event-based communications so that caches are invalidated in response to certain events. It's also possible to go one step beyond this and use events alone to build up a view of the data that only a specific application relies on, rather than using a core API for a single point of truth. This is an advanced technique!

Designing for Failure

The final thing to consider are the failure modes of this system, such as what happens when a single component fails or otherwise becomes unavailable. For message-queue-based approaches (whether as an asynchronous action, or in an event-based system), it's important to understand what happens if a message is received more than once, in the wrong order, or not at all, and to choose the underlying platform based on these requirements. For example, when adding a new component to a system that responds to events, consider whether it needs to have received all previous events that have occurred in the system to be up-to-date, or whether it will respond appropriately only to new ones.

Most responses to these failure modes can be handled in the individual applications themselves, and there are good techniques for doing this. For RESTful communications, the circuit breaker pattern is useful for protecting against failure of the underlying services, alongside caching layers (especially making use of functionality like stale-on-error). If possible, making synchronous communications asynchronous is also effective, as the messages remain on the queue until processed.

THE CIRCUIT BREAKER PATTERN

In real life, a circuit breaker is something that trips when it detects failure. The software circuit breaker is fairly similar. When the circuit breaker is "closed," everything operates normally, but when failure is detected, the circuit breaker "opens," stopping any requests to that backend service. After a period of time, the circuit breaker lets through a single request to see if the back end has recovered. If that request is successful, then the circuit breaker closes and things return to normal—otherwise, it waits again. The waiting is often some sort of exponential backoff with a random delay, to avoid accidentally flooding the back end the moment it recovers.

The method of determining failure can vary. A common method is incrementing a counter every time there is an error, and resetting it when there is success, with failure being detected when the counter passes a certain number. This has the downside of letting a partially broken service go through unprotected, so an alternative is to instead measure the percentage of failed to successful requests over a period of time, and determining failure based on a percentage of failed requests over a certain period of time. Remember to differentiate between expected and unexpected failures though! A 404 could be a valid response from a back-end service if you're requesting a resource you're not sure exists, and shouldn't count as a failure.

This is especially useful if the failure of the back-end service is related to load, and it needs some time to recover. Also, if the back-end service is failing by timing out, then not bothering to do the request can speed up the render of the page, especially if it's a non-critical part of the application that's failed.

Finally, it's also important to understand the effect of these failures on your user stories, and when designing the user experience. For example, if your site is an e-commerce site, but the component that determines whether an item is in stock or not is down, what should be presented to the user? There are a number of options, such as allowing orders and then refunding if the item turns out not to be in stock, or simply refusing to accept orders. The correct answer depends on the context of your organization.

It might seem that the need to handle many of these requirements would disappear if a monolith was built, rather than microservices, but in reality that system would be more brittle, as a failure could propagate to unrelated systems in the same monolith, so failure handling could not be avoided, although the cases to handle are different. The benefits of having a flexible system architecture, consisting of small, single-responsibility modules with well-defined interfaces, vastly outweighs the downside of having to manage failure modes between those modules, and you will end up with a more robust system as a result.

Designing Modules

In addition to designing the architecture of your entire system, you should also consider the structure of the individual components and modules within that system. The main difference between the design of an individual component and that of a system stems from different overheads relating to each of their constituent pieces. In a system, making a component too small introduces overhead for coordinating that component, but making it too big increases flexibility for scaling or building resilience into your system. Inside a single component, however, breaking it down into many smaller pieces introduces very little in the way of overhead, giving you the flexibility and simplicity of having many parts that do one thing well, without the coordination downside.

Another aspect to consider is that, inside a component, it becomes trivial to refactor across module boundaries (as long as they do not stray into other parts of the system), which means that you can minimize up-front architectural planning inside an individual component, as the cost of correcting mistakes is smaller. The cost is not zero though, so putting some thought into application structure is beneficial.

One major upfront decision about an individual component is which technologies to use: programming languages, frameworks, and libraries. In a perfect world, choosing the best technology and language to implement the requirements of a particular component would be the obvious answer, but a component always exists as part of a larger system. Using languages and frameworks that are already in use in other components can maximize the efficiency of a team because they do not have to context switch. In a greenfield build, this can be a risky choice. In web development, the two dominant approaches are to use a framework such as Angular, Rails, or Django, or to instead build something by bolting libraries together (perhaps with a relatively small framework facilitating this). Frameworks can be extremely powerful, but inflexible. For example, Rails lets you create monolithic CRUD applications very easily, but only if you work in the way that it expects you to work. If you don't, you may encounter resistance, and it may actually be slower than not using the framework at all. On the other hand, using libraries can be slower to initiate, and involve writing more code to glue the libraries together, but if you need to build a very domain-specific type of application, this gives you the flexibility to configure your application as you wish. Frameworks are also harder to move away from, as almost all code must be built in the style of that framework, whereas libraries are easier to replace in an application because only the parts that interact with that library are dependent on it.

When choosing a framework or deciding which libraries to use, make sure that you fully understand the capability and use case of the framework or libraries you pick, and that they actually meet your needs.

Designing individual components is much better understood than designing the kind of complex, distributed systems that many organizations now use. The concept of microservices didn't come around until 2011, whereas design patterns for applications were first discussed in the 1980s, and the famous *Design Patterns* book published in 1994. Of course, since then, the field of developing applications has continued to evolve and be further refined. A design pattern is a recommended (and tried-and-tested) approach for solving a particular type of problem in application design. When using frameworks, you are often forced to use particular patterns, but when using libraries, you will often need to implement the patterns yourself.

There are many design patterns, but there are subtleties to the context in which you should apply them. Many of the design patterns in the eponymous book were developed in the context of the C++ language, and others in early versions of Java. In other languages, features that do not exist in C++ or older versions of Java can make a design pattern superfluous.

Design Patterns is also mostly concerned with patterns for object-oriented programming, which has been the dominant programming paradigm in recent decades—however, it is not the only one. Languages like JavaScript and Python allow you to mix procedural and functional styles alongside OOP, but understanding object-oriented principles of design allows you to apply the same concepts to these paradigms too.

In addition to design patterns, many principles have evolved that help drive good design and engineering. Many of these have adopted catchy acronyms like KISS, DRY, and SOLID. "Keep it simple stupid" (KISS) encourages developers to write code that is approachable for an average developer to help with future maintainability, rather than adding in additional layers of abstraction that may be elegant but are unnecessary to solve the problem at hand. "Don't repeat yourself" (DRY) encourages you to only implement needed functionality or concepts once, and then use them across multiple modules where appropriate. Correct application of DRY is discussed later in this chapter. SOLID refers to five different concepts:

- Single responsibility principle

- Open/closed principle

- Liskov substitution principle

- Interface segregation principle

- Dependency inversion principle

The SOLID principles scale up or down depending on the scale you're working at. The larger components of a well-architected system could be said to be SOLID, as well as the individual classes or functions within each component.

The *single responsibility principle*, for example, is one of the driving factors behind microservices. The principle states that each individual class in your system should only take responsibility for a single thing. A corollary to this is that for each responsibility your system takes on, there should be a single part of your system responsible for handling it. For example, if a part of your system calculates VAT costs, then if the VAT rate changes, then you should only need to update a single part of your system, and that same class should also not be concerned with other tasks, such as calculating delivery costs.

According to the *open/closed principle*, a particular bit of code should be open for extension but closed for modification. This is mostly applied to reusable bits of functionality. It dictates that each other class that uses your class should be able to extend its functionality beyond what is provided to satisfy its use case, without having to modify the module it is inheriting from. In object-oriented programming, this is often taken to mean inheritance, but it can also mean that any dependencies specified are done so using interfaces, so alternative implementations can be used.

Barbara Liskov originally described the *Liskov substitution principle* in her 1994 paper as "Let $\phi(x)$ be a property provable about objects x of type T. Then $\phi(y)$ should be true for objects y of type S where S is a subtype of T." (Barbara Liskov and Jeannette Wing, "A behavioral notion of subtyping," ACM Transactions on Programming Languages and Systems (TOPLAS), vol. 16, #6, 1994). Although this mathematical description can seem intimidating, it simply means that if you extend a module, or provide modules with the same interface and intend for them to be used interchangeably, then the assumptions that the user of that class has about how to interact and use it must hold between everything that implements or extends that interface. For example, if you have different modules for calculating delivery costs that implement the same interface, but one of those requires you to enter the total weight of the shipment, and the others do not, this can be said to violate the principle. All modules must also require the total weight to be known, even if nothing is done with it, in order to keep the interface and the assumptions the same. If you do not use this, then any time these classes are used in your codebase, you will have to be aware of an edge case, rather than it being a truly reusable component.

Some programming languages allow you to formally specify these cases in the form of preconditions or postconditions, and to test them. A precondition is an assertion that must be true for you to be able to correctly use an interface, and a postcondition is something you can assert about the output of a function or method, if the preconditions were satisfied. For example, in our VAT calculator case, we could express a precondition that the input must be a list of objects that consist of a price, which is a non-negative, and whether or not it's VAT exempt, which is a boolean. The postcondition is that it will give you a non-negative integer. Some computer science theory goes further than this to fully specify pre- and postconditions in mathematical form in order to make systems that are mathematically provable as correct, but this is something you will be unlikely to come across on a day-to-day basis.

The 'I' in SOLID is the *interface-segregation principle*, which says that a user of an interface should not be required to depend on more methods than it actually needs in order to complete its task. This is related to the single responsibility principle of keeping classes small and focused on a single thing. If a class gets too big, or an interface does too much, then it's best to break it into smaller classes with more tightly scoped interfaces.

For example, a shopping cart can be added to or read from, but during the checkout process, it only needs to be read from. If the interface for your shopping cart gets too large, you could split it into two—one that deals with adding and another with reading—and then have a class that implements both interfaces.

Dependency inversion is one of the more famous components of SOLID and, especially in frameworks for strong object-oriented languages like Java, one you are forced to tackle head-on, especially if you want to do any unit testing. The approach to building a running system out of components that implement dependency inversion is called dependency injection. Dependency injection can also be a headache for new developers, those who are not used to enterprise environments, and those who are coming from weaker OO languages, but this is more due to overly large and onerous dependency injection frameworks than the concept itself. With dependency inversion, you are not responsible for finding the classes or modules that you need to do your tasks; instead, you are given them. Sometimes this is done using dependency injection frameworks like Spring, but you can also write code that injects the appropriate methods directly (known as wiring code), without using a framework.

As a result of dependency inversion, you do not depend on concrete instances of your dependencies, but instead on the interfaces. For example, a class that talks to a backend service, rather than instantiating its own HTTP client, can be given a client that implements the same interface. In development mode, this could be a client that implements the need to work through corporate proxies, but in production mode, which may be deployed to AWS, it could be one that does not use proxies, but perhaps implements a caching layer instead.

Although the SOLID principles are formulated around object-oriented programming, they can be repurposed for other paradigms too. For example, in dependency injection, dependencies are often passed to the constructor, but in functional programming style, the dependency inversion principle can be implemented using closures.

Take the following example in JavaScript. A naive non-dependency injection approach might be the following:

```
import { getProduct } from '../db/products';

export default (request, response) => {
  getProduct(request.params.productId)
      .then((product) => {
```

```
    if (product === null) {
      response.status(404).end();
    } else {
      response.json({
        name: product.name,
        description: product.description
      });
    }
  })
  .catch((err) => {
    response.status(500).end();
  });
};
```

However, at the very least, this can be hard to unit test. In this form, we might actually have to stand up a real database and fill it with test content. We want to replace the import with a way of choosing which getProduct to use. We might do this as follows:

```
export default (getProduct) => (request, response) => {
  getProduct(request.params.productId)
    .then((product) => {
      if (product === null) {
        response.status(404).end();
      } else {
        response.json({
          name: product.name,
          description: product.description
        });
      }
    })
    .catch((err) => {
      response.status(500).end();
    });
};
```

Instead, the exported function is a factory that returns the real controller function. This additional level of abstraction can seem confusing, and you now need to wire up your controllers to their dependencies at the point you instantiate them (normally at the point you add the route), which does give you a high degree of flexibility. However, you do not always need to inject everything. For example, if you rely on a pure function that has been abstracted out for reusability, you can import that directly rather than expect it to be injected in. Another common exception is a logger. Loggers tend to be universal, so almost everywhere in your code needs one, so rather than injecting it in, you can import it from a file (this is known as a singleton) to keep your code tidy.

Refactoring

When it comes to the system-wide architecture, stability and some up-front design is important, but within the individual modules, you should feel free to alter the internal structure and implementation without worrying about affecting the interface. This process is called refactoring, and applies to anything between the level of an individual function/method, to a class, to an entire module.

Refactoring is often done at the end of a bit of work to clean up cruft that has accumulated, or in advance of a new piece of work to get the code into a state that's more amenable to change. Refactoring works well with test-driven development, where making each test pass gives an opportunity to tidy up the code, and having good test coverage allows you to refactor with confidence, as you know you won't inadvertently break something. Refactoring usually doesn't change the interface, and shouldn't change the functionality.

Robert C. Martin's book *Clean Code* defines what clean and tidy code should look like, and is worth a read for any software engineer. Regardless, the purpose of refactoring as you go is to make sure that when you, or a colleague, come back to code that was written many weeks, months, or years previously, you or they can easily follow the flow and intent of the code.

Removing duplication is a common reason to refactor code. If you're duplicating the same thing in several places, it's useful to extract that into a shared place, so that in the future there's only one place you need to change code. This concept is known as "don't repeat yourself," helpfully abbreviated as DRY (and code that reduces repetition is referred to as "dry code"). A misconception of DRY is that the thing that shouldn't be repeated is the code. In fact, repeating code is okay—it's concepts that should not be duplicated. If you refactor two similar, but separate, concepts together because their code is similar, you may make it harder to follow and unpick later if one concept changes but another doesn't. Similarly, if you've reduplicated code to the point where it becomes hard to follow the logic, that can often mean that you've made your code too DRY.

Tools

Once you've designed a system architecture, you must go and build it. And although the architecture of a system may be its foundation, foundations still need to go into the ground, and the way you build something is linked to what it is you're trying to build.

Every organization needs some sort of development platform. This might be a comprehensive suite of cloud-hosted tools for source control, continuous integration and deployment, or a well-configured IDE on a single developer's machine. Unless you're re-designing everything from the ground up, it's likely there will already be something in place. However, applying systems architecture techniques to your development platform is also valuable. Platforms that have been developed ad-hoc can often by the weak part of an otherwise strong architecture; poorly secured CI servers have been the entry point into secure architectures of major hacks in the past. At the very least, a development platform should have some way of managing source code, building deployable packages, and deploying those onto development, staging, and production environments in a secure and easy-to-use way.

What you should not do, however, is design an architecture with any specific implementations in mind. Once you have conceptualized the way the system will work, you can then find the right tools to use to realize it. A system architecture should not, for example, dictate a particular database technology or programming language. Instead, the desirable characteristics of a component should be expressed, and then appropriate tools and frameworks that satisfy those characteristics identified. This should always be considered in the context of the team, and any implementation details should be used to feed back into the architecture. For example, if a software development team is very familiar with Microsoft technologies, but the only database that fulfils a requirement is Oracle, then it may be wise to adjust the architecture to find something that's more realizable. Similarly, sometimes the "best" option may be a particular programming language that no one is familiar with, in which case a compromise may be found that still satisfies the requirements of the brief.

An architecture must also be realizable within the context of the organization that is building it—so, although a system architecture should not be tied to specific technologies, there will come a point where those implementation details must reflect back on it. This is especially true when designing a system architecture that may be part of a number of interconnected systems, in which case consistency is quite useful.

Changing Your Architecture

A system architecture is harder to change than individual bits of code, as it is the foundation for all the components of the system. However, it is impossible for you to determine the future of your system, so it is inevitable that some degree of change will be required. Changes to your architecture also need to be done while your system is live, which requires careful management.

Some of these changes are simple and straightforward, such as adding new components to support new functionalities. Almost all systems should allow for adding to it, but often adding new things to a system can highlight problems or bad assumptions in an earlier design. Perhaps a separation of concerns is in an incorrect place, or there's a previously unidentified issue related to scaling a component of the system. In these cases, you need to not only add a new component, but change the structure of what is already there.

This is one advantage of a monolithic system. As the system is deployed as one unit, you can fairly easily refactor the monolith to change those assumptions and all the internal components at once, in a large deployment. With microservices, an iterative approach to these types of changes is needed. One way to achieve this is to run old and new components in parallel for a period of time, then refactor the services that use any deprecated component to stop using it, eventually removing the replaced component. We can also use the patterns discussed above when moving from legacy systems, by now dealing with the bits that need changing as legacy and placing facades in front of them while moving to the changed versions, eventually decommissioning the old ones.

The actual details of the way changes are made of course depends on what the change is. But when using microservices, constant small steps should be possible, eventually leading to the big changes you need.

Summary

Systems architecture is about designing a suitable structure for a particular system, and how that might integrate as a sub-system. The goal of a systems architecture is to act as the most effective way to solve a problem, while remaining flexible enough to respond to future change. Changing the architecture of a running system is much harder than changing the detail of individual components within that system.

The two extremes of systems architecture are that of a monolith—one application that does everything—and microservices, where a series of smaller services work together to implement a goal. Monoliths are good for small systems, but can become unwieldy as they grow, whereas microservices offer a great deal of flexibility in exchange for a higher overhead of coordination and distribution.

Systems architecture begins with identifying the core functions to be handled by the system, and then the possible actions that may be taken by the users of the system. We can then use this information to derive the boundaries of individual components of the system, and the nature of inter-module communication between them. Most module communication can be classified as either request-response or asynchronous/queue-based.

Architectures should also take into account cross-functional requirements like security, performance, and resilience. Patterns such as caching or circuit breakers can be leveraged to help realize these needs. The architecture should also be realizable, with appropriate tools such as databases identified based on the requirements of a component.

The SOLID principles are five important concepts that each component in your system should respect on both the high-level and low-level scales, as they ultimately result in reusable and loosely coupled components.

CHAPTER 5

Ethics

Software engineering as a profession has a shockingly immature grasp on the ethics of engineering, and the impact we're making on the world. In other engineering disciplines, ethics and codes of conduct are baked into the professional bodies that represent practitioners. Software engineering as a discipline has largely sidelined professional bodies, preferring best practices and coordination to emerge naturally, rather than from a professional body. It's as rare to come across a chartered engineer in a digital organization as it is to come across one without (or not working towards) the qualification in civil engineering.

The pros and cons of these professional bodies can be debated at length, although the consensus seems to be that they do not add much value, and qualifications (certainly for developers) do not hold much weight with employers. In some countries, "engineer" is a protected term, and only qualified individuals can use it—similar to medical doctors, or lawyers. This is to protect the image of an engineer, doctor, or lawyer as someone who can be trusted. In these countries, software engineers are often referred to as software developers instead.

A defining feature of a profession is that a professional should be someone you can trust, and this is either achieved by baking it into the training of that professional (the most famous being the Hippocratic oath for medical professionals) or by either legislative or industry-led registration and certifications (in the UK, for example, a CORGI registered gas fitter implies a high degree of trust, which is especially important when dealing with something as dangerous as gas).

The one thing these approaches to ethics have in common is that people who undertake roles in these professions aim to do no harm. The software development industry has a much less formal route to entrance than many other professions, and no widely recognized certification schemes. Combined with its lack of professional bodies (which have their own ethical codes), this is a potentially dangerous situation, as we are not effectively self-regulating either.

© Chris Northwood 2018
C. Northwood, *The Full Stack Developer*, https://doi.org/10.1007/978-1-4842-4152-3_5

There have been some visible efforts to address these shortcomings, the most visible of which are the Geek Feminism and diversity in technology movements, but these are only focused on a few aspects of ethical behavior. The Code Craftsmanship movement similarly focuses on a set of ethics around the approaches taken to actual coding, but doesn't address the whole breadth.

Ethics is an important component of any society, and are generally most effective when they emerge as practices through consensus rather than through legislation. So, what does an ethical code look like for a software developer? At its core, it is the same as the ethics we should be practicing as individuals in society, and the more formal codes of other professions: we should strive to do no harm, or at least minimize harm.[1]

Although on the surface it may seem easy to achieve this—after all, if a shopping app crashes due to a sloppy engineering approach, it won't have the same impact as a bridge collapsing (though of course, there are many safety-critical software systems too)—but the impact our apps have on society is often more abstract. This does not make it less important to consider.

Privacy

One of the major tensions personal computing has introduced has to do with privacy. Computers, and especially mobile phones, have become intensely personal devices, and they and the services they interact with hold a wealth of data relating to users, who likely won't want to share it with everyone. As a professional, you are expected to respect your users' privacy, but at the same time, this data can be valuable to an organization and inform your decisions to build a better product or increase effectiveness of strategies such as advertising.

An analogy that often arises in relation to user data is that of oil, often focusing on the perceived value of data and how it's desirable to "mine" it. When refined, oil is very useful and valuable, but the flip side is that in its crude form, it is toxic, and if spilled, can destroy entire ecosystems. Collecting and processing data should be considered risky, and the easiest way to reduce that risk is to reduce the amount of data you are collecting. This gets especially tricky when some level of personal data is technically necessary—for example, IP addresses could be considered personal information, but an IP address is required for users to establish a connection to a server.

---

[1]Why not simply "do no harm"? Sometimes minor individual "harm" is unavoidable to minimize societal harm. Issac Asimov's *Robot* series explores this in an interesting way.

Just because you *can* collect data does not always mean that you *should*. A "big data" craze has perpetuated the idea of collecting all the data you possibly can and then seeing if any trends emerge from it. However, the process for analyzing all of that data is complex, and for many organizations, this dream has never fully been realized. Instead, collecting more focused and meaningful data is both easier to analyze and easier to practice ethically.

Legislators are also increasingly reacting to what is perceived as a failure of the industry to self-regulate, and are implementing new laws to protect citizens from over-collection and questionable use of their data. The EU's General Data Protection Regulations (GDPR) has called into question the business practices of many online advertising providers and organizations that rely on advertising for revenue, and are forcing large-scale changes to those practices. Still, many consumers are surprised at how widely their data is being sold and shared, and the lack of oversight of the practice. This was further underlined by the scandal of Cambridge Analytica, which surreptitiously collected Facebook profile data of Facebook users, which was then used to target ads as part of political campaigns, including the Trump presidency and the Brexit vote.

When determining the necessity of collecting data, you must also think like an attacker. What would happen if the data you're collecting was leaked, or your company got acquired by another one? The reason you're using the data now may be ethically acceptable, but in another context, it might be morally dubious. For this reason, it's important not only to get consent from a user to collect their personal data, but consent also to process it in certain ways, and to record this consent explicitly alongside the data. Ensuring that this consent is tightly scoped can protect you from changes in your organization's mission or policies, although an attacker will not respect this consent for processing. You may decide that, in those cases, holding data at all is too risky. For example, charities dealing with refugees may decide to limit the data they collect in case a hostile government administration subpoenas it to deport those refugees.

Even when anonymizing data, care must be taken, as it is possible, given enough data points, to still link some data to a specific person. One method for anonymizing data is to give users a random ID that is not linked to their actual identity, and then tie personal data to that. This method is more accurately described as pseudonymity, as people still have an identity within your system—it is just now tied to the random ID rather than one that relates to their individual identity. Given enough data points, it can be possible to tie this back to an individual. One famous example of this was in 2006, when AOL released the search logs of users of their search engine, tied to anonymous IDs. However, looking at the search terms was sometimes enough to tie those anonymous IDs to an individual, because users will sometimes search for their own name, or for businesses geographically close to them, schools their children attend, etc. A number of users were able to be positively identified by journalists for press purposes.

This dilemma can be difficult for large organizations, especially where people may interact with them in many different ways, as this results in more data across the whole organization which, if correlated, could identify a user. A developer on a product team may be hard-pressed to confidently say whether or not their users' data is being used responsibly across the entire organization, but should be able to ask the important questions.

True anonymity would mean that no data points in your system are tied to any sort of identifier. This allows you to still develop aggregates and averages, but not correlations. For example, if you were examining the cities where people had items shipped, then you might be able to tell that people from Slough made more orders from your website than people from Ashford, but you would not be able to tell that the people from Ashford actually spent more in total, as you couldn't correlate across different data points.

Expectations of privacy change across time and cultures. The early Internet had a much lower expectation of privacy, and the people using it left much more information open to the outside world than they do today. In some cultures, sharing a constant feed of photographs of yourself traveling is acceptable and encouraged, whereas other cultures would shocked by that behavior, as it would reveal that your house is empty, putting you at risk of being robbed. Fully understanding all of the cultures you operate in and their expectations, as well as legal ramifications, is a necessity in the modern world.

For many, privacy is expected at all times, but for others, there are cases where a lack of privacy is acceptable. The cultural relationship between the state and its citizens is one example of this, highlighted by stereotypical differences between political parties and between places like the US and Europe. On one hand, many perceive the role of the state as that of a helping hand that cares for the citizenship, and having good data allows it to do that better. Others believe that the state should be minimized, and individual freedom trumps all, so the state collecting data on a large scale is an invasion of privacy.

An example of this is the UK's National Health Service (NHS), where a program known as "care.data," which aimed to link together a citizen's interactions and health records, was rolled out. Privacy activists campaigned against this, and many individuals were opposed to it, as they saw privacy as a core principle to be upheld. The NHS believed that this system would not only improve individual care (for example, patient records would be available at any hospital), but allow data to be shared with researchers to monitor health trends of a whole nation, and possibly detect new correlations between different lifestyles and health conditions. The cost-benefit decision here was difficult, but ultimately privacy won over and the NHS shut down the scheme, although many health researchers regret the result.

This tension, like many others in ethics, does not have a straightforward answer, but requires careful reflection as you grow in your career. It is worth taking some time to reflect on the NHS care.data example given above to determine which argument you find more convincing and how you might respond if it were your own personal data at stake, perhaps on a smaller scale inside your own organization.

Cognitive Load

"Your app makes me fat" was the claim made in a famous blog post by Kathy Sierra,[2] who highlighted an academic study showing that people who have to do more difficult tasks (hence, have a higher cognitive load) show less willpower (for example, the ability to reject unhealthy food) than those who do simpler tasks.

This simple observation is very important when it comes to our role in developing the solutions that people use. We should aim to decrease the cognitive load for our users to minimize any negative consequences of using our applications. Good usability also aims to achieve this, but sometimes can conflict with business goals. Sometimes, you may be asked to design a user interface that puts the needs of the business above the needs of the user. These are sometimes called dark patterns, and include things like making it hard to delete an account, or hiding an option to decline travel insurance when purchasing a flight. As professionals, we have a responsibility to push back on features that have negative consequences for the people who use what we build.

Similarly, we also have to think about the human cost of our products. If we're building an app for employees, then they may potentially be spending a considerable portion of their day working with your app, and you can have a large impact on their life. This goes beyond technical decisions to include entire product decisions, especially in the case of "gig economy" apps, where we have a professional responsibility to treat the

---

[2]Kathy Sierra, "Your App Makes Me Fat," http://seriouspony.com/blog/2013/7/24/your-app-makes-me-fat, July 24, 2013.

users of the apps (for apps like Uber, this is the rider as well as the driver) with respect, and to avoid misleading them or making their life more difficult. Ultimately, these users are still individuals, and this category of product can have a significant impact on their lives.

There are entire classes of products that developers may have to make a personal ethical judgement on. For example, the potential for working on military systems may require careful consideration about whether or not to accept a job, but projects that may seem more benign, like a social network, could be used to cause harm if used incorrectly by its owners. Ethical consequences can be subtle too. For example, a face recognition app may help a social network user quickly and accurately tag photos, but if used by a totalitarian state, it could be used to persecute citizens.

There is no right answer to these questions, but they are issues that as professionals we must consider, and re-consider if the context of our work changes. We not only have the right, but also the responsibility, to say "no" to our work being used in unethical ways.

Energy Usage

The design of Bitcoin's blockchain is mathematically brilliant, and has certainly garnered a lot of attention, but it is flawed in an engineering sense. As the blockchain is decentralized, a transaction has to propagate through the blockchain for it to appear in the record of truth. At the time of writing, each transaction uses the same kWh of electricity as a typical house uses in a day.

The expenditure of energy, and other physical resources, is certainly a visible part of the impact IT has on the world, but it also feels very abstract from the perspective of an individual developer, especially with the move to the cloud. When organizations ran their own data centers, energy usage was at least visible to that organization, often as a cost to be minimized, in addition to any environmental impact. In the cloud, it's hard to see this impact, much less consider it, but it is important to do so.

Of course, there are good engineering and business reasons to minimize energy usage as well; increasing performance/efficiency and reducing costs can be big drivers too. Evaluating whether or not unnecessary load and resources are being used, and whether or not capacity is sufficient (is much of your server capacity being left idle for a long time?) can go a long way.

Trust

The people we work with, whether that be clients, colleagues, or users, place a high degree of trust in us to do our jobs. They trust that we will do what we say we will, usually for an agreed price, and for us to do that to the best of our abilities.

They also trust that we do not misrepresent ourselves, and behave honestly. Selling yourself as an AWS expert after launching a single EC2 instance on the free tier, or as a Ruby specialist with several years of experience when in reality all you've done is follow the Rails tutorial, undermines that trust. We should not be scared to admit it if we truly believe that we don't meet the expectations of those who ask us to do something, although, at the same time, stepping out of our comfort zone to try something new is okay as long as those expectations are made clear.

We should also trust our colleagues, and be trusted by them. Undermining, playing politics, or bullying is completely unacceptable— yet all too common—in any profession. When a team undertakes a retrospective, the prime directive is a good principle to follow in most interactions with people: "we assume that everyone did the best job they could with the knowledge they had at the time."

Diversity is a factor here, too. Technology is not quite reminiscent of scenes from *The Wolf of Wall Street*, but there are still too many pockets where "culture fit" (i.e., looking like the people who are already on the team) is valued above skill set. This still happens explicitly, but unconscious bias is even more dangerous. Research has shown that more diverse teams perform better than monocultures. Many organizations are capitalizing on this by mixing functions on a digital team, but it is also our responsibility to make technology a welcoming industry for all who want to contribute, and to foster teams where all members can contribute to the best of their ability.

Software engineers also have a fairly unique style of interaction with our peers through the mechanism of open source. Open source is often the result of volunteered time, and the result of this work is often made available under fairly permissive licenses. Some of these, like the famous MIT or BSD licenses, are completely permissive, whereas others, like the GPL, are more nuanced, and require that any changes or work that builds on top of their work is also made available in a "share-alike" way if they are distributed.

What the GPL enforces in its license often becomes a societal expectation of people who use more permissive licenses. For example, taking an open source component and selling it for profit is a fairly rare occurrence, as to do so would jeopardize the entire nature of open source. Using an open source component as a library within a commercial product is often seen as acceptable, but any improvements or changes made to the library itself are expected to be contributed back to the main project, so others can benefit from them. Web development blurs the lines, as code is not shipped directly to users as a product, but the same responsibility is still there: if you make improvements or fix bugs in an open-source library, the societal expectation is that you will contribute those back. Together as an industry, we can then make each other better, and avoid betraying the trust placed in us by those who make these libraries available, who then might turn to alternative methods such as digital rights management, or just not make their work available at all.

It is also worth remembering that open source is often built on the efforts of volunteers, and that we should also treat maintainers and contributors to open source projects with the same rule of thumb that applies to our colleagues, as discussed earlier.

Summary

Ethics is an important part of most engineering disciplines, but is not talked about enough in software development. This chapter looked at four ethical concerns that you may come across: privacy, which is being increasingly legislated due to perceived ethical failings of the profession; cognitive load, where we can inadvertently introduce negative side effects to our userbase when we focus solely on other goals; energy efficiency, which can sometimes seem abstract in the work we do, but has a direct real-world effect; and trust, within our profession and to those who we work for.

Ethics lives in a world where there is no right answer; rather, it can be personal and highly subjective, depending on individual circumstances. Nevertheless, it is something we should consider at all points when building systems in order to build a better world for everyone.

CHAPTER 6

Front End

Different teams will often have very different ideas of what part of their app is the front end. For some teams, the front end is literally just the HTML, CSS, and JavaScript that makes up their app. For others, this can include the logic and server-side code that generates the HTML too, with the "back end" being simply the APIs. So, to avoid ambiguity, this chapter defines the front end as the bit of your server that generates the HTML, as well as any code that runs in the browser.

There are three key technologies to keep in mind when it comes to code that runs in the browser: HTML, CSS, and JavaScript. JavaScript is such a large topic that it is broken out into its own chapter, but below we cover HTML and CSS, which are specification languages that specify the structure and presentation of your web page. JavaScript is a fully specified programming language that allows you to add interactivity to the browser and manipulate the structure and presentation.

For a back-end developer coming to front end, everything can seem a bit too foreign. All of a sudden, you're using new languages and new toolchains, and you have to target multiple runtimes. But it's important to remember that any back-end techniques you know and love can apply to the front end too. Don't panic; just start copying snippets of JQuery from Stack Overflow into a single .js file, as you're writing legacy code from the start.

For the front-end developer, this might feel like home turf, but there is much to be learned from the techniques that may traditionally live in the domain of the back-end developer.

HTML

Hypertext Markup Language is the language at the core of the web. It is not necessarily a programming language for building applications, but instead a language for describing documents. There are two fundamental approaches to expressing structured documents in software engineering: markup and standoff. In markup languages, like HTML, the structure and annotation are inline with the text and contents of the document.

© Chris Northwood 2018
C. Northwood, *The Full Stack Developer*, https://doi.org/10.1007/978-1-4842-4152-3_6

HTML annotates sections of text with tags, denoted by angle brackets that give the corresponding section a meaning, or as a way of embedding non-text elements within a page. Standoff annotation mechanisms instead leave a document as is, and then have a second file that describes the structure. For example, you may have a plain text file containing the text to be described, and then a second annotation file describing things like "the characters between positions 112-118 are bold." The benefit of markup over standoff is that keeping the document and the annotations in sync is much easier, as they can be manipulated as one, but the downside is that if you want to have text in your document that happens to look like a tag, you must encode (or escape) that text to indicate it should not be treated as a tag.

Hypertext is a specific form of a technology called hypermedia, which was of much interest to researchers in the 1990s when HTML was developed. Hypermedia refers to any non-linear media—for example, a video that you can navigate in any order you want, rather than following only one path. The navigation occurs by following hyperlinks, which are references to other documents or bits of media. Tim Berners-Lee thought of this as a web of documents, hence the term World Wide Web.

This book will not teach you HTML, but there are many other good resources out there, and it is important to be aware of the basic principles when building an HTML page. HTML tags are used to express the structure of a document, and although they do also imply a specific form of rendering in a browser, this structure and meaning are also used in other ways—search engines, accessibility tools, and more rely on this structure being in place and being meaningfully applied to a document in order to correctly interpret a web page.

From Server to Browser

At the core of any web site or application is some way of creating HTML and delivering that to the user via a web browser. This used to be done by hand-writing some HTML and just serving those as files from disk, and this is still a valid technique today, but it limits the amount of "dynamism" available, as the same page must be served to everyone. Although JavaScript can be used to add some interactivity and dynamism to the client's browser, it is very common for the actual HTML that is delivered to the browser to be generated on the server side in an application in response to a request, rather than simply serving a static file from disk. Even when a dynamic application is not required, it can be useful to generate static HTML on disk by assembling them from common templates on disk, using a tool known as a static site generator (one example of this is Jekyll). These tools work similarly to the dynamic server-generated code, but instead generate all possible outputs up front, rather than on request.

When constructing a web page, you will often encounter different concerns for various different parts of the page. For example, a common navigation bar or footer might be the same on every single page, but other components might need some information from a database, or another system, to be inserted. For static components, like the footer, it is very common to simply write fragments of HTML that are assembled together by the web browser, but for dynamic components that can change, there is a dazzling array of libraries and techniques for doing this. To further complicate things, the dynamic content in the database might also hold its own styling data, in addition to how the component which presents that data is styled—this is referred to as rich content.

The approaches for building an HTML document server-side generally break down into the following techniques: auto-generation, tree transformation, and string interpolation. There is some crossover between these three techniques, and they can be combined.

Auto-generation happens when an underlying library automatically creates the HTML for you, perhaps by directly serializing a class. Auto-generation can often lead to problems and should only be used in very small doses—for example, if you're using a tool like Django's forms, which renders out a model to a simple HTML form. With auto-generation, you often have limited control over what the resulting HTML looks like, and as that HTML is your integration point between not only your content, your styling, and your front-end logic, but also your users, it's important for you to control it. The method is quick, and can seem useful if you're working in a "full stack" framework, but as discussed in the Designing Systems chapter, it's often better to pick multiple smaller tools and wire them together to make something more than the sum of its parts than it is to use a one-size-fits-all solution. Auto-generation can be considered an anti-pattern, something that seems good at first and will help you move quickly, but as time goes on will cause you an increasing amount of pain.

One exception that is worth calling out is Facebook's React. Although React takes an auto-generation approach, using the JSX extension to JavaScript, there is a strong link between what you write and what is output that mitigates most of the downsides and offers considerable upside. Indeed, when using JSX, React appears to have more in common with a string interpolation technique than a traditional auto-generation approach.

Tree transformation is a technique that takes content or a template written in some other non-HTML language and translates it directly into an HTML tree, without going through an intermediate stage such as being parsed with classes into models. Sometimes the source document is itself represented as a tree (like XML or HAML), and other times it's just flat content (like Markdown or BB Code).

WHAT IS THE HTML TREE?

The term "tree" comes from computer science, referring to a particular type of data structure. A tree consists of a set of nodes and a set of pointers associated with those nodes. The root of the tree is a single node that has pointers to other nodes, and these pointers are known as branches. Eventually, a node does not have any pointer and this is known as a leaf. Additionally, no node can point to a node that another node points at, so there are no loops, or nodes on multiple branches. If you sketch out a diagram of this, you end up with something that looks like a tree (although often computer scientists start with the "root" at the top, so you get an upside-down tree). Relations between the nodes in a tree are expressed in the same terminology as in human ancestry, as is shown in Figure 6-1. The node that points to another particular node in the tree is called the parent, and the nodes it points at are the children. Nodes that share the same parent are referred to as siblings.

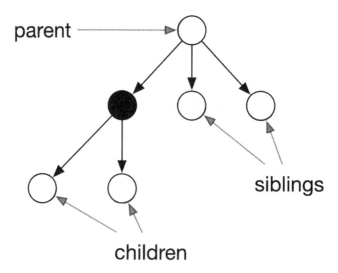

Figure 6-1. *A tree structure. From the point of view of the node shaded black, the parent and children are labeled.*

HTML conforms to this tree-like structure. An HTML element can have other elements nested inside of it, which you could call the children of that node, but this reflects the branches in a tree. Take for example the following HTML:

```
<html>
    <body>
        <div>
            <h1>An HTML tree</h1>
            <p>Hello world</p>
        </div>
    </body>
</html>
```

If you represented that as a tree, as in Figure 6-2, you would end up with a structure like this:

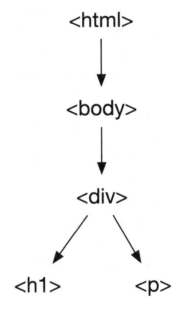

Figure 6-2. *An HTML document structured as a tree*

Trees are common data structures, and other syntaxes for writing HTML can also be represented with this kind of nesting structure, which can be transformed into a tree and then output as HTML.

For dynamic rich content, tree transformation is a powerful technique. It often does not make sense to store content in a database as HTML, as this can leave it brittle or linked to specific implementation details, such as CDN URLs or CSS class names, that are hard to migrate. Instead, you should consider using another markup language (such as Markdown, BBcode, or wiki syntax), which is then translated to HTML at render time. For simple cases, where the source syntax is well-known, there are many libraries that can help you do this. The downside here is that you often have limited ability to hook in any extra HTML attributes (such as class names), which can make writing CSS selectors or JavaScript against those elements tricky.

Although there are many libraries that will do the translation for you, there are others that require you to implement the translation rules yourself. The most well-known example of this is XSLT, which has native support for translating XML into HTML, although the exact matching rules have to be written in "XSL," or Extensible Stylesheet Language (which itself is XML). Although XML has developed a poor reputation, generally due to inappropriate usage or over-complicated schemas, it is very effective at certain tasks. XML itself grew from the HTML standard as a more generic language, and there was even an aborted attempt to deprecate HTML and replace it with an XML-based variation known as XHTML.

XML is very adept at annotating text inline, and other formats, such as JSON, can make the process clunky. Creating your own XML schema—with tags that have semantic meaning in your domain—and storing it in your database can sometimes work better than storing HTML. In this scenario, when this content directly maps to the HTML output, XSLT should be seriously considered. Listing 6-1 shows how you may store content as XML in a database, but then map it to some output HTML as shown in Listing 6-2.

Listing 6-1. Sample XML that refers to an image by ID

```
<article>
        <paragraph>This is some example content.</paragraph>
        <image id="a9be99f7" alt="Example" />
</article>
```

Listing 6-2. An example of what that XML may be translated to when rendered to HTML

```
<article>
      <p>This is some example content.</p>
      <img src="https://cdn.example.com/images/a9be99f7.jpg"
        alt="Example">
</article>
```

You may consider storing the HTML directly, but this can be problematic. For example, if your CDN URL changes, you may then have dead image links in your database, or if you refer to CSS classes, it will be harder to refactor your CSS without breaking content.

There are scenarios where content is not stored as HTML, but where direct tree translation isn't the best approach. For example, instead of writing something that translates JSON directly into HTML, it can be beneficial to load those into models that are then passed to the view. Then, string interpolation is used.

Although tree transformation is an effective technique for handling dynamic and rich content, it is less effective when it comes to managing static components. Template languages such as HAML or Jade have become common as a mechanism to write an abstracted version of HTML, which is then translated into HTML at render time. Although this has the upside of enforcing the validity of the generated HTML, there are often downsides. The most important one is that it adds a layer of indirection between the code you see in the browser and the code you see on disk, which can make debugging harder. Often, these languages make inline tagging (such as annotating a single word in a sentence) clumsy, as shown in the following example, as well as hiding important HTML details, such as whitespace collapsing. In complex systems, it is often necessary to fall back to inline HTML in addition to HAML, which can clutter your code, and styles of different engineers between two different languages mixed together can conflict.

```
%p
  This is how you insert
  %a{:href => "foo.html"} a link
  with HAML.
```

Given these downsides, and the limited upsides of using such a tool, it is best to avoid this kind of HTML generation style for your actual templates. If you're especially worried about the risk of introducing invalid HTML into your codebase, you can incorporate HTML validation into your automated tests (and it is probably a good idea to do so anyway) to still reap the benefits of these transformation layers.

String interpolation is by far the most common way to create templates. This technique works by taking a typical HTML file and adding a special type of tag that is interpreted by a library. This template is rendered by passing a number of objects to a renderer, as well as the template name, and these can be referred to within these tags—for example, calling a method on an object in order to return a string that is echoed into the view.

```
<article>
      <h2 class="title">{{ title }}</h2>
      <p class="abstract">{{ abstract }}</p>
      <a href="{{ link.href }}">{{ link.text }}</a>
</article>
```

PHP deserves special mention here, as the entire language is based on the idea of string interpolation. However, in an MVC world, mixing the domain logic with the templating language can make the code harder to maintain due to working in different domains in the same file. As such, many modern PHP frameworks actually come with their own templating language, rather than using PHP's support for this interpolation directly. This introduces an artificial constraint on how much logic can exist in the template to enforce these good practices. Most other web frameworks in other languages will come with their own templating languages too, such as Ruby's ERB in Rails, Python's Jinja in Django and Flask, or Handlebars in JavaScript. Although the exact syntax may vary between these templating languages, the overarching principles remain the same.

Although it is common to hear that templates should not contain any logic, this is impractical in most real-world applications, and most templating languages include simple logic, such as if statements and loops. Even with these limited constraints, it can be easy to introduce significant logic to a template, violating the single responsibility principle and making that logic hard to test. These should be refactored into a more appropriate place such as the controller (for example, computing the value of an if statement and passing the result through as a boolean to the view), or on the model or view model being queried.

Another common feature of templates is the ability to include other templates. This is a powerful technique that can help with code organization and minimize re-use. Although it may not seem like it, many refactoring techniques for logic code also apply here. A particularly long page can be broken down into a series of smaller templates, even if they are not reused, which can make the intention and structure of the page easier to see.

One important feature of some templating languages is support for template inheritance. Template inheritance is somewhat similar to inheritance in object-oriented classes. A base template will typically define a full HTML document, with some common header/footers, and then will include gaps, which the individual templates can fill with their content (typically the page body). This can be a good technique for reducing duplication, although in template languages that do not support this, a common solution is to have "header" and "footer" template files included at the top and bottom of the file to provide that level of functionality.

In addition to generating HTML in a server-side application, or all at once with a static site generator, there is a technique known as server-side includes, or edge-side includes, that will assemble pages from individual components for presentation to a user's device. In server-side includes, the server that reads a file from disk will parse it and dynamically include another file to create a new composition to the user in response to a directive in the file. In edge-side includes, this is done using an intermediate proxy server. This approach can be powerful if you want to decouple the applications that produce the different components of a single web page, and also include different caching rules for each component.

Styling

HTML specifies the structure of a web page, and CSS (Cascading Style Sheets) specifies the styling and presentation of it. At the core of CSS are selectors and rules. The selectors specify which HTML elements these rules apply to, and the rules describe the value of the presentation properties that get applied to any element that the selector matches.

```
.header {
    background-color: #eee;
}
```

The preceding code is an example of CSS. The selector is `.header,` which indicates that the rules in the block below should apply to any object with a class of `header`, and that it should set the `background-color` property of those objects to #eee, which is a way of expressing a light gray color. The syntax of pure CSS is very regular and follows this format, and this book doesn't aim to cover the whole range of CSS properties and values, but the Mozilla Developer Network (MDN) is a good resource that does cover the whole range.

In addition to classes, CSS selectors allow you to target elements by their tag name (e.g., with a selector of `p`); an element with an ID (#body for an element `<div id="body">...</div>`); or by attributes (`[href]` for all elements with an attribute of `href`). A special selector of `*` exists that applies to all elements, and attribute selectors can also use operators to test the contents of a value, not just the presence:

- `[attr="foo"]` where an attribute equals the value `foo` (e.g., `[data-languages="en"]` would match `<span data-languages="en">`)

- `[attr*="foo"]` where an attribute includes the substring `foo` (e.g., `[data-languages*="en"]` would match `<span data-languages="german english">`)

- `[attr^="foo"]` where an attribute starts with the substring `foo` (e.g., `[href^="https"]` would match any secure link, but not one that might have https elsewhere in the path)

- `[attr$="foo"]` where an attribute ends with the substring `foo` (e.g., `[href$=".pdf"]` would match any link to a PDF file)

- `[attr~="foo"]` where an attribute includes the whole word `foo` (e.g., `[data-languages~="en"]` would match `<span data-languages="fr en de">` but not `<span data-languages="english">`, as in the latter `en` is not the whole word)

- `[attr|="foo"]` where an attribute is exactly `foo`, or a `foo` followed by a hyphen and some other text (e.g., `[data-language|="en"]` would match `<span data-language="en-GB">`)

Any attribute operator can also be used case-insensitively by adding an `i` before the final bracket (e.g., `[data-languages*="en" i]` would match `<span data-languages="English">`).

Selectors can also be nested—for example `.body` p says to apply to all `<p>` tags that occur under an element that has a class of body, and combined, for example, `p.author` applies to `<p>` tags that specify a class of author. An HTML tag can carry multiple classes—for example, `p.author` would still apply to `<p class="author large">`, as would `p.large` and `p.author.large`. Nesting and combination can be used together— e.g., `.body p.author` for all `<p>` tags with a class of author that have an ancestor in the DOM somewhere with a class of body.

Methods of nesting can also be made more specific. In the previous selector of `.body p` there can be many elements nested between the element that has the body class and the p, but using the operator `>` we could say `.body > p` which means only the p tags that are directly children of a tag with a class of body are targeted.

Other operators target siblings in a DOM tree. Take, for example, the following HTML:

```
<div class="article">
  <p>some introductory text</p>
  <img class="figure" ...>
  <p>Some more text</p>
  <h3>A sub section</h3>
  <p>Line 1</p>
  <p>Line 2</p>
</div>
<p>Continuing text</p>
```

If we had a selector in our CSS of `.article img + p`, then the p that immediately follows the img would get styled according to the properties specified in that definition. The other `<p>`s would not, in contrast with `.article h3 ~ p`. The ~ here means to style all subsequent siblings, so the two lines that come after the h3 heading would pick up that style, but not the line that comes after the div, as moving up a level of nesting means they are no longer siblings (the parent DOM node is different).

CSS also allows us to target "pseudo-classes," which corresponds to how a state may change. For example, `a:hover` would apply when an element is being hovered over (for instance, changing the style of a button). There are many pseudo-classes, and online sources such as the MDN cover the full list. Similarly, there are pseudo-elements, the most famous of which are `::after` and `::before` (for compatibility reasons, these can be specified with one colon, like pseudo-classes). These pseudo-elements refer to elements that do not exist in the DOM, but can be made to behave like them—for example, `:before` can be combined with a `background-image` to make an icon appear inline that is purely defined in CSS. A detailed description of these is beyond the scope of this book, but there are many good reference materials on how to use them.

It is the "C" of CSS that causes issues. Multiple style sheets can apply to a document, and if there are multiple selectors that target a specific instance of a HTML tag on a page, then the cascading aspect of CSS comes in and a set of weightings is used to determine which property should "win" and be the one that is actually applied.

All browsers have a default style sheet, which causes a page to at least have some styling (default fonts, different sizes for headings, etc.), rather than just render a blank screen when a document is loaded, but this will always lose out to any style sheets specified by the site itself. The original intent was for users to be able to specify their own stylesheet that would override anything else (for example, to increase font size for those with vision impairment), but this was never well used in practice and ended up being over complicated. One of the main issues with CSS is that it can make scoping hard, so it's easy to add a rule that has an unintended side effect on another component, or an odd interaction. These types of bugs are generally referred to as specificity bugs, and there are a number of techniques to deal with these and to minimize the risk of introducing them in the first place.

Another confusing part of CSS is that some properties not only apply to the element that the selector specifies, but also any elements nested inside it. This can be useful in avoiding large amounts of duplication—for example, if you have a heading and a paragraph inside a div, then you can set a font color on the div and it will apply to the heading and the paragraph, rather than causing too much duplication, but this can sometimes cause unexpected side effects.

CSS also lacks the ability to directly express certain concepts in a straightforward way—the most famous example of this is vertical alignment of a series of blocks (although this has improved somewhat). These concepts have to be expressed by building the desired effect out of a more fundamental set of properties, which can lead to common code patterns (sometimes called "CSS hacks") that can make it hard to see exactly what the direct effect of each property is, as it is the combined effect that is wanted. Another fundamental limitation is the inability to write a selector in a form that says, "apply to this element, but only if this element has a child node that this selector matches." That is to say, you cannot write a selector like `.product:has-child(.price)`, which would style an element with class `product` if it had a child class `price`. This is due to CSS being applied in a top-down way. If you could style a parent based on its children, then the renderer would have to look ahead to see which elements are coming up in the render, which has a significant performance overhead, or go back and re-render the parent when the child is being rendered. The most common workaround for this is to have classes like `.product--has-price` added in the server-side code and styling that, rather than attempt to do it in pure CSS.

These restrictions are a source of frustration for many developers, but the simplicity of CSS means that there is not much to learn, even if some of it is not obvious. This simplicity has become de-facto enforced, as it is hard to make significant changes to the language in a backwards compatible way. New properties and values can be added, as browsers will simply ignore those it does not recognize, but any more significant change to the language's syntax is harder to introduce. As backwards compatibility (supporting older browsers) is often an important concern in web development, writing CSS often requires writing "lowest common denominator" CSS, which lacks developer niceties, like variables and mix-ins.

To work around this, the concept of CSS pre-processors was introduced. These are transpilers that accept some other language and output valid CSS. Common transpilers are Less and Sass, which all support specifying selectors and rules like normal CSS, but have a different syntax for declaration and add additional features to the language over base CSS. SCSS is a variation of Sass that allows you to write Sass, but in a syntax that is closer to normal CSS than normal Sass or Less. For this reason, SCSS has become very popular, and when most people refer to Sass, they specifically mean the SCSS variation. One reason SCSS is popular is that plain CSS is also valid SCSS, so it offers an easy upgrade route for people moving from traditional CSS-only front ends, and is also familiar to developers.

An early powerful feature of Sass and other pre-processors was the ability to support variables for reuse, although CSS has now itself adopted variables. For example, you could have one file that defines your color palette, and then reuse that variable to create multiple themes. Listings 6-3, 6-4 and 6-5 define 3 SCSS files, and when rendered with Sass this will output two CSS files, one of which declares white-on-black, and the other black-on-white.

Listing 6-3. dark.scss

```
$background-color: #000;
$text-color: #fff;

@import "main";
```

Listing 6-4. light.scss

```scss
$background-color: #fff;
$text-color: #000;

@import "main";
```

Listing 6-5. _main.scss

```scss
body {
  background-color: $background-color;
  color: $text-color;
}
```

@import is another useful feature of SCSS files, allowing multiple files to be consolidated into one. The underscore in _main.scss indicates that it is a partial file, so only exists to be included by the top-level SCSS files, and will not be rendered into a CSS file.

Other useful features include functions, mixins, and extensions. For example, you could have a base class that is defined in SCSS as:

```scss
%button {
  ...
}

.add-button {
  @extends %button;
  background-image: url('add.png');
}
```

This creates a class called %button, but unlike normal CSS classes, it cannot be used directly in HTML. Instead, it must be extended by another selector, and anything defined in %button is also available in .add-button and anything else that extends it. On the flip side, you can also use includes. The two might seem functionally similar, but can suffer from performance issues. A class that is extended many times can have very long selectors when rendered into CSS, which can impact performance, whereas an include is simply repeated every time it appears in the final CSS, which can increase size. Which one to use in any given circumstance is hard to assess, and can require benchmarking to figure out the actual performance impact. An include in SCSS looks like this:

```
@mixin button() {

    ...

}

.add-button {
  @include button;
  background-image: url('add.png');
}
```

Mixins and includes also allow function like behavior, as they take parameters. For example, you might re-write the previous example as follows:

```
@mixin button($icon-url) {
  background-image: url($icon-url);

    ...

}

.add-button {
  @include button('add.png');
}
```

Parameters can also take default parameters, which makes them very effective. To override attributes that are inherited through @extends, you can specify the attribute in the selector that extends it, but this also complicates the final rendered CSS by having extensions and overrides rendered side-by-side.

PostCSS has a similar approach, in that it starts with plain CSS, but it supports plugins that add extra features to CSS. Some of these plugins enable SCSS-like features, whereas others simply enable new, non-backwards-compatible, CSS language features, so you can write pure CSS, but then output it in a backwards-compatible way.

There is an alternative to using features like SCSS's extends and includes: using pure CSS and then mixing together CSS classes in the DOM. To do so requires some level of discipline, and a technique known as BEM is one method of achieving it. BEM stands for Block Element Modifier, and may just be seen as a naming scheme, but it goes beyond that. In BEM, a high-level component is called a block, and corresponds to a reusable or distinct component within your page structure. A block is usually made up of other HTML elements, which may look like this:

```
<div class="product-card">
  <h3 class="product-card__name">...</h3>
  <img class="product-card__photo" ...>
  <p class="product-card__description">...</p>
  <p class="product-card__price product-card__price--discounted">...</p>
  <a href="product-card__link button button--primary">...</a>
</div>
```

In the preceding example, we have a block, `product-card`, and then a number of elements within it, `name`, `photo`, `description` and `link`. The link is itself a block of type `button,` and that button is modified by being a `primary` button.

These class names demonstrate BEM's naming scheme, which is "**block__element--modifier,**" where element and modifier are optional. The CSS definition for this example would then define `product-card` as the high-level component and each element within it appropriately too, although there is an implicit contract dictating that the element may only be used inside of that block, which can simplify your definitions. Sometimes you may need to vary the behavior of a block, and this is where the modifier comes in. Instead of having multiple classes, such as `primary-button`, `secondary-button`, etc., for variations on a theme, which can result in duplication (or use SCSS extends/includes, which results in duplication in the rendered CSS), you can abstract common functionality to the block (or element) level and then only specify the differences of that specific variation from the base. This is demonstrated above by modifying button at the block level (in which case the elements may inherit that modification by specifying nested selectors in the CSS), or at the element level itself, as in the price element.

Even though BEM can be used alone, it's also common to use it with SCSS and other similar tools, as it is a way of dealing with CSS's specificity issues by avoiding excessive nesting, and dealing with namespace issues by ensuring elements are namespaces within a block. There are other approaches for dealing with CSS's flat namespace, the most common of which is to simply prepend the name with a namespace. For example, if you are creating a shared module that can be embedded on other pages, like a "Share" button, you might start all of your classes with the name of your tool and a hyphen to avoid clashing with any names the site which contains your embed may use. Other technologies have emerged that dynamically tie CSS to DOM nodes, either in JavaScript or HTML, by being aware of which CSS classes are used by a DOM and then rewriting the names to include a unique identifier.

A useful tool to have when writing CSS is an "autoprefixer." When a new CSS property or value is introduced, there is often a period when some browsers support an experimental version of it, which may have subtle differences from the final standardized version. In order to avoid introducing broken syntax for these experimental features, a browser manufacturer will introduce a "prefixed" version of the rule of value. For example, when a method for introducing rounded corners on boxes was created, you could support this in WebKit browsers by specifying `-webkit-border-radius: 5px`, until the final standardized specification was approved. With an autoprefixer, you can simply write the standardized version, and it will generate the prefixed versions too to support older browsers that allow the experimental versions but not the standardized version.

When doing front-end work in CSS, it is also likely you'll come across CSS frameworks. When using build tools like NPM with SCSS, these act as libraries and utilities that you can import into your code, but are also standalone CSS files that you can embed, providing many classes for you to use in your HTML.

CSS frameworks can range in their scope from relatively simple ones—like `normalize.css`, which tries to "reset" the CSS to a stripped-down set of defaults that are the same across all browsers—to larger ones, which define helpers to build grid layouts and typography rules, to fully-featured ones like Foundation and Bootstrap, which also include styling for many common elements such as forms, menus, etc. Many organizations will develop an in-house CSS framework that complies with their house style and includes components and styles that are reused across many different pages.

CSS is called Cascading Style Sheets because multiple rules can apply to a particular DOM element, and the process of figuring out the exact value of a property to apply to a DOM element is known as the cascade. Sometimes, there will be a conflict when the same property is defined multiple times, so the cascade must figure out the most specific rule to apply, and there are a number of limitations in doing this.

The first has to do with ancestry in the DOM. If you defined a `font-family` in an HTML selector, and then override that in a p selector, then any text inside a `<p>` tag will take the font defined in the p selector, as that is closer to it in the HTML tree structure. Note that not all CSS properties are inherited by child nodes; many only apply to the exact node being targeted.

If there are multiple selectors that apply to the same node, and that node is either the exact node (or at the same level of ancestry, for properties inherited from a parent), then we must look at the actual selector that defined that property and compute a specificity value.

To compute the actual specificity of a selector, you first count its number of IDs, then the number of classes, attributes, and pseudo-classes, and finally the number of elements and pseudo-elements. You then compare, in that order, the counts of each type, and the first count that is higher is the most specific. For example, a selector with two IDs is always more specific than a selector with one, even if the latter has more classes specified, as IDs are always more specific than classes. In another example, if neither selector specifies an ID, or if the number of IDs in the selector is the same, then classes do matter, and the selector with the most classes is the most specific. Continuing, if the number of IDs and classes in a selector is the same, then it is decided by elements.

The final rule for determining which to apply, when all else is equal, is which one comes last in the CSS definition file. So, if you have two p selectors, the one that comes second will override any values set in the first.

There are specificity calculators that can be used to determine the specificity value for a selector, which can help with debugging. However, avoiding using complex specificity rules is preferable, as it can get very complicated quite quickly, so it's important to choose a selector carefully, making sure it is the lowest specificity it needs to be to accomplish a task. BEM encourages using very flat CSS, where most selectors are a single class (perhaps with pseudo-elements) to manage specificity in this way. This can lead to verbose HTML, as an element might need many CSS selectors if it combines different classes, but BEM proponents believe this is a good trade-off. The use of IDs is also commonly discouraged in CSS.

A special case rule exists in CSS known as !important, e.g., specifying a rule such as font-weight: bold !important. The ! may look like a negation, but it's a form of declaring that this rule is the most important and should be more specific than any other declaration. Use of !important is considered bad form, as it can lead to inflexibility when trying to work on the same code base at a later date, and normally indicates that there have been some other badly managed specificity rules that need to be addressed, since you might have quite a tangled code base. One of the few scenarios in which to consider using !important is when you need to override a foreign stylesheet, but in all other cases, you should continue using normal specificity rules instead. !important is itself bound by specificity rules; if you have two rules that are !important that apply to a

DOM element, the same process as above is applied, and the most specific `!important` gets applied. `!important` does not allow you to bypass specificity—it just creates a new type of specificity to consider.

The final special case to consider is that of the inline style, e.g., `<span style="...">></span>`. In this case, the properties defined inline are always the most specific.

Components

The UX chapter covers approaches to designing front-end experiences, and a very common one is to break down a single web page into a series of reusable components, which can then re-appear on other pages. Sometimes this reuse can span multiple web sites across the same organization too. This makes sense for someone coming from a development background, who may try to structure code as reusable modules, classes, and functions, and it's something we can do when building UI components too.

The challenge with UI components on the Web is that it's hard to define it as a single self-contained package, unlike in other areas such as mobile development, where you can link a library and import a class. Take, for example, an e-commerce web site, which might want to show thumbnails of an item on both a search results page and in a "similar items" box on a product result page. At the very least, you need to insert some common HTML onto both pages, and this can be achieved by using an "include" directive or similar in a templating language (where the template could be parameterized), but you'll almost always then want to include some styles and potentially supporting JavaScript. You could include the script and CSS inline with the HTML template, but this leads to performance losses, as it can result in lots of duplication if a template is used several times, slowing down performance, and CSS styles should be declared in the `<head>` of the page to be compliant with the specification. Some frameworks, such as WordPress, allow these templates to declare any additional styles and JavaScript to be loaded, which are then correctly included in the rendered page and deduplicated, but this can also lead to performance issues, especially on less reliable connections such as mobile, as the browser now has many small CSS or JS files to fetch.

The most common way to work around these performance issues is to bundle the styles and any scripting for all the components used on the site into a single file for CSS and JavaScript for the entire site, and then serve that to the user. This works well for small to medium style sites, because although the first visit to the site might require downloading a script file that contains unused JavaScript or unused CSS, that file can then be cached and reused as a user navigates a site. There is a slight overhead on each page, but this approach normally offers the best balance between performance and overheads, as long as the single files do not get too bloated.

This approach may seem to violate the "don't repeat yourself" principle, since a component may need to be specified in several places: in the HTML where it's used, in your CSS file to be imported, and in your JavaScript file. However, this is normally the least complex thing to do.

When building a shared component, there are two predominant ways to actually structure the code, your choice of which can be influenced by the frameworks you're using or the preferred style of the community. The first is to have a folder per type of resource, and then a file for each part of your component. For example:

- `templates/thumbnail.html.j2`

- `assets/styles/_thumbnail.scss`

- `assets/scripts/thumbnail.js`

The other is to group them together into a directory, e.g.:

- `components/thumbnail/template.html.j2`

- `components/thumbnail/_component.scss`

- `components/thumbnail/component.js`

Sometimes there may be other assets to consider. For example, you may want to split a particularly large component up into a number of JavaScript files or CSS components, or sub-templates, but you may also need to include any image assets, such as SVGs or custom fonts. The basic method of doing this remains the same, but the exact details will depend on the build tool you are using. Some will automatically copy them into the right place or transform them to inline when they are included, but others might need additional steps.

Both of the approaches above assume that your entire site is in a single code base, but for larger sites, or when there are shared components, you will often want to make them available as packages that can be installed using your package manager. NPM (and compatible alternatives, such as Yarn) have become the largest ecosystem for front-end component sharing (as well as for back-end JavaScript code when using Node). NPM is discussed further in the JavaScript chapter, but it is a repository of published packages and a command line tool for installing these from a package definition. NPM supports private repositories, which can be an effective way to share your code, either through directly linking to Git repos, using a hosted service they provide, or self-hosting your own repository. Many JavaScript build tools integrate directly with NPM-installed JavaScript modules, but other tools like CSS or a template loader might require you to either specify a full path to the file to be included or adjust a setting to look in the right directories.

Using NPM, you can split out a particular component to its own folder and repository, publishing it to a place where other projects depend on it. One downside here is if you need to always have the exact same version of a component deployed across your entire site, it can be difficult because you will need to update the version in every place it is used when a dependency is changed, and then deploy that change. This is a fundamental flaw in every component that ends up being bundled in a specific web site, where you cannot update that component in isolation. If this use case is important for you, it is best to avoid bundling it at all, and bring it in directly into a page through `<script>` and `<link>` tags, or using the `<iframe>` approach, discussed below.

As sites get larger, the overhead of having a single bundle for the entire site can be overwhelming, and the most common technique for dealing with this is called "code splitting." Code splitting is a feature of your build tool, and when used it will create multiple bundles of code (CSS or JavaScript) instead of one. You can then choose to include only the relevant bundles on a particular set of pages, often selecting a basic-level bundle for common components across all pages (like navigation), and then a bundle for any page-specific functionality that gets loaded in. A naive approach to this method might create two distinct bundles, but often several bundles will have some shared libraries or styles, which will result in the library or components being bundled several times—one in each bundle. Some build tools are smart enough to identify this scenario and will automatically create other bundles that contain the common functionality. Implementing code splitting does require you to define the bundles or how they are split up, and this can become complex to maintain, so it's advisable to only introduce this if performance benchmarks actually identify significant issues with the single-bundle approach.

For single-page web apps, there are other approaches that can simplify the developer experience. In a single-page web app, HTML templating is often done in the client with JavaScript, bringing the templating and scripting into one place and becoming closer to the model used in most non-web development. Further approaches, classified as "CSS-in-JS," also bring the styling into the JavaScript code base. At the time of writing, these approaches are fairly immature, and can cause performance issues or require heavily tying your code to a particular build tool, thus adding a new substantial dependency.

One approach to CSS-in-JS is for the styling to be managed at run-time by the JavaScript, which can have extremely negative performance implications, especially for responsive designs. An alternative approach is to have the build tool look at where the styles have been defined in JavaScript and extract them into a CSS file, which then behaves like a traditional bundle in the browser. The latter approach is extremely promising, although the tools to do so are currently immature and adoption (at the time of writing) is still limited. With the CSS extraction approach, you often get additional benefits, such as rewriting class names to avoid conflicts if two different classes have the same names (working around CSS's global namespace).

A radically different approach to sharing components between different web pages is to use IFrames. Although frames have been long thought of as a problematic technology, these weaknesses do not necessarily apply to IFrames. IFrames can be accessible and interact well with web pages, with the only real complications coming into play if you have to dynamically size an IFrame to fit its contents. An IFrame is essentially embedding an external webpage into a page; the parent page needs only know the URL of the component to be embedded, which takes it completely out of the bundling process above, and allows for the component to be deployed and managed independently of the page that uses it. It does introduce another set of risks if the server hosting the IFrame component goes down, in which case it will show as an error on the parent page, but does leave it otherwise unaffected.

Creating an IFrame component is similar to creating any other web page on a site, in that it needs a URL that renders HTML, but this URL is normally not directly exposed to users because the component by itself is not meaningful. IFrame components are also useful if you want to share content to be embedded directly by third-party web sites that may have many different build systems or styles (in which case it would be hard to otherwise provide a component for them), or if your component needs access to cookies or similar on your domain that third parties will not be able to access due to cross-origin rules.

In the event a component needs to be parameterized, this can be done by passing query parameters in the URL and then letting the component that renders the contents of the IFrame react appropriately. A JavaScript API (`window.postMessage`) also allows the parent page to communicate with the embedded IFrame if further interactivity is required, but otherwise access to the DOM of the parent or the child can be limited unless they are hosted on the same domain. This can cause some issues, so IFrames are often only used for relatively self-contained components, and not those that need to interact significantly with the state of the parent page.

There is no perfect answer to the problem of building a componentized web UI. The web community has recognized this and has started working on a set of specifications known as web components, which has a "native" way to solve this. With web components, you can define a custom element using JavaScript in the head of your document (or in a bundle), and when you want to include that component, you can use it as if it were a regular HTML element, passing any parameters as attributes to that tag.

Web components are a complex and evolving beast. Styling is handled using something known as the shadow DOM, which allows you to specify styles that only apply within the scope of that HTML element, but also stops document-level styles from affecting the contents of the custom element. As web components become more mature and browser support improves, it seems sensible to expect these to become much more common than they are at the time of writing.

Responsive Design

Responsive design, or responsive web design (RWD), is a technique used to design a web page that will adapt itself to the specific capabilities of a particular device. This technique was mostly enabled by a feature of CSS known as media queries, and before responsive design was widespread, it was common to build multiple versions of a site— one for desktop and another for mobile—and then serve different HTML based on the user agent (the string the browser sends to indicate the version) of the browser. This often required maintaining two similar but separate code bases, and as a result many mobile sites were simply limited versions of a desktop site, and as users moved more and more to mobile, this became unsustainable. The expansion of the kinds of screens that web browsers could appear on (mobiles, tablets, laptops, watches, TVs, fridges) resulted in the practice of creating one version that can adapt to many devices.

It is not without its downsides, though. You often end up having to code for the lowest common denominator (mobile phones do not have the processing power of laptops, for example), which can lead to some compromise for higher-end devices. A technique known as progressive enhancement, which is discussed later on in the book, can be used to overcome this, but this is often not as simple as having one plain version per site. Sadly, this trade-off between multiple simple sites, which require a lot of work to maintain, versus one complex one persists to this day, but the consensus appears to be that the additional complexity is still less work than even creating just two versions of one site.

There may be circumstances where responsive design is not needed—for example, an internal app that is only being deployed by a call center can probably be desktop only, so it is always worth considering that option.

When designing a responsive web site, it is useful to categorize the different screen sizes needed and then create designs that work on those screen sizes, although some sites simply have one basic layout and ensure that the content scales to all screen sizes equally, which is a quick and easy solution if possible for your content and design. For others, you may want to separate the layout of a site into different categories. This can be as simple as "mobile" and "non-mobile," but often includes intermediate categories such as "tablet" and might consider device orientation as well. Each category is not a fixed layout, but possibly covers a wide range of devices and screen sizes in each category, so variable width is often considered here. Often, the largest category has a maximum width set when it becomes a fixed-width design.

The boundaries of each category are known as breakpoints. A breakpoint is where the layout of a page changes from one category to another. For example, you might want to set a breakpoint of 400px, where below 400px is the mobile category, and equal to or above 400px is the tablet category. Note here that a pixel in CSS does not necessarily correspond to a physical pixel on the display. This is discussed further in the UX chapter, but as a reminder, in CSS, 1px corresponds to a pixel if the device's display is 96dpi, and the physical pixel usage is adjusted if it is higher (or lower).

Radically changing the layout at every breakpoint can be confusing if a user switches between them (for example, if they rotate a device, or resize a browser window on a laptop), and would be much more difficult to implement. Small changes to the layout (perhaps moving from a single column to several) rather than reordering an entire page is normally preferred.

Other assumptions often get baked into these different screen sizes. For example, one might assume that mobile and tablet screen sizes will be used for touch, and any buttons or other clickable areas should be scaled up for that, but smaller laptops (or side-by-side web browsers on a desktop) might not be touch screen, and conversely, touch-screen laptops and desktops with bigger screen sizes are increasingly common. Similarly, mobile devices are often assumed to be held closer to the face, so text can be made relatively smaller. These assumptions are baked into designs between each breakpoint, but it's important to be aware of them, and that it's actually device width/height/orientation being used as a proxy for these wider assumptions, and relying on those factors alone will sometimes steer you wrong.

CSS media queries are a way of defining a block of CSS that only applies when the screen characteristics match a certain set of criteria. For example, if you wanted to say that text should turn blue on mobile, you might write the following:

```
@media (max-width: 400px) {
        p {
           color: blue;
    }
}
```

The preceding code dictates that the CSS applies when the browser width is less than 400px.

You can combine multiple statements into a single query, so that the inner rules only apply when all are set. Combining min-width with max-width therefore allows you to specify ranges:

```
@media (min-width: 401px) and (max-width: 1024px) {
  ...
}
```

The above would then only apply between 401-1024px. It's important to highlight that we start at 401px for a reason! If we reused the 400px value, as we did in the mobile-only query, then if the device happened to be at exactly 400px, then both sets of media queries would apply. This would be an odd edge case to catch, as min-width and max-width are inclusive (equivalent to "more than or equal to" and "less than or equal to," respectively), so they do overlap.

In addition to width, you can also specify height in the same way, as well as device-width and device-height, which allows you to specify the absolute size of the device you are on, rather than the current size of the browser (so you can, for example, always render a desktop site on a desktop, even if it's made smaller), but this is not necessarily a good idea. orientation is another property of use, and can be specified with values of portrait or landscape to further target a particular configuration. There are many other properties, including aspect ratios, and newer features such as whether or not a user can hover with their current input device, that can be used to be more explicit about assumptions made about touch screens, etc. Media queries can also be constructed using operators other than and, including or which behaves as you expect, and not which can only be used to negate an entire query, rather than a particular parameter within it. Commas can be used to specify multiple different queries that apply (similar to the way a normal CSS declaration can specify multiple classes that match). Finally, it is interesting to note that the original purpose of media queries was to specify a "print" stylesheet—one that only applies when a page is printed out.

The actual breakpoint values are worth breaking out to variables when using a CSS variant that supports it, as they can be duplicated and might need to be tweaked during development. This also makes it easy to keep them consistent, having a single set of break points across an entire site, rather than different components having their own set of breakpoints applying to them.

Responsive design with media queries is often combined with a technique known as "mobile first," which is discussed later in this chapter.

Progressive Enhancement

At the core of the very identity of the Web is the metaphor of documents. Each web page was one document, and web sites consisted of a collection of those documents. Each document had a globally unique reference—a URL—that could be used to look it up, and documents were hyperlinked together using these references. It was truly ground-breaking, and for years this documents metaphor prevailed. Many standards were written based on the idea that web pages were simply documents, and then tools arose that exploited this, such as accessibility toolkits and search engines.

Then, people started putting things on the web that weren't documents. Web sites such as Hotmail launched, and didn't quite conform to some of those core principles of the Web. Nowadays, we call these types of sites web apps. These happily coexisted with the original web and worked well enough with the document metaphor that it didn't break too many of those tools. This harmony was achieved using a technique called progressive enhancement.

Progressive enhancement is the idea of layering functionality on top of a simple document to give a richer experience. And it wasn't only these new web apps that used progressive enhancement; traditional document-driven web sites started using it too. In the early days of the web, well-formed documents with very little styling were the norm. Then CSS came along, allowing people to style their documents, and it wasn't unheard of for people to apply custom stylesheets in their own browser. For example, users who had trouble seeing might increase the default font size or add high color contrast to their default experience. When JavaScript came along, the same scenario applied. Web sites worked without JavaScript, and for browsers that supported it, JavaScript improved the user experience.

However, in the late 1990s and early 2000s, Windows started dominating the scene, along with Internet Explorer. Although sites that were content based continued to conform to standards and to the technique of progressive enhancement, web apps, especially intranet web apps, stopped doing so, as it was easier to assume the user was browsing with Internet Explorer. This was exacerbated by Internet Explorer's adoption of proprietary extensions, which enabled new types of web apps. Progressive enhancement usually requires more engineering discipline than not using the approach, and in those environments, there was no need for it. With the rise of mobile browsers and the breakup of Microsoft's monopoly on the web browser, these web apps suddenly became a large chunk of legacy code.

Similarly, with the rise of the mobile web, many sites that had been built around that particular environment struggled to adapt to mobile phones. Many organizations had to suddenly build a separate mobile site and then, years later, merge them back together using the rising technique of responsive web design. Sites that had used the technique of progressive enhancement had an easier migration to deal with. Many simply served a mobile version of their CSS template, but could leave their HTML documents as they were.

The early days of mobile web were similar to the early days of the Web on the desktop. Dozens of different devices, with different browsers and capabilities, made progressive enhancement the only game in town. However, like the consolidation of the desktop market to a smaller number of players, the mobile browser market has become dominated by Android and Apple. At the same time, JavaScript's capabilities increased to a point where the browser could do more and more, and a web app could rely on the server less. A slew of frameworks arose, embracing the idea of building these kind of web apps (Angular and Meteor, among many others). These were generally incompatible with the idea of progressive enhancement, and in some use cases that was okay. However, these tools also got used in many situations where it *wasn't* okay. The abandonment of progressive enhancement in these cases suddenly caused problems when things that you could previously take for granted on the web if you were standards compliant—search engine discoverability, compatibility with accessibility tools—were no longer there. Additionally, these type of web apps can have long startup times, causing a slow page load, and this was especially true on smartphones.

To Progressively Enhance, or Not?

Progressive enhancement is all about identifying the core functionality of your web site and making it available to all, and then applying any additional functionality or nice-to-haves as layers beyond that. As web technology and browsers have improved, the core experience has gotten richer. For example, ensuring that your page works without CSS is no longer strictly necessary. On the flip side, devices on flaky network connections, or issues with your server, can cause web pages to load without any style sheets.

You may think the same argument applies to JavaScript—few browsers nowadays do not support JavaScript, and unless there is a shaky connection, JavaScript should be loaded. However, not all search engines will execute JavaScript, or will only execute a limited subset of it. Furthermore, although it is completely possible to build fully accessible web applications with JavaScript, having to implement those semantics yourself is harder than using the built-in functionality of the browser. Also, JavaScript has more failure modes. A typo in a CSS file will not break all of your styling (although it may break part of it), but an error in your JavaScript could hinder critical functionality, or completely alter how the page is displayed.

Regardless of what type of web site you're building, at its core is the HTML document you deliver to the user. For search engines and accessibility tools, this is still the most important element. Most will understand some of the layers on top, but only to a certain extent. For content-heavy web sites, this document should contain the very essence of your page, and it should be renderable before any JavaScript gets applied to it. For web apps, this is much harder to do, as for many, the essence of what the site does cannot be expressed using only the simple building blocks of HTML, or often to do so would require significant server-side effort. For some web apps, a decision is made on a component-by-component level as to whether progressive enhancement is used or not, but for others, the decision is made to not attempt at all. The single-page application pattern is one example where progressive enhancement is abandoned.

The decision of whether or not to use progressive enhancement is fundamental to the entire front-end experience, so it should be considered with care. For most content web sites, any decision to not apply progressive enhancement techniques can cause long-term issues with the web site. In some circumstances, short-term engineering gains can be made, but this is offset by the higher cost of implementing search engine optimization and re-adding the appropriate hooks for accessibility purposes. Progressive enhancement has stood the test of time, and has shown value again and again, but like many things in software engineering, the answer to the question "should I progressively enhance?" is, "it depends." The decision of whether or not to not apply the technique should be made carefully.

Not using progressive enhancement, combined with techniques for performance, such as only loading the JavaScript when a page has first rendered (to speed up time before the page becomes usable), can leave the page in awkward half states, where a button may be visible, but clicking on it does nothing, as the JavaScript has not added any events to it yet. In a progressive enhancement context, this is less annoying, as it can fall back to the non-progressively enhanced version (such as submitting a form the traditional way, rather than with AJAX). However, when there are entire features being delivered using JavaScript, if these are only added after page load, this can cause annoying flashes as the page re-renders, or cause the content to jump around. To deal with these, you can use a small inline script tag to add a class to the <body> tag, and then use CSS to hide them by default until that script runs. If the inline script is the first thing in the body, elements will be immediately visible as they are rendered on browsers that support it, perhaps in a "disabled" or "loading" state, until they are completely enabled once the JavaScript has been loaded.

Mobile First

Complementary to progressive enhancement is a technique known as "mobile first." This technique starts with the assumption that browsers on smartphones are the least-capable browsers: the hardware is under-powered, network connections the least reliable, and interaction mechanisms the most limited. This technique is often used in the interaction design stages too, where the designs are developed with the most constrained environments in mind first, and as those constraints are lifted, more can be added. Many teams find it easier to add functionality to supported devices than to have to shoehorn an experience for bigger or more capable devices into a smaller one.

With mobile first, it's useful to establish a baseline. A decade ago, a BlackBerry or Nokia smartphone might have been the starting point, but nowadays it's more likely to be a cheap smartphone, which can be running a very capable browser but be constrained by either how out of date it is, or the performance of the device. Once you have established this baseline, you can design and build a version that targets that device, and then figure out what other, more capable, classes of device you want to target. A more capable smartphone might be very similar, perhaps with a bigger or higher definition screen, but then you might move to a tablet, where the screen is much bigger, and the way people hold and interact with the device completely changes. The last class of devices to consider are desktop or laptop devices, where users navigate using a mouse (or trackpad), which gives you much finer control over interactions with the UI, as well as features such as hovering.

If we try to apply the technique in reverse, then the value of mobile-first becomes clear. If we assumed desktop first, and then used hovering as part of the UI, then when a mobile variant is developed, either a workaround to enable the same interaction would be needed, which may not be obvious for mobile users, or significant rework would need to be done to the interface to take into account the fact that the user will not always be able to hover. By addressing designs in a mobile-first context, we either eliminate the use of desktop-only interactions like hover, or only use them for additional "nice-to-haves" rather than critical parts of the functionality.

Mobile first goes beyond the way you approach building the UI, though. By dealing up front with the fact that a network may be unreliable, you can build with those constraints in mind from the start, rather than having to go back and retrofit or rewrite code.

Most web sites nowadays will also reference external media, and mobile first encourages you to provide assets that are an appropriate size or quality for mobile devices. Take the example of images. There's no point in downloading a 4K image for a phone with a low-resolution screen on a slow connection. As mobile phones generally have smaller screens than laptops, it may make sense to generate `<img>` tags with an `src` of a small resolution of the image appropriate for a mobile phone as the lowest common denominator. JavaScript can then be used to check the size of the actual screen and replace that `src` with a more appropriately sized image, but starting with a small image gives the fastest experience on mobile, while enhancing it for less constrained devices later. This kind of behavior is becoming increasingly abstracted away in the HTML specification. For images, `srcset` now does this without requiring any JavaScript, and for media like audio or video, formats such as MPEG-DASH also support adapting the media size and bitrate appropriately.

Mobile first, when used with responsive web design, normally involves defining all your mobile styling without using any media queries, and then overriding any mobile-only styles with media queries for larger devices and screen sizes.

Feature Detection

For many, the simplest level of progressive enhancement is "does the core of the experience work without JavaScript?" and this is not a bad starting point. However, as discussed above, there are some experiences, especially in web apps, where the core essence is not expressible using HTML and CSS alone. But progressive enhancement is not about the binary notion "is JavaScript there or not," and can cover much more.

Take, for example, geolocation. Although the JavaScript API exists in modern browsers, there is no guarantee it will actually work (for example, if the device has no GPS chip, or it cannot get a signal and GeoIP is inconclusive), so you should not rely on that API for the core experience of your site. For example, if you are building a "find a store" feature, then you may want to start with a simple search form that has no dependency on JavaScript, and only expose a "Use current location" button if the Geolocation API is available. This is a technique called feature detection, where a certain area of functionality on your web site is only enabled when a corresponding feature is detected in the user's browser. Implementing detection for a particular feature is dependent on the particulars of that feature, but there are libraries that can abstract this away.

Another technique that has seen significant use is the "cuts the mustard" technique. This goes beyond the simple "does JavaScript run" approach; instead, a test is run to determine if the browser has a baseline support for modern JavaScript. Using this kind of technique can help with testing, because instead of a large combination of browsers and devices with different features to test, testing can be divided into browsers and devices that "cut the mustard" and those that don't. Browsers that don't cut the mustard get a non-JavaScript experience, which is better than having a subtly broken web site, and gives you an easier way of confirming your site works for search engines and in other situations where JavaScript cannot be relied upon.

Progressive Enhancement of Styles

Progressively enhancing CSS is more of a binary affair. It's usual for a site to minify all CSS down into one file, and for that to be loaded—therefore, either the page is completely styled, or not at all. When a CSS file has not loaded, it is usually very obvious to the viewer that something has gone wrong (and if they're using it on a mobile device with a bad signal, they possibly think the problem is on their end, not the site's), but even here you can make the best of a bad situation with progressive enhancement. When building a site, by focusing on the structure and content of the page in HTML, if CSS fails to load, then at least users can still read whatever you've published (even if it's not pretty). This is good for search engine optimization too. A good rule of thumb is if the page still makes some kind of sense without CSS being applied, then a search engine can probably get some meaningful data from it.

Unfortunately, CSS is not quite as simple as an all-or-nothing process of loading a file. Like JavaScript, there are differing levels of support for features and CSS properties in different browsers, but unlike JavaScript, CSS has no feature detection. Fortunately, browsers will ignore CSS statements they do not recognize, which can eliminate most of the need for progressive enhancement. For example, if you need to support legacy Internet Explorer, you would be wise to accept that elements will not be pixel perfect in those older browsers. Similarly, some browsers only accept "prefixed" versions of properties (sometimes with different syntax for values than what was eventually standardized). Tools like an autoprefixer can behave like JavaScript polyfills to allow you to access these.

It is slightly harder to manage significant changes in CSS that browsers can just not parse. The most famous example of this was for legacy versions of Internet Explorer (prior to 9) that did not support media queries. As developers embraced mobile-first progressive enhancement and responsive web design, this gave IE users a significantly poorer experience. The common workaround was to produce an IE-only stylesheet, corresponding to the "desktop" break point, and then use IE conditional comments to include that only on IE. This was definitely not progressive enhancement in its purest form, but a hack where the trade-off made sense.

When Not Using Progressive Enhancement

For web sites that have not been built using progressive enhancement, there is often a need to retrofit the advantages of progressive enhancement. The most common example is the need for discoverability by search engines, and for fast load times.

Additionally, one of the more common arguments against progressive enhancement is that it can increase engineering costs; functionality has to be implemented on both the server and client sides. The solution to both of these is server-side rendering, but the mechanism for doing so varies radically.

There are many proxies and servers out there that will render a page using a headless browser and then serve the resulting content directly to the user, but this can interfere with single-page application frameworks, which do not assume any content already exists. Some frameworks can bind themselves to server-side rendered content and use that as their initial state, speeding up build time. Sometimes these proxies will only do so if they detect a user agent belonging to a search engine, a technique that is often penalized by search engines if they discover it.

One technique that has emerged as a result of the popularity of NodeJS to reduce engineering costs (building the same logic and views server- and client-side) is "Isomorphic JavaScript" (or "Universal JavaScript"). Using JavaScript on the server, this renders the views using the same JavaScript code that is used in the client, with some initial state. Modules can then be shared server- and client-side, without having to re-implement the core of the view.

Search Engine Optimization

Search engine optimization (SEO) can often be seen as a dark art, but is a necessity for any content-based web site in this day and age, as search engines are a primary way that people browse the Web. In reality, most people will be coming to your site either via a link on social media or a web app, or by searching for it. Entering URLs by hand has become the preserve of power users.

SEO is essentially the mechanism of making the content of your site easily understandable by search engines so that they rank your site highly for relevant terms, as well as adopting any other positive technical signals the search engines use to rank. The water has been muddied by ethically questionable SEO agencies that apply short-term hacks like adding loads of unnecessary keywords onto a page, or even more dubious techniques like hidden text, or serving search engines different content. Another important way search engines rank content is the number of incoming links from reputable sites. Again, some questionable agencies might spam your URL onto sites via comments in an attempt to boost your ratings, but these kinds of hacks are short-term at best, and often damaging in the long run.

Search engine optimization is definitely needed for content-type web pages, but even for application-type pages, some can be useful. Although many of these pages may be hidden behind a login and aren't directly searchable, it is possible that things such as landing pages will be, so applying these kinds of techniques will help there.

The search engine market is unquestionably dominated by Google, which does not reveal exactly how results are ranked, but has indicated that some specific factors are important. The ethos of Google and other search engines is that the things that matter to humans are the things that matter to the engine. Ultimately, technical methods cannot correct for bad content, so getting the right content, including effective headlines and a good standard of English, is the single most important thing you can do. The second is to make sure that Google can understand your page. Although search engine crawlers can execute some JavaScript, it is not clear how much of the language they support. Fortunately, making a site easily parseable by browser—using techniques such as progressive enhancement—and ensuring that it is accessible means that search engines can also parse it, so a web site that is well-designed for human users should also work well for SEO purposes.

However, it isn't just the actual content of the page that can be beneficial to search engines. There are specific bits of metadata and structured tags that should be added to your HTML to help boost your results. The `<title>` tag in HTML is one such example, as this is the name of the document as it shows up in search results. The simplest level beyond this is what is called a meta tag, which can be added inside the `<head>` of your HTML document to indicate additional bits of data, such as a summary of the document, known as a meta description. Specific search engines and social media also support more specific tags, such as "rich snippets," to indicate media or other elements that stand out on a results page, or when sharing on social media to generate a small preview window. Adding these kinds of tags will make your site stand out over ones that do not, but almost everyone uses them, so not having them is more likely to mean that your content will have a low rank, rather than their inclusion guaranteeing a high rank.

Beyond the content and metadata, there are other signals that search engines take into account when ranking results. For example, if your site is not responsive to the size of a mobile screen, it will not appear as high for searches conducted from a mobile phone. Speed and security are important, too. Google in particular will punish sites that are slow to render and load, because users often will not wait more than a few seconds for a site to load. This makes it doubly important for you to manage the performance of your site. Web sites that are not HTTPS will also not perform as well on Google as those that are served over a secure connection. Google often uses these signals to push the web in the direction it would like it to go, towards a faster, more secure future, and it should not be surprising that Google pushes more technical improvements as search signals to improve the quality of the Web in general.

The final set of important signals for search engines, as discussed above, is the number and quality of incoming links to your site. If you have the same content split over many pages, then there are often multiple URLs that people can link to, simplifying your site design so there's only piece of content with one address that is linked to means that that one link will get a higher rank than having a larger number of links each with a lower rank. In terms of actually getting those external sites to link to yours, this is a completely non-technical problem! Linking to the site from social media and using press releases to link to your content, or even other sites linking back, will help.

The final word on managing URLs for SEO is that if your URLs change, you will often find your search rank dropping as you lose incoming links. It is possible to mitigate this with correct use of HTTP redirects, but there will always be some intermediate phase between adding the redirect and the new page or URL getting the appropriate rank. In this case, it is important to have a good and sensible URL structure up front. There will be times when you find you have to delete content and change redirects, and when that happens, it might seem at first that you can just restructure your internal navigation and the site will be fine, but don't forget about any incoming links, and always set up redirects appropriately.

This is only a brief overview of SEO, as it is a fast-moving field that changes from day to day. Any book that tries to cover anything other than high-level concepts will become outdated very quickly. However, it is not a dark art that can only be implemented by specialists from SEO agencies; it's something that a full stack developer should be able to do with minimum fuss by understanding these principles.

Build Tools

When using a tool like Sass, and even when not, there are often steps we should take in order to transform our source code into the version that gets delivered to the user's browser. This is similar to the way compiled languages might need some sort of build tool in order to compile and assemble Java classes into a `.jar` for distribution, and indeed some of those traditional language tools have developed some capability to handle front-end code. However, the most mature and common tools for building front-end code are those that were designed specifically for that purpose. There are many tools, each with their own philosophies and approaches, and many new ones appearing all the time.

Some of these tools are targeted towards one task—for example, Compass is responsible for building a CSS file from Sass input—but others are more general and orchestrate a number of tasks—for example, Webpack tries to satisfy all front-end building concerns. There are also task-running tools that can orchestrate the different parts of your build tooling into one command. Some popular tools include Gulp or Grunt, which might combine a number of the more-focused tools, or tools like NPM scripts or makefiles, which are often used with tools like Webpack.

Given that the front-end world evolves very quickly, I will not give any concrete recommendations here, as they will undoubtedly become outdated very quickly, but I will discuss a general approach to the types of activities you may want to live in your build tool. Often, you will configure your build tool to use a pipeline, starting with source files and outputting a final build, with each stage taking the output of the previous. These stages will vary, but will often develop as follows:

- Starting with an entry point, processing it to find all the imports, and concatenating them together into one built output

- Transpiling each import (for example, converting JavaScript into a backwards-compatible variant, or Sass into CSS)

- Generating source maps that can be used to help debug the final build by mapping it back to the original code (a source map describes how the compiled code relates to the original, and is supported by major browsers to allow you to debug the original code, rather than the compiled version)

- Minimizing the code or images, through compression or removing white space to minimize the file size, which can improve performance for the end user

Your build tools will also want to run any tests against your code. These could be unit and integration tests, style checkers (sometimes known as linters that ensure your code matches best practices and your preferred style), or other analysis tools that identify common bugs.

Most build tools will have two modes—one to output a "production" build, and another to better support development. Keeping the difference between your production builds and development builds as small as possible can minimize bugs that only crop up in production, but some are necessary. For large projects, minification can take a long time, so that is sometimes skipped in development mode in order to minimize waiting time after making changes. On the flip side, source maps that are invaluable for debugging can be large and slow down production, so are skipped. Some libraries go further, sometimes by including extended debug logging or checking values at runtime, which are then skipped for performance reasons in the production build.

Another common difference between development and production builds is that often production builds will run once with the output being uploaded to a CDN, whereas development builds will happen in a "watch" mode, where a build tool will watch the source files for changes and then automatically rerun the build. This process can make use of caching in order to be much quicker than a full build or test run. Some build tools support the ability to go further, using techniques such as live reloading or hot module reloading. In these cases, the build tool will start up a web server to serve the built assets, but insert additional code that will cause your web browser to connect to that web server using a web socket or similar. The web server will then tell the browser to automatically refresh the page if the code has changed, or, in more advanced cases, reload a single component of the page for even faster development.

Do not underestimate the complexity or power of a well-tuned build tool. Correctly configuring the build can have real performance impacts for your end users, as well as greatly enhance your workflow. Do your research to find what works best for your stack, and spend some time setting up a skeleton that works for you and that you can reuse.

Summary

The front end of your application is the bit that your users actually interact with. On the web, HTML determines the layout of your document, CSS dictates the visual styling, and JavaScript can be used to give a degree of interactiveness by manipulating the HTML structure and CSS rules.

All apps start by delivering HTML to a web browser, even if it's only a small amount to bootstrap a rich web app. For many sites, the bulk of the HTML is generated server-side, and there are different ways of generating this: automatically using libraries and frameworks, which has limited flexibility; tree transformation, where some other data structure such as XML or HAML is translated directly into HTML; or string interpolation, where the HTML is built using file- or string-based templates.

CSS is structured into selectors and rules. The selectors describe which parts of the HTML the rules should apply to, and the rules then specify the exact effect on the rendered content. Some rules, such as fonts, cascade such that they apply to children of the targeted element, and when several rules can apply to a particular HTML element, specificity is used to determine which one takes precedence. CSS can also target pseudo-elements and pseudo-classes, which do not exist in the HTML but represent virtual content or distinct states.

CSS has for a long time been a fairly limited language. Other languages have been introduced, such as Sass or Less, that compile into CSS but provide additional syntactic sugar, such as variables or inheritance, over the plain CSS language.

It's common to take a component-based approach to building your front end, and this plays well with the approach of many UX designers. There are several approaches to this-such as handling the HTML template, CSS and JavaScript separately-although in some rich applications, you can bundle these together with some potential performance cost. These components can be bundled as shared code or hosted and embedded as IFrames.

Two important techniques for the front end are responsive design and progressive enhancement. Responsive design is where the styling of the site uses media queries to change based on the size of the user's screen, and is often combined with a mobile-first methodology, where the basic design is mobile-friendly and the site responds as the screen gets larger. With progressive enhancement, all users get the same basic experience, and then JavaScript is used to improve the user experience when the device supports it. This increases the reach of your application by not depending on particular features, but making use of them when they do exist.

The final part of front-end design to consider is non-human users of your web sites. This can include search engines, which index your site and allow it to be searched, and many of the techniques that make sites usable and accessible can make your site attractive to search engines.

CHAPTER 7

Testing

At some point during every project, there will inevitably be two questions that need answering for each change you make: does it work, and has it broken anything? Testing can be used to answer these two questions, although there are subtle differences between the types of testing used to resolve them.

Test-Driven Development

Test-driven development (TDD) is a well-established technique for developing software, although it is often misunderstood. The purpose of TDD is not to generate high test coverage, but to use tests to help drive the design of your code; TDD is really about development, not just tests.

TDD is based on a cycle of "red-green-refactor." At first, you write a test for the new functionality you want to add, which should fail (go red), and then you write the simplest bit of functionality to make the test pass (go green). Once you have done this, you can refactor your application and test code to tidy it up and remove duplication.

In test-driven development, it is common to write tests that only address a single module at a time. These types of tests are known as unit tests, as opposed to integration tests, which are discussed further later in the chapter, and which test multiple modules at once. Some people, especially those who practice behavior-driven development, will often start by writing a test that's wider than one particular module, and then write the necessary tests with a smaller scope that satisfies the requirements of the bigger test—this is the outside-in approach. Others prefer to start at the smallest unit and then write integration tests to wire the modules together once they have been built, referred to as the inside-out approach. It is often a matter of personal style as to which approach you go for, although proponents of the outside-in approach say it helps them decide which components need to be written, and proponents of the inside-out approach like the flexibility of not having to design the interfaces of the individual modules in advance.

141

© Chris Northwood 2018
C. Northwood, *The Full Stack Developer*, https://doi.org/10.1007/978-1-4842-4152-3_7

If you have issues writing tests that only target one module, that might suggest that there are several highly coupled modules that might actually be better joined as one, or, if there are multiple distinct types of tests for that one module, that your one module should in fact be split into multiple smaller ones.

"Arrange-act-assert" (sometimes called "given-when-then," especially when used with behavior-driven development, discussed later in this chapter) is a common pattern for arranging your test code. Take the example below:

```
it('should increase the size of the shopping cart when adding a new
item to it', () => {
        const cart = new ShoppingCart();
        const product = fetchTestProduct();

        cart.add(product);

        expect(cart.size()).toEqual(1);
});
```

Here, the arrange-act-assert process is shown using white space, which is a common pattern that can help readability when scanning a test file. The "arrange" part of the test involves setting up the objects and bits of data you want to test into the right state, and then "acting" upon that by running the function that's being tested. Finally, "assert" checks that the act step was successful.

There may be times when this style does not work for the type of test you want to write, but be careful—a test that follows the arrange-act-assert-act-assert pattern should often be broken down into two separate tests, perhaps abstracting the "arrange" steps out into a helper function that is used in several tests.

Each test you write should test one logical bit of functionality: the part of the code you're testing. This might mean there are multiple assertion lines in a test, but there should only be one *concept* that is being asserted. The value in this is that if a test begins to fail, you should know from the name exactly why it is failing. If there are different concepts being checked in one test, some failures can mask others, so you might not get a full picture of why a change has introduced a regression until later on.

In the process of running the red-green-refactor cycle, you'll end up with a comprehensive automated test suite. With this kind of suite, you can go a long way toward answering the second question: has this change broken anything? A passing test suite should give you a high degree of confidence. One could argue that any good test suite should give you this degree of confidence, but a test suite developed using TDD allows you to build in this confidence from the start; seeing a test go from red to green lets you know the tests are working.

Not having any automated tests at all is a very dangerous practice. Skipping testing completely is often too high a risk for any organization to accept, but without automated tests, manual QA is needed, and it is too slow and expensive for the fast-changing nature of a digital organization. Test automation, especially for rote checks, is therefore an essential part of modern product delivery.

ALTERNATIVES TO UNIT TESTING

The functional programming language Haskell uses an alternative approach to unit testing than the arrange-act-assert method described above. Instead of writing code with explicit examples for the input and expected output of a particular function, you instead write assertions that should be true for whole ranges of inputs. The testing library (in Haskell's case, this is called QuickCheck) then randomly generates input from the allowed ranges to try and find cases that fail.

For example, when testing a sorting algorithm, you may want to specify that, when the input is an array of integers, each item in the array is less than or equal to the next element.

This is known as "property-based testing" and is especially useful when developing more algorithmic aspects of code (such as sorting algorithms), where there are a large number of edge cases in the input data.

Test Pyramid

Test-driven development is an effective way of developing a test suite that can help protect you from accidental breakage, but there are many different ways a system can break which unit tests developed using TDD will not cover. Although an individual class may be behaving correctly according to the tests, there's no guarantee that any other class that relies on this one is making the correct assumptions about how that class behaves, or if any changes have caused a responsibility to be lost. Because of this, it's important to test at various levels within your application, from the smallest units (which could be an individual function or class) to the individual modules, and even the whole system.

Ultimately, all the organization cares about is whether or not the system as a whole works, and it can be very tempting to write the majority of your tests at this level. However, there is a downside to testing the system as a whole. It is often much slower than running an individual unit in isolation, and when external dependencies are involved, it can be brittle due to circumstances outside the direct control of the system.

The test pyramid shown in Figure 7-1 highlights the different layers to test. When your tests are considered at all levels of the pyramid, you should have a high degree of confidence in the performance of your application.

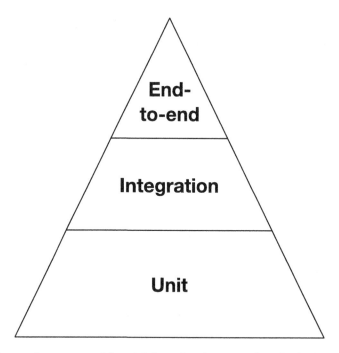

Figure 7-1. *The testing pyramid, with height showing level of abstraction and breadth showing coverage at each level*

At the bottom of the pyramid are unit tests. These test a single unit in isolation but test each system exhaustively. When it comes to unit tests, it's important to test only an individual system in isolation. However, many classes will have dependencies on others, and in this case, a technique known as mocking is used. Many testing libraries have built-in support for mocks, which are objects that have the same interface as the dependency. Mocks can be used to ensure they are interacted with in the correct way, or return canned responses to easily but exhaustively test that a class behaves correctly under all conditions.

Dependency injection is a technique where a class (or function) is given its dependencies, as opposed to instantiating them itself. When using dependency injection, when the system is being tested, instead of real instances of the dependencies being given to a class (for example, in its constructor), the mocks are given instead.

However, there are times when not all the dependencies can be mocked out—for example, a class that has to read a file from disk, or is responsible for actually making a database connection. It is important to make these classes as small as possible, so they are little more than wrappers around the external dependency. Then, for classes that need that functionality, mocks can be used instead. When it comes to testing these units, the integration testing level can be used.

Integration testing is used to ensure that a cluster of modules actually interact together in the expected way. When using mocks, it can be easy to introduce an assumption to a mock that does not reflect the way the real dependency operates. This is especially true in languages that do not have strong typing, such as JavaScript, Ruby, or Python. Integration testing allows a test to run against real instances of their dependencies, such as real files on disk, a real database, or other dependencies. However, integration testing does not need to be as exhaustive as unit testing. Rather than testing each possible configuration of inputs and outputs, the value from integration testing comes from ensuring the assumptions on the interactions that have been mocked are correct, so it's only tests for these interactions that must be tested.

Integration tests are not as quick as unit tests, because they may have to do more computations rather than return a pre-canned answer, or have to communicate with a real database. Regardless, they are still fairly fast. Individual unit tests can be expected to take less than a few milliseconds to complete, whereas integration tests can take tens or hundreds of milliseconds. The slowest type of test is the end-to-end test, where each test can potentially take several seconds to complete.

End-to-end tests offer significant value, and because they are equivalent to the tests a human can run, it can be tempting to run a large number of them. This is a common pitfall for teams with someone in a traditional QA role who starts to embrace test automation.

End-to-end tests interact with systems in the same way a user would. For an API, this could be by simply making HTTP requests from a separate program, but for a web site, this can involve using either a headless browser (a type of browser that can be controlled programmatically, but never needs to show a visual representation of the web page to a human). However, headless browsers are not truly representative of how a user interacts with a site, especially as there is no browser with a perfect implementation of HTML standards. A popular tool called Selenium allows for real web browsers to be controlled remotely, and to query the state of a web page to make assertions on the state. It is also common to run the same test suite against different browsers to ensure cross-browser compatibility.

As these tests interact like a real user, they give the highest degree of confidence. But they are also the slowest. You should write as few tests as possible at this level, but enough to cover the most important parts of the system, similar to the approach taken with integration versus unit tests. For example, if you have an HTML form, it is important to test the success and failure cases at the end-to-end level, but testing every single validation, and every way in which a validation can fail, is best performed at a lower level of the pyramid, such as the unit test level.

Integration and unit tests interact with classes directly and must be written in the same language, and interact directly with the code of the system under test. The same does not apply to end-to-end tests. It is not uncommon to see end-to-end tests written in a different language from the application (for example, using Ruby with Capybara to drive a browser), and end-to-end tests can grow in complexity considerably. A technique known as the Page Object Model allows you to organize your code, which can simplify the actual tests. In this process, a layer of abstraction is placed between the browser and the tests, in the form of classes that abstract interactions between the pages. This technique is very helpful in clarifying exactly what the purpose of the test is, as well as reducing any duplication of identifiers such as CSS selectors, which can make the end-to-end tests quite heavily coupled to implementation details of the page being tested.

Using the Page Object Model, you create an abstraction layer over your UI to hide any implementation details, and then create a test using that abstraction layer. This allows you to change UI implementation details without breaking a large number of tests at once, as you can refactor the abstraction layer at the same time, as well as adding clarity to your test code. The example below shows how you may use Page Object Model alongside Capybara in Ruby.

```ruby
class HomePage
  include Capybara::DSL

  def visit!
    visit '/taster/' if category.nil?
  end
```

```ruby
    def pilot_filter
      PilotFilter.new
    end
  end

class PilotFilter
  include Capybara::DSL

  def visible?
    not container.nil?
  end

  def opened?
    container.find('.taster-filter__list', visible: :all).visible?
  end

  def open
    page.execute_script("$('.taster-filter').focusin()")
  end

  private

  def container
    first('.taster-filter')
  end
end

describe 'Pilot Filter' do
  before do
    @home_page = HomePage.new
    @home_page.visit!
  end

  it 'should appear on the home page', smoke: true do
    expect(@home_page.pilot_filter).to be_visible
  end

  it 'starts off closed' do
    expect(@home_page.pilot_filter).not_to be_opened
  end
```

```
  it 'opens when selected' do
    @home_page.pilot_filter.open

    wait_for(@home_page.pilot_filter).to be_opened
  end
end
```

Behavior-Driven Development

When it comes to answering the first question—whether or not a change works—automated testing introduced by developers often isn't quite enough. The main issue is that it's the developers who are defining both what the change is and whether or not it works. This is fine if the developers and the organization are in total agreement on what a successful change looks like, and what the desired change even is, but this is, unsurprisingly, rare. As discussed earlier, a lot of desired change at an organizational level is actually fairly abstract, but the product and UX functions of the team should have a fairly good idea of what concrete actions are needed in order to implement those changes, and it's those concrete actions that fall to the development team.

In the world of waterfall projects, requirements are often specified in large Word documents known as functional requirements documents, with requirement identifiers. These documents are handed over to the development team, which does what they think they're being asked to do, and then to a separate test team, which creates test cases and scenarios that satisfy each requirement. The main issue with this approach is the speed, checking that the developer and tester understanding of the requirements align comes at the end of the project. Most agile frameworks try to introduce the idea of a common understanding at the start of the build of a feature, and behavior-driven development (BDD) is a specific technique that can help with this.

Like TDD, BDD is often misunderstood, largely due to a growing number of BDD tools. Using a BDD tool like Cucumber, without fully understanding the rest of the BDD process, can become a more complex way of doing unit testing without giving you any additional benefit. Many BDD tools are based on the idea of executable specifications—that specification written by non-coders is responsible for executing your tests. These executable specifications are then parsed and matched against specific rules, which leads to real code being executed.

There are a lot of problems with this approach. Natural language is a bad proxy for code, so you either end up with a lot of ambiguous prose that is hard to parse, or, in order to make writing the parsers easier, you constrain the language of the specifications, which can frustrate business representatives. Executable specifications were designed to help business representatives and the development team communicate, and to ensure that the tests do actually cover all the requirements of the organization. There are other ways of achieving this same goal, though.

Waterfall projects often use requirement identifiers and the concept of traceability to ensure coverage—that is, you should be able to see which requirement caused some tests to come about, and that there are sufficient tests to cover a requirement. This can then be audited to ensure coverage. By stripping back this process to the essentials, we can re-use this in an agile project and get the best of both worlds. By giving each acceptance criteria an ID, and then putting a code comment by each automated test that implements the checks for the criteria specified in that ID, we can maintain traceability. These IDs can be trivial to generate. I often use a numbered list on a story card (either the back of a physical card or on a system like Jira), and then an ID can become simply the number in the bullet point plus the ticket number—e.g., #24/6 for the 6th bullet point on card 24. Instead of a full audit, a simple code review can then be used to double check the coverage.

Separating the specifications from the test code while maintaining traceability will make it easier to write the tests at the appropriate level of the test pyramid, which can help avoid many problems experienced by teams that are attempting to introduce executable specifications.

Three Amigos

So, how can we generate those acceptance criteria in the first place in order to gain a shared understanding? Getting this right is actually the very essence of BDD, and most people who focus purely on the tools may see their attempt to use BDD as a failure as they have failed to understand this point. The best way to achieve this is through shared authorship between all the parties involved. A technique known as the "Three Amigos" is a very effective way of doing this. The three amigos are a product representative, a developer, and a tester, the idea being that the product representative is the one who knows and understands the problem, the developer can ask questions in order to elicit a shared understanding, and the tester can guide the amigos to explore the whole problem space and interactions with other parts of the system to ensure all parts are covered.

In reality, the roles are a bit more blurred, and there can be more than three people involved; other business specialists, UX specialists, and project managers are commonly included. It's also okay for the specification to evolve as questions are asked, and it's completely acceptable for a developer to propose alternate solutions that may be simpler to implement as long as the essence of the requirements is still met.

The most important part of a three amigos meeting is that, at minimum, the people who will build the solution and the business people who know what is needed, have those conversations together, and are empowered to make and act upon decisions in these meetings. An amigos session with just a tester and a developer will end up simply guessing at the requirements. Similarly, one where the amigos are not empowered to make decisions will end up playing committee tennis, where the proposals go to another board to be reviewed and signed off, possibly with alterations added.

Often the outcome of an amigos session is the executable specification, but a set of acceptance criteria can be just as effective, especially if it's easier to use the expressiveness of natural language to say what the expectations are. These acceptance criteria are not the only point of reference, though. The developers and testers working on a story may not be the same as in the amigos session, but communication can help, especially because the avoidance of ambiguity in natural language is hard! It can be helpful to build a glossary on a wiki page over time, so stakeholders understand what a specific term means. This can be especially useful if there are fairly generic names in use (for example, an app may have an "about" page for the app in general, and an "info" page for each specific item).

The conversation is just as important as the outcome. Therefore, it's often unhelpful to develop the acceptance criteria for a story much in advance of when the build starts, partly because the business needs may have changed, and partly because people forget the discussions. Nailing those discussions down in the form of code is the ultimate goal.

One popular technique for specifying acceptance criteria is to use the Given-When-Then form of specification. This form starts by setting up the preconditions or assumptions for a particular part of the story, then specifies what actions the user takes, and then the post-conditions, or what should happen when a user performs those actions.

- Given I have an empty shopping cart

- When I add an in-stock product to my shopping cart

- Then the shopping cart should show that it is not empty

If you are taking this approach, it can be easy to fall into a trap of over-specification (this is especially true when these Given-When-Thens are being used as the basis for an executable specification). The above scenario can be considered a fairly high-level specification that still captures the essence of what is needed. When combined with a set of wireframes from a designer, it will often show exactly what is needed. The following example shows the same scenario but is over-specified.

- Given I have an empty shopping cart

- And there is an in-stock product in the database

- When I visit the page of the in-stock product

- Then I should see an "Add to Cart" button

- When I click the "Add to Cart" button

- Then the shopping cart icon should change to show a full cart

- And the number '1' should appear on the shopping cart icon

The issue with over-specifying like this is that it makes it hard to see the essence of the scenario, which can disengage business stakeholders.

An alternate style for Given-When-Thens is to use concrete examples. I personally prefer the more abstract ones, but it is just a matter of preference. The above scenario could be expressed like this:

- Given I have an empty shopping cart

- And carrots are in stock

- When I add carrots to my shopping cart

- Then the shopping cart should show that it is not empty

For teams that are considering adopting BDD, it's important to start with the essence of it and then choose tools based on their needs. You can do BDD without using Cucumber, and you can do BDD without using the Given-When-Then format for your acceptance criteria. Experiment and find what works well for your team!

Manual Testing

Regardless of how much you automate, there will always be a need for some form of manual QA. Automation removes the rote of simple testing (does clicking on this button do the right thing?), allowing testers to focus on more complex and emergent behavior. This can be a quick sanity check on a new feature, or an attempt to reproduce some unexpected behavior a user reported, or an aid to developing automated tests (if an automated test is failing, does a manual test pass, or when developing new automated tests, knowing the automated steps can come from first testing manually).

Most complexity in a system comes from interaction between components. When a whole system is tested together, those components can interact in unexpected ways, giving rise to unexpected behaviors. These behaviors often need to be kept in check, and identifying them is what manual testing excels at.

The two major parts of manual testing are functional testing and regression testing. Functional testing checks that any changes that have been made behave as expected, and make sense within the context of the whole; regression testing checks that any pre-existing functionality has not been broken by the new feature. Regression testing is the area where automation can have the most impact, as this is the most repetitive type of testing. Automation by itself is often not sufficient, and this is where close collaboration between a developer and a tester can help. A developer will be aware of which code paths they may have touched in implementing a feature (which may sometimes be non-obvious), which allows for testing to focus on the areas that are most likely to have been changed.

It is common for testers to write a test plan that lays out what they are going to test and their approach to doing so, and historically this document can be quite large. A particular test case might break down the steps to follow and the expected response, but at that level it becomes somewhat similar to writing code, so this level of detail is now often expressed in code. Especially when using behavior-driven development, the test plan can simply reference those acceptance criteria and focus on high-level approaches, if a test plan even exists at all.

It used to be common for dedicated test teams to sit apart from development teams, who accepted builds at the end of the sprint and then spent a test sprint testing the previous release—this led to incredibly slow feedback cycles. A more modern approach is to sit testers down with a development team and work alongside the developers, testing features incrementally as each component is developed. Bugs are raised in the same sprint and can be fixed while the work is fresh in the developers' minds. A more dysfunctional model could involve completely outsourcing a function like regression testing to an offshore facility where the testers simply follow test scripts expressed in a test plan. This kind of testing is ripe for automation.

Test automation might seem to eliminate the need for a tester, but the responsibilities and mindset of a tester still play a valuable role on modern teams. To that end, it's quite common for testers to refer to themselves as QAs, or quality analysts, who take a role more akin to a business analyst than a traditional tester. Where the difference of this role is best exemplified is in a three amigos-type situation, where the critical eye and perspective of a tester can help flesh out additional acceptance criteria. Another area where a QA can help is "exploratory" testing. In exploratory testing, the QA takes on the mindset of a user, and does complete end-to-end tests of various parts of functionality, ensuring that everything happens as expected (not just as specified). The QA has to understand the product and its customers to be able to do this effectively, and although testing the "happy path" (the most common use case that a user is expected to follow) is useful, a QA should also diverge from these paths where appropriate and do things that may seem strange, but are perhaps something a confused user would do. This kind of exploratory testing, especially when combined with user testing in the UX process, is where testing adds significant value. It is not just bugs that can be found, but also deficient specifications.

Visual Testing

Another area where manual testing excels is "eyeballing" a page to ensure it is visually effective. There have been many attempts to automate this process, with various levels of success, and there is no general solution that satisfies the question, "does this web page look like it's supposed to?".

Selenium is useful for testing whether or not content appears on a page and is visible, and it is possible to write tests that make assertions regarding the position (in terms of x and y coordinates) of a particular element on a page, but these tests will be very brittle. Small differences between browser versions, or available fonts, can introduce small errors, and changes such as introducing a new component on a page may cause a large number of tests to be updated. Unreliable tests will often be ignored, and combined with the amount of work required to maintain those tests, it usually means it is not worth writing them.

The human eye is therefore the best tool to verify the look and feel of a web page, but as a web application grows, running regression tests can get tiresome when all are done manually. Fortunately, there are tools that can help here, although they often have a high maintenance cost and are not used often. The general idea is to take either entire pages or individual components on a page and take a "known-good" screenshot of that page or component. As changes are made, the tests are then re-run and new screenshots taken. If any screenshots have changed, then the user of the testing tool is informed, and either approves the change or flags a regression. Adoption of these tools should always be taken with caution, as they will often flag false positives.

Cross-Functional Testing

So far, we have discussed ways of checking how your application behaves and whether it satisfies the requirements placed upon it. This kind of testing is often called "functional testing," but there are other attributes of your application that you will want to test. These don't relate to any particular feature (or function), but instead deal with attributes of your application as a whole. The types of requirements in this category are often called "non-functional" (as they don't relate to any one function of your application), or, perhaps less confusingly, "cross-functional" (as they cut across each part of your application).

Testing these cross-functional requirements is just as important as testing the explicit functions of your application. The kinds of things you may classify as cross-functional include security, usability, accessibility, performance, ability to handle load, and device compatibility. For the most part, these kinds of cross-functional requirements are common to many web applications, although some of the details may vary. Because of this, there is a large suite of common tools available to help you test your application, and many of them just need appropriate configuring.

However, these tools are not always necessary. For example, if you establish a requirement that an API call returns in less than 200ms, then you could write an HTTP request wrapped in a timer and make an assertion on that timer, like any other test. But if your requirement is that a page loads and renders to a usable state in less than 2s, then writing a test to do this becomes more complicated due to the complexity of rendering. A performance testing tool can be configured to make this type of assertion.

For other cross-functional requirements, such as security and accessibility, tools can help, but like functional testing, it often requires a bespoke approach, and there is no automation silver bullet. The general testing approach to these kinds of factors is often very much like normal testing, but is across the whole product (or focusing on where the changes have occurred) and may require specialized skills. More details on how to quickly check accessibility can be found in the Accessibility chapter, but simple security checking can be executed in a similar way to checking other features—by trying negative test cases and checking that they work as expected. The Security chapter will discuss some security aspects to watch out for, which can help you develop test cases, but security testing often requires you to try very non-obvious ways to break the application, which can benefit from specialized skills for apps with particularly stringent security requirements.

Like any other type of testing, testing non-functionals like security and accessibility does not prove the absence of bugs, but performance and load testing operate in a completely different way. Whenever you run these tests, you always get a result that can be evaluated against a benchmark, rather than it simply being a "pass" or "fail" scenario. These types of tests are also very environment specific, which can make them hard to run regularly as part of your normal development cycle.

Load testing (sometimes called volume testing) is a type of testing where the application is given a lot of simulated traffic to check that it behaves correctly under load. However, a load test running against a local development environment might not give meaningful results, as the hardware the application is running on may be significantly different. Some organizations configure their testing environments to have the same hardware as their live environment to allow these environments to be used for load testing, but this can be prohibitively expensive. Cloud computing can be helpful in this area, allowing you to spin up an environment that mirrors production for load testing. Some organizations feel confident enough to run their load testing on their live environment without negatively affecting their customers.

Load testing is often done at scale, and therefore uses quantifiable metrics to determine its success or failure. To set these metrics, you must first determine the baseline performance for your application, which is how it performs when it is not under any load—often with a single user. You should then determine the application's typical level of use—often based on real-world metrics if modifying an existing system, or a best guess based on what the organization knows—and the acceptable deviation from this level. This could be expressed in terms of percentage increase, or specific targets if hard metrics are known. Whether or not a system passes or fails a load test is then evaluated against these metrics. Load tests can also be modified to test "until destruction," where the number of requests or volume of traffic increases until the system completely fails, to give a good indication as to how much headroom your system has.

With this kind of testing, it is often useful to track the test results over time to identify trends, as well as checking for hard passes/fails against benchmarks.

Due to the unpredictability of environments when running load and performance tests, it is often necessary to repeat the tests to get meaningful results. Many tools will do this for you—for example, a performance testing tool will often render the same page 100 times and take an average that will give you more confidence than running it only once.

It can also be useful to check for these requirements by analyzing the behavior of real users, especially for performance and load tests. By monitoring real user performance, you can get a much better idea of the actual performance of your site than by simulating a load test (although load tests are still important for gaining early confidence). Monitoring things like server response time and CPU is discussed in further detail in the In Production chapter. For testing the performance of your front-end code, a suite of testing tools known as RUM (real user monitoring) allow you to capture analytics on statistics from real devices, which can be much nosier but give you a better idea of how your site performs on a wide range of real-world devices.

Summary

Testing is key to any software project, and should be used to not only ensure that a system works correctly, but that the correct system was built. Some level of testing can be done automatically by writing test code that runs individual components of the system in isolation (unit tests), or wired together (integration tests) in various states, and asserting that their responses or actions are correct.

Test-driven development is a mechanism for using tests to help structure your development. Tests are written first, and then the code needed to make it past second, finally once the functionality is proven correct the code is tidied up (refactoring). This allows a problem to be broken down into small, individually testable pieces, and can add up to be an effective suite for checking that nothing has accidentally broken or regressed.

Manual testing occurs when a user drives the application and checks that its behavior both meets the spec and makes sense. This can have some level of automation applied to it, where test code can drive the application as a user does—these are known as end-to-end tests. Manual testing is also effective at spotting visual errors, which end-to-end tests can miss. They can also be relatively brittle toward changes. Manual testing is best applied when the elements to check are ill-defined or abstract, and human creativity takes precedence. Exploratory testing is also something humans can undertake, where a tester takes a free-flowing journey through an application to test scenarios on the fly, rather than those which are pre-defined as requirements.

Behavior-driven development takes test-driven development a step further and adds specification at a higher level of abstraction. TDD might focus on unit testing, but BDD usually looks at integration or end-to-end testing. BDD is mostly used to ensure that there is a shared understanding between the developers, testers, and product representatives (the "three amigos"), who document the different scenarios the product is used in, often expressed in the Given-When-Then form.

The final aspect of testing to consider addresses components that go across all the functions of your application. This can include performance testing, security holes, or accessibility flaws. Like functional testing, automation can assist, but applying human skills to testing these will help catch areas that automation can miss.

CHAPTER 8

JavaScript

Famously designed in 10 days, JavaScript has quite a mixed reputation among software developers. However, if you're doing anything on the web, you will need to have some JavaScript skills.

JavaScript was originally designed as a language for manipulating web pages using an API known as the Document Object Model (DOM). Originally created at Netscape, it was named JavaScript as an attempt to ride the wave of hype behind the increasingly popular Java language, a decision that has caused confusion for new developers for years, as the language has little in common with Java. The early days of the web didn't help, with Microsoft developing its own variant, known simply as JScript which added new features, such as XMLHttpRequest (now part of the main language, and commonly abbreviated to XHR), which allowed developers to make requests to external servers to refresh the information on a web page. The European Computer Manufacturers Association (ECMA) finally decided to attempt to merge these competing implementations into a new standard, called ECMAScript. Therefore, what is called JavaScript nowadays is actually various implementations of ECMAScript, which is why you might hear terms like "ES6" or "ES2018" used in reference to JavaScript (previously it was versioned by number, but is now by year—ES2018 is the ninth edition of JavaScript). These refer to the different specifications published by ECMA, which different browsers are compliant with. In this chapter, I will reference the ES2018 version of the language. For developers who have worked with JavaScript before, ES6 introduced some significant language changes, such as the introduction of arrow function, with the yearly iterations beyond that introducing smaller, but still significant, changes.

JavaScript may have come from a rushed past, but as the language is constantly refined, some of the biggest thorns in the sides of developers (especially those who come from other languages) are disappearing. Some still remain, however, and I'll call out those issues below.

159

© Chris Northwood 2018
C. Northwood, *The Full Stack Developer*, https://doi.org/10.1007/978-1-4842-4152-3_8

For a long time, JavaScript on the browser was only used to add extra enhancements to a page, such as inline form validation, or simple animations. This was partly because the JavaScript engines in the browser simply weren't fast enough to support complicated operations; although there were some early apps that did, they were highly tuned for performance and were therefore complicated to build. Google changed all this with the introduction of the V8 engine, which significantly sped up JavaScript and allowed for much more complex code to be introduced to the page. Later on, the Node project was launched, which allowed JavaScript to run on a server, along with a new standard library to support server-side requirements. In addition to enabling the same language on both the client and server sides, this also enabled code-sharing between the two, introducing a new style of app known as isomorphic—or universal—JavaScript, where code is agnostic as to where it's run.

Asynchronicity

This book isn't the place to cover the huge range of events and APIs available in a browser, as they are rapidly evolving and there are many fantastic resources out there already. However, there are a few important things to understand. The main thing to understand about JavaScript is that it is single-threaded and relies on the concept of asynchronicity extensively. The downside is that, while JavaScript is executing, the runtime is "blocked." In the browser, this means that the whole browser will not react to any interaction from the user while a JavaScript function is running. On the server, it means no other connections will be accepted or handled.

Many JavaScript applications are IO-bound, rather than CPU-bound—that is, most of this time is spent waiting for an external event to occur, rather than doing heavy number crunching. In these kinds of environments, this single threading approach makes a lot of sense, because Node does not need to actively wait for these external events to occur. It can just execute a function, then when that function ends, it can use callbacks and event listeners for various asynchronous activities. When the events those handlers were set up for occur, those functions can then execute. In between those two instances, any other callbacks or event listeners can execute in response to events that have either occurred while the original function was running, or that happen while there is no active method.

This makes life simpler, because concepts of thread safety do not need to be considered, which eliminates an entire class of errors and complexity. If you are handling a callback, you do not need to worry that suddenly another function may start in the middle of your context and leave some shared state in an inconsistent or unexpected mode.

For a more concrete example of what this means, take, for example, some theoretical code for making a web request:

```javascript
function fetchAndLog(url) {
    const request = new XMLHttpRequest();
    request.open('GET', url, false);
    request.send();
    console.log(request.responseText);
}
```

The issue here is that it might take several seconds for the request to complete, and during that time the user can't interact with the page—to them, it almost appears to have crashed. Even when the request is quicker, it can seem to make the page slow.

An asynchronous approach might look like this:

```javascript
function fetchAndLog(url) {
    const request = new XMLHttpRequest();
    request.open('GET', url, false);
    request.onreadystatechange = () => {
        if (request.readyState === 4) {
            console.log(request.responseText);
        }
    }
    request.send();
}
```

While the user is waiting for the HTTP request to occur, they can continue to interact with the page as appropriate. This can cause complications with the user interface. If the user has performed an action that requires something asynchronous to occur, it may not always be obvious that their action has worked, so they click on it again. Updating the UI to include an intermittent "pending" or "in progress" state in response to an action is needed to avoid this.

CALLBACKS, PROMISES, ASYNC & AWAIT

For complicated functions, nesting callbacks to such an extent can result in "callback hell," where there's a deep level of nested callbacks. Take the following example for downloading a video file, transcoding it using ffmpeg, and then deleting the original file.

```
function downloadAndTranscode(url, outputFilename, callback) {
    downloadFile(url, (err, downloadedFilename) => {
        if (err) { callback(err); }
        ffmpegTranscode(downloadedFilename, outputFilename, (err) => {
            if (err) { callback(err); }
            deleteFile(downloadedFilename, (err) => {
                if (err) {callback(err); }
                callback(null);
            });
        });
    });
}
```

Every time a new asynchronous operation occurs, a further level of nesting is added, which can make the code hard to follow. Promises are a technique that can avoid this by building a chain of individual promises that each respond to the one before it. In the example above, we could rewrite this using promises to instead look like so:

```
function downloadAndTranscode(url, outputFilename) {
    return downloadFile(url)
        .then(downloadedFilename =>
            ffmpegTranscode(downloadedFilename, outputFilename))
                .then(() => deleteFile(downloadedFilename))
        )
}
```

In the example above, assuming that the functions themselves also return promises, a chain is set up. A promise can be thought of as a placeholder for an asynchronous function that will either resolve to some value or reject if an error has occurred. The promise object itself does not actually change, but instead handlers can be added to it by calling .then() with a callback. The return value of .then() is then a new promise, which can then be chained further. Promises are a very rich subject, and the Mozilla Developer Network provides a more in-depth introduction to promises and how to use them. `Promise.all()` has particular advantage over the previous callback style of asynchronous handling, allowing multiple asynchronous actions to happen in parallel and then succeed or fail as one, with the results being made available to the following `then()` in the chain.

`async` and `await` are also language features introduced to JavaScript that work behind the scenes to handle the construction of promise chains and can further simplify them. Using `async` and `await`, the chain above could be further simplified to:

```
async function downloadAndTranscode(url, outputFilename) {
    let downloadedFilename = await downloadFile(url);
    await ffmpegTranscode(downloadedFilename, outputFilename);
    await deleteFile(downloadedFilename);
}
```

The main issue with asynchronous actions is that it is often hard to refactor an API that previously worked synchronously into an asynchronous one. This is sometimes necessary when the way the API works under the hood has changed to an asynchronous one. However, refactoring an asynchronous API to a synchronous one is much simpler, as the callback can simply be called synchronously. With this in mind, it can often be easier when designing an interface in JavaScript to make it behave asynchronously, if there's any chance whatsoever that it will need to become asynchronous in the future.

This approach can create subtle bugs with regards to ordering and race conditions. Even if you can evaluate an asynchronous function immediately (for example, calling an error callback immediately on a method that makes an HTTP request if the parameters are invalid, whereas sometimes the callback is called asynchronously if it has to wait for a response), it can make sense to force it to always behave asynchronously, using mechanisms like `setImmediate()` or Node's `process.nextTick()`.

JavaScript in the Browser

JavaScript was designed to run in a web browser, and for a long time, that was the only place it did run. But JavaScript was never a widely loved language, and for a long time, people have used alternate languages for the Web. This was partly because of perceived shortcomings in JavaScript, and a desire to standardize on one tech stack. This caused the rise of browser plugins like Flash (which was supposed to address the former) and

Java (to address the latter), but these plugins have grown out of favor as the tension between closed source, proprietary plugins and the open nature of the Web intensified. JavaScript also evolved to address many of the issues that made it unappealing to become the powerful language it is today.

Another driving force for alternative languages was that many bits of functionality had to be implemented twice—once on the server (to validate form requests, for example), and again on the client (to provide a better user experience and faster responses). Some frameworks responded by automatically generating JavaScript for the page based on the server-side logic, but this created issues. The automatically generated code was inflexible and hard to debug, and it often performed poorly. With the rise of Node, the holy grail of writing DRY ("don't repeat yourself") code was in sight, as modules could be shared between the client and server. This has had varying levels of success, as the contexts of execution on a server and execution in a browser are very different and required careful engineering to get right.

An alternative approach was languages that compile to JavaScript. Google's GMail service has its front end written in Java, with a compiler that outputs JavaScript. Other languages, such as TypeScript and CoffeeScript, have taken the same approach, and occupy significant niches, but most web development is still done in JavaScript itself. This is partly because these alternative approaches can make debugging hard, but also because mixing libraries between different languages and the additional build work needed can often add more complication than saved effort. A feature known as asm.js was created to ease the ability to compile to JavaScript, allowing a simple subset of JavaScript that these compilers can target that, in theory, offers a high level of performance. This original idea has evolved into a standard called WebAssembly, a kind of low-level assembly language for the Web, which can be high performance but lacks access to the DOM, so cannot completely replace JavaScript.

One notable exception where compilation has taken off is in the case of JavaScript being compiled into another form of JavaScript, a process known as transpilation. For a long time, JavaScript didn't support modules or packages. Asynchronous Module Definitions (AMDs) were the first attempt to solve this, and ran natively in the browser simply by the addition of a library, but Node used an alternative method for module loading known as CommonJS. CommonJS wasn't natively compatible with the browser, so tools were needed to package CommonJS modules into browser-compatible scripts (Browserify is the most popular tool used to do this). This meant there was no longer a direct mapping between code written in an IDE and code running in the browser. Even before this, minification tools were used to boost performance, applying optimizations to the code and providing a single downloadable file. As with other languages that compiled to JavaScript, this made debugging more difficult. Fortunately, a technique known as source maps was introduced that allowed in-browser debuggers to help map the minified or transformed JavaScript back to the original.

With this in place, then came the next step in JavaScript transpilation. Although many people were using the latest browsers and were, thanks to auto-updating, remaining up-to-date, there was still a considerable chunk of people using older browsers, and either couldn't or wouldn't update. For some individuals, this can be a result of using old and unsupported devices, but for organizations, policy often dictates a conservative approach to rolling out new software until it has been thoroughly tested, meaning browsers can lag behind. As the pace of evolution of the web increased, developers wanted to use these new features, but were constrained by older browsers. At first, a technique known as polyfilling was used. Polyfills are scripts that provide pure-JavaScript versions of new APIs that are available in JavaScript, and were effective in letting people use new JavaScript APIs in old versions of JavaScript. However, they can't cover all the holes—for example, adding something like the Geolocation API to a browser that simply doesn't support it is impossible. Another limitation of polyfills is that they can't actually change the underlying language. As newer versions of JavaScript evolved, the syntax changed, introducing new ways of expressing classes and defining anonymous functions. The introduction of transpilers allowed for developers to use these new features in the code they wrote, but for them to be translated into a less readable, but backwards-compatible variant to allow for execution in older browsers. This can be thought of as a more advanced version of the autoprefixers used in CSS.

However, with these transpilers, an increasing number of technologies have arisen that are closer to the traditional compiler approach. Facebook's React extends JavaScript to "JSX," which allows you to specify the HTML structure of a React component using an HTML-like syntax. Carefully considered usage of such a technology can be beneficial— in the case of React, as you can only use JSX to write React components, then you aren't introducing a new dependency beyond using React. However, extensive use of similar technologies for other purposes can lead to vulnerable situations, since you are then heavily dependent on a non-standard approach for vast portions of your application, rather than only in a carefully scoped area.

Before the introduction of polyfills and JavaScript, a different approach was taken for backwards compatibility. This was partly because of a lack of standardization between the dialects of JavaScript, which did not emerge until much later. Some of these differences were fundamental, such as Mozilla and Internet Explorer having very different models for dealing with JavaScript events. To cope with these, it was much more common to use a library to abstract away the differences, so that library became your interface to the browser. By far, the most common library used to do this was JQuery, which became ubiquitous across the web, present on the majority of web sites at its peak.

As the Web has developed, this practice has become problematic. In modern browsers, the layer of abstraction offered by JQuery slows things down considerably, and many features that JQuery offered are now offered directly by JavaScript itself. Additionally, JQuery works in a global namespace, which can cause tension when you're trying to develop loosely coupled components. JQuery is still a useful tool and shouldn't be discounted, but in simple cases, it is not uncommon to see modules that interact with the DOM directly, rather than developers relying on JQuery. Use JQuery when needed, but know that it is no longer necessary to default to it.

As people are building richer and richer JavaScript applications, the original design decision to only have one thread, and to use an asynchronous model to keep the UI responsive, has started to cause issues. Front-end developers often refer to this problem as "jank." A site is janky when it isn't smooth to respond (for example, slow animations, or unsmooth scrolling, often caused by a "scroll" event handler). Fortunately, new browsers support "web workers," which are a way of bringing a thread-type structure to JavaScript. Web workers can be thought of more as background processes than as threads. They run in a more constrained environment, without access to the full set of browser APIs. Most importantly, the web worker does not have access to the DOM to alter the page directly. There is also no shared state, though messages can be passed back and forth between the main JavaScript context and the workers.

Offline-First Development

The Web is an inherently connected medium. If you have no network connection, you can't load web pages. Native applications have always had this advantage over web applications, as the code and content are held locally on a device. As increasingly complex applications are now being delivered over the Web, and with the rise of smartphones that may have patchy connectivity, a solution to this gap was required.

HTML5 introduced the concept of application caches, where manifest files determined which resources a browser should cache, which were "online only," and whether any offline placeholder content should be used when the network is unavailable. This approach proved hard to work with and was deprecated from the standards. A much more flexible alternative has now sprung up, known as service workers. A service worker is a JavaScript application that runs in the background of the browser, without access to the DOM. It behaves like a proxy server, in that all requests for the page or domain it was registered for go through it, meaning that the service worker can decide how to handle caching for requests.

Service workers are inherently asynchronous. They receive events from the browser, and then call `respondWith()` on the event with promises that either resolve with a response to the request that event signifies, or reject if there's an error. For example, the `install` event happens when a service worker is first loaded. In this case, it is common for a service worker to download all the static assets and add them to the browser cache.

Often the most important event, once a service worker is installed, is the `fetch` event. This is called when the browser wants to make a network request. It is up to you to then handle this appropriately. You could choose to return from the cache instantly if it exists, resulting in performance improvements but potentially presenting stale content to the user, or to instead make a network request to get fresh content, only falling back on the cache if the browser is offline.

Caching is a complicated area, with many different approaches depending on your exact goals. Caching in general is discussed elsewhere in this book, but specifically for browsers, a Cache API exists. The Cache API in browsers does not handle expiry of items in the cache, which means you will often need to write some code yourself (or use a framework) to handle this for you, in addition to implementing appropriate patterns such as "stale-while-revalidate" if desirable (see the Systems chapter for more information on caching techniques). You should also be careful about what you cache. A photo-sharing web site could quite easily fill up a user's disk if everything is cached indefinitely. To avoid this, browsers limit how much can be cached for an individual site. If you cache too much, browsers will prune the cache of important elements and your site may not work appropriately offline.

Offline-first goes beyond just using service workers to handle caching. Much like mobile-first web applications are designed to work with the most constrained screen sizes and interaction style first, web applications that are offline-first are designed to work without a network connection as their primary mode (usually by synchronizing the local caches with a server and then only accessing those local caches), rather than having an offline-only mode added on at a later date. This can add complexity to some types of apps, but will ultimately result in better performance and a more robust experience for the user. In the case of content web sites, the complexity of being offline-first may not matter; having the entire archive of a site synchronized to a device would be overkill. There are always exceptions, however. A travel guide being used out and about on a mobile phone without an internet connection would be a good fit. A news web site would not.

For read-only web sites, offline-first can be quite simple, requiring periodic downloads of certain data. This data can then be stored using the IndexedDB API from the service worker and accessed in the client. The Background Sync API was designed for exactly this use case, but at the time of writing, it is an extremely new API without widespread support.

For web sites where a user is expected to contribute data, the complexity can increase significantly. For example, in a hospital, it could be useful for doctors to use tablets for issuing prescriptions. However, wi-fi coverage at a hospital may not be consistent, so although the medicine database may be synced locally, the actual prescription could be stored until the device has once again connected, and then issued, similar to the way e-mail applications work. This kind of application could be handled fairly straight-forwardly by the Background Sync API by behaving opposite to the sync of server-side content. When a sync occurs, the service worker would check for messages in a pending or outbox table in IndexedDB and then fire them, marking them as successful when completed. User experience is important here, as the doctor would need to know if they've successfully issued a prescription, or if it has failed.

Other use cases become even more complicated. Take, for example, collaborative document editing, where multiple people are editing a document and want offline access (perhaps to edit an important presentation on a train or plane). Every software developer who has worked on a team is familiar with merge conflicts, when two people have worked on the same code and their changes have clashed with each other. The appropriate way to deal with this depends on your use case. Sometimes, "most recent wins" is a simple way to solve this, especially when combined with versioning to allow for mistakes to be corrected. A technique dating from the 1980s but popularized more recently by Google Drive, known as operational transformation, is a much more complex but effective way of dealing with this sync, as it can deal with any asynchronous operation, not just offline ones.

Regardless of the complexity, if you are building an application that is expected to be robust on mobile devices where connectivity may not be guaranteed, offline-first will allow you to tackle that complexity head on, rather than deferring it to another time.

Document Object Model

If you're working in browser-side JavaScript, you will at some point have to interact with the Document Object Model. The DOM is basically a tree of JavaScript objects that is exposed on a global object called `window` that represents the HTML structure of the page (starting at `window.document` for the `<html>` tag) and other HTML APIs. You manipulate the page by altering this tree—for example, inserting a new node as a child of another one to create new content, or by grabbing a node on the tree and altering its properties (for example, `innerText` on a `<p>` tag). Each HTML element has a corresponding class in JavaScript that offers an API, as well as some common APIs that apply to all elements (such as querying to find a child element, either on `document.body` to query the whole page, or inside an element for more scoped queries).

Another important concept related to the DOM is events. Until fairly recently, there were fundamental differences between how events were handled in browsers, but fortunately nowadays modern browsers implement the standard. DOM events occur in response to user interactions, such as clicking on part of the page or scrolling through it. You can bind functions to events that happen on particular DOM elements by calling `addEventListener()` on the DOM element you want to listen to. An older approach is to assign a function to an attribute of the DOM element you want to react to—for example, `target.onclick = myFunction`—but this has the downside of only having one handler per event.

DOM events differ from other types of events that require passing a specific callback to an API, as there is no DOM element to listen to. For example, calling `setInterval()` or `requestAnimationFrame()` both accept a callback with the result of the operation. Another difference in DOM events is the concept of event capturing and bubbling. When a user clicks on a button, the event is first "captured" through all of the parent nodes until it reaches the target, and then "bubbles" up, so that the event listeners on the button, then on the parent node of the button, then on its parent, and so on, are called, all the way back to the root of the DOM tree. You can use `event.target` to see which DOM element actually triggered the event. For example, if a click handler is on a `<p>` that has a `<span>` inside it, perhaps the user actually clicked on the `<span>`. Most event handlers run in the bubbling phase, and it is rare to see capture phase handlers in actual code. You can use addEventListener to specify whether a handler runs in the capture or bubble phase. Event handlers can also prevent further bubbling or capturing by calling stopPropagation() on the event object the handler is called with, but this can have unexpected consequences. preventDefault() is a more useful alternative that serves a similar purpose, by stopping the browser from perform its default action while still letting the event propagate to other listeners.

The number of HTML elements, events, and their interfaces is changing rapidly, although the most common of these are by-and-large stable and form a core of the HTML standard. Even covering these in detail would require a whole book, and I recommend the Mozilla Developer Network and many other resources that offer an extensive and up-to-date reference for all of these.

Server-Side JavaScript

Like JavaScript in the browser, server-side JavaScript is asynchronous, but the side-effects of this manifest themselves slightly differently. If the JavaScript in the browser is busy, the user can't interact with the page, but if the JavaScript on the server is busy, then the server will not process any other connections at all—users will have to wait until that one operation has completed. Although this asynchronicity can at first seem hard to understand (especially for a back-end developer used to dealing with threads and other techniques for parallelizing work), it is in practice a much simpler, and safer, approach than alternatives in other languages such as threading, when the work needed to be done by the application is IO-bound (that is, waiting for responses from other systems such as disks, databases, or API servers) rather than CPU-bound. Many web applications follow this pattern.

The major downside to JavaScript's single-threaded nature is that on a multi-CPU server, it is limited to using only one CPU, and if you want to utilize all the CPUs on a multi-core system, you will need to start up multiple processes of the app (fortunately, Node's cluster module allows you to share a port between all of these processes). This does mean that anything kept in-memory will not necessarily be available in response to future requests from a user, as a different process on the same box may serve that request. For storing any information that may need to persist beyond multiple requests, an external caching server such as Memcached or Redis is used. Using this approach is good practice, because if your application becomes popular, you may want to scale it onto multiple servers behind a load balancer to handle all of the requests.

With an external caching server in place, it is as easy to scale to multiple boxes as it is to scale to different processes. This approach is called horizontal scaling, and is discussed further in the Systems chapter.

The biggest difference between JavaScript in the browser and JavaScript on the server is the DOM. There simply isn't one on the server (nor would it make sense for there to be one!). Instead, Node has a completely separate standard library that provides functions that make sense on the server, but not on the browser, such as opening raw TCP sockets and accessing files. The language and syntax are otherwise the same, but for front-end developers new to server-side coding, it is sometimes surprising to realize that things such as a global `window` object actually aren't part of the JavaScript language, but just the DOM.

Of course, you can still render HTML, but this is done using templating techniques (as discussed in the Front End chapter) rather than by building a DOM, or by using a virtual DOM library that behaves like a DOM but renders out a string of HTML. The libraries and frameworks used by JavaScript are in a high level of flux that almost certainly means anything you read here will be out of date by the time this book is printed. However, server-side JavaScript seems to have developed a culture of small, loosely coupled libraries, as opposed to other server-side languages where there are much larger all-encompassing frameworks (such as Java's Spring or PHP's Symfony). It is not uncommon to have a large number of dependencies on your application. This can make a quick-start slightly harder, since you have to wire together a number of things before you start, but also gives you a great deal of flexibility to build exactly what you need.

JavaScript Modules

For a long time, JavaScript didn't employ the concept of modules—simply different files that all acted in the same way in the same environment. JavaScript doesn't have a standard library like other languages—all functions are available at all times—and the DOM was a single global object called `window` that new APIs kept getting added to over browser releases. If you wanted to bring in other functions that weren't built into the language, you would normally add another `<script>` tag to your HTML before your code was loaded, and then those libraries would at best add something else to the window object (like JQuery), and at worst leak a bunch of internal functions everywhere, and you would just have to hope they didn't clash with anything else.

The very first solution to that was to take advantage of JavaScript's scoping rules to only expose what you wanted to leak. One way to do this is a mechanism known as an immediately-invoked function expression, or IIFE. When something is defined inside of a function, it only remains visible inside of that function, so to avoid putting everything onto window, modules were instead wrapped in a function that then became immediately invoked:

```
(function() {
        function somethingPrivate() { ... }
        function externallyUsableFunction() { ... }

        window.MyLibrary = externallyUsableFunction;
})();
```

This defines a function and immediately calls it, which means that when a file containing it is dropped onto the page, it gets run straight away and `window.MyLibrary` is made available, but none of the private functions are available.

However, there are flaws here. What happens if two libraries accidentally pick the same name, or you want two different versions of the same library? You also have to hope that if you make a distributable library that has other dependencies, any HTML page that includes your code correctly adds the other `<script>` tags before you are called. This relies on users following some documentation, as opposed to the library declaring its own dependencies in code.

Following this, a new mechanism known as asynchronous module definitions (AMDs) was used. This was an agreed syntax for defining a module and then importing it into another module.

```
define('MyLibrary', ['dependency-1', 'dependency-2'], function(dep1, dep2)
{
        function MyLibrary() { ... }

        ...

        return MyLibrary;
})

require(['MyLibrary'], function(MyLibrary) {
        MyLibrary();
});
```

The first example above defines a library called MyLibrary, which exports a single function (called `MyLibrary`) and has access to two dependencies. This can be thought of as a step up from IIFE; functions are still used to ensure that the scope can be controlled, but instead of attaching things to the `window` object directly, they are returned from the function and stored until the library itself is depended upon. The definition also allows you to add the names of any dependencies you need, which are given as arguments to your defining function, so they are made accessible only to the modules that explicitly ask for them.

What the function actually returns could be anything. It could be a function, or it could be an object with many things on them, or perhaps even a simple string (if being used to define concepts like config settings or translations).

A library is then needed to provide a way of managing these dependencies, the most popular of which is called RequireJS. When you specify a dependency, RequireJS will then load it from the network as needed, which can reduce pre-load time, and is why these module definitions are asynchronous. A common optimization was to bundle all the dependencies together, so only one file needed to be downloaded at runtime.

NodeJS introduced another method of introducing modules, known as a CommonJS module. Instead of requiring IIFE, NodeJS by default ran each file in its own environment to avoid polluting the global namespace. A file therefore becomes a module by default, and to make something available to other modules, you added `module.exports = MyLibrary` to the end. Another module could then important that using syntax similar to `const MyLibrary = require('./my-library.js')`, as a path to the file that defines it (or if a non-relative path, like a path relative to a special folder called node_modules where all your dependencies live, often managed by a dependency management tool). This `require()` function, unlike the one in AMDs, is synchronous, therefore returns immediately, rather than requiring a callback. This is fine on a server where all files are local (although it can cause blocking), but gives you reduced flexibility on the desktop, as all possible dependencies must now be delivered as one bundle in advance, rather than loading in part later (there are now some tools that try to work around this restriction).

In an attempt to bridge the gap between AMDs and CommonJS modules, another approach known as a UMD (Universal Module Definition) is also used, although most often as the output of a build tool for a library, which is compatible with both.

The final type of module you will come across is the ES6 module, which was introduced in the JavaScript ES6 spec. An ES6 module is similar to a CommonJS module, except the syntax for importing and exporting modules is now language keywords, rather than special variables and functions.

In ES6 modules, you can have a default export defined like this:

```
export default function() { ... }
```

And then you can import this in another module:

```
import MyLibrary from "./my-library.js"
```

This makes the function available in the second module as MyLibrary.

ES6 modules also add the ability to export multiple things from a module, rather than a single thing, as with CommonJS. In this case, we can expand the first module as follows:

```
export default function() { ... }
```

```
export function utility() { ... }
export let configurationKey = '...';
```

and now in the second module:

```
import MyLibrary, { configurationKey } from "./my-library.js"
```

which makes MyLibrary and the configurationKey string available, but not the utility function. We can also avoid the default import completely:

```
import { utility } from "./my-library.js"
```

If the name of an export clashes, then it is possible to give it a different name when you import it:

```
import MyLibrary as AnotherLibrary from "./my-library.js"
```

The main drawback of ES6 modules is that, because they are a feature of the language, the module name must be a string literal. The following example is not allowed:

```
let libraryName = "./my-library.js";
import MyLibrary as AnotherLibrary from libraryName
```

This is because all imports in ES6 modules are done before the code executes, unlike the other module loading approaches, where the module loading happens at runtime. This is because loading a module might require downloading code in a browser, so all the referenced modules are downloaded at once, rather than having to be preloaded.

Structuring Your JavaScript

Before the mainstream adoption of JavaScript modules, it was common to have a small number of files containing large segments of functionality, or sometimes JavaScript inline in the HTML. This worked when JavaScript was mostly used for small functionality improvements, but modern JavaScript applications tend to be larger, and using a single file for your entire application is hard to manage. Nowadays, using modules to structure your application is normal.

Knowing how to structure your modules can be quite hard. There are two leading methods for dealing with this. One is to have folder structures for each type of component—for example, grouping any UI modules in one place, and modules for managing state and business logic in another, perhaps with further separations based on models, views and controllers for MVC apps, or actions, reducers and state for Redux applications. This method has been criticized for being an arbitrary separation that requires looking in lots of different places when changing a single feature. Another option is to have a directory per feature or functional component with all the different parts of that feature (models, views and controllers, or similar) in that folder. One issue with this method is that often models and other common concepts will be shared across many features.

As with many things, balance is key. It is widely considered good practice to have the components relating to your views be free of any non-view logic. Taking state out of a view component also makes it easier to reuse it, potentially across other modules. In React with Redux, it's also useful to keep a separation between the two types of view components: the component itself, and the component bound to the state.

In this case, all your views can be grouped together, perhaps with subgroupings for complex view components that might themselves have subcomponents, and business logic areas grouped based on functional domains. This means a view might take from many different areas of the state to render a UI component, but for the state, all the logic for manipulating that part of the state are kept together.

JavaScript Types

For many developers who are experienced with languages such as Java or C#, JavaScript's approach to data types can be surprising. JavaScript is known as a weakly typed language, in that it does have types, but these are implicit, and if something is in the wrong type, the JavaScript run time will try to implicitly cast something to the expected type. This behavior can be surprising, and can throw off a new JavaScript developer, and is the butt of many jokes about JavaScript.

For example: `1 + "2"` will result in `"12"` as + is overloaded to mean string concatenation as well as addition, and the integer 1 will be coerced to a string to make the types match. `+[]` will end up being 0, as the + operator attempts to make something positive, but a list has no sensible value and ends up being 0.

The biggest issue this causes arises when checking for equality. When using `==` (and `!=`), JavaScript will try to coerce both sides of the equality operator to match. For example, `"1" == 1` will evaluate as true, which is normally unexpected and undesirable. When using the identity operator, this type coercion does not happen, so both the types and the value of both sides must match. This can result in an idiosyncratic look to JavaScript code, where the identity operator of `===` (and its counterpart `!==`) appear frequently.

Fortunately, with the correct use of equality and identity checks, you can avoid hitting most of the pitfalls of this loose typing. Despite the fears of developers who are used to working in strongly typed languages like Java, it is rare to uncover bugs that result from this automatic type coercion. That said, you should also aim to avoid writing code that uses this loose typing, as that can introduce subtle bugs. It is sensible to call `.toString()` when concatenating strings when there is any doubt over the type of a variable, or run input through `parseInt` to ensure it is indeed an integer. The exception to this is often in `if` statements. As null, undefined, or empty strings become `false` when cast to a Boolean (these values are referred to as "falsey"), it can be a quick shortcut to write an if check such as `if (!input) { return; }` at the start of a function. Conversely, a number of values evaluate as true when considered as a Boolean, and these are called "truthy." You may see syntax such as `!!input` used, which negates a value twice and, as a result, converts a truthy or falsey variable into a literal true or false.

JavaScript, as of ECMAScript 6, has seven data types. Six of these are considered to be primitives, and they are Boolean, null, undefined, number, string, and symbol.

Booleans are `true` or `false`, and they behave as you would expect. There is only one value that has the type null, and that is `null`. Undefined is similar, having only one value: `undefined`. The difference between `null` and `undefined` can be confusing, but the main difference is that `undefined` is used to represent a variable that has never had a value assigned to it, whereas `null` is used to indicate that something has been deliberately given no value. Null also behaves confusingly when used with the `typeof` operator.

Despite null being a type, typeof null === 'object' is true. This is a result of a bug in the initial implementation of JavaScript that was left too long, and now cannot be fixed without breaking legacy code.

Also, unlike other languages, JavaScript only has one type for numerical values: number. This can simplify code, although if you are used to languages that do separate the two types, you must remember that the way elements such as integer division behave will differ from the way you are used to—it will become a float.

Strings should also be a familiar concept. In JavaScript, strings are immutable, meaning any operation you perform on a string does not change the original string. For example:

```
const url = 'https://www.example.com';
console.log(url.slice(0, 8));
```

This will print out the first eight characters of the variable url, but does not actually modify it. Instead, a new string is returned.

In implementation terms, JavaScript strings consist of UTF-16 characters (known as code points), which can act strangely when working with Unicode characters. In Unicode, some characters have IDs that are too long to fit into the space of UTF-16, so two UTF-16 characters are used, known as surrogate pairs, to represent a single character. This can manifest itself as strings appearing longer than they are. "🖊".length would return 2, rather than 1 as expected, as emoji exist in the area of Unicode known as the "astral plane," so require two UTF-16 characters. Other operations also require caution. For example, if you wanted to reverse a string, a naive approach would be to iterate over it backwards, but this would result in an invalid string, as the individual UTF-16 code points would be inverted, in this case referencing invalid Unicode characters. There are libraries that can help you work with these kinds of strings, but further detail is beyond the scope of this introduction.

The final primitive is the latest addition to JavaScript. Symbols were added in ES6 as a way of uniquely identifying keys on objects. The main difference between strings and symbols is that two symbols are not identical even if they have the same value. Although "example" === "example" evaluates to true, Symbol("example") !== Symbol("example") requires that the comparison is a not-equals in order to be true, unless the symbols on both sides are the same instances of the objects.

Objects are the workhorses of JavaScript, and can do many different things. Objects essentially map keys to values, behaving like maps or dictionaries in other languages. Functions are also objects, which means that objects can be executed. Objects are also used to implement other higher-level types, such as linked lists (known as arrays in JavaScript) or sets. A JavaScript array is an object with numerical keys and other helper methods.

Different objects always have different values, even if their contents are the same. For example `{ foo: 'bar' } !== { foo: 'bar' }` will evaluate to true, as in this case, the two objects that were created are different instances of the object. As arrays are also objects, this means that `[1, 2] !== [1, 2]` too is true. JavaScript does not provide a built-in way to check for equality in these cases, but there are simple approaches to implementing these kind of equality checks. For arrays (or objects where the order of keys is guaranteed), using `JSON.stringify()` to translate something into a JSON string and then doing a string equality check is a quick way to check this. For more complicated checks, such as deeply nested objects, there are many utility libraries available.

JAVASCRIPT OBJECT NOTATION (JSON)

When data is transferred between systems, it often needs to be converted into a string, or binary file, to allow it to be transferred across a network. This process is known as serialization, and often this can be used to serialize arbitrary objects. For example, in Python, this is known as pickling. JSON is JavaScript's equivalent, although it only supports serializing fundamental data types, not classes or similar, unlike other languages.

JSON was proposed in the mid-2000s by Douglas Crockford as a lighter-weight alternative to the XML-based serialization format that JavaScript originally used. JSON is a limited set of the syntax JavaScript uses to declare Boolean, object, string, number, and array literals. For example, it only supports double-quotes (") for strings, and does not support trailing commas in objects or array items. This was intended to make the language simpler and easier to use— to parse, you could use JavaScript's `eval` function to run it as JavaScript, and the result would be the parsed object. However, as `eval` allows running arbitrary JavaScript, this opened up a security hole if there was any chance the JavaScript was malformed or untrusted, so later versions of the language introduced `JSON.parse()` and `JSON.stringify()` as methods to convert JavaScript objects to and from JSON strings.

As a result of its relative simplicity and support for types that are also fundamental in other languages, JSON has become a common serialisation format for other languages and systems too, and there are many libraries for other languages to serialize and parse JSON—even those where neither server nor client is JavaScript.

As a result of JSON's lack of support for more complex types, both server and client must agree on how to convert anything more complex into JSON and then back into the more complex type, so JSON by itself cannot completely self-describe data. It must be paired with some additional type information. This is a source of criticism for JSON, especially from the XML community, where XML schemas can be used to more strictly define the form and meaning of the encoded data. There are tools available for JSON that help define the meaning and check the validity of serialized JSON—JSON Schema is one of the more commonly used options.

The biggest advantage of JavaScript's weak typing is that duck typing can be used when passing objects around (i.e., if an object behaves in an expected way, even if it isn't defined in terms of the expected type, such as if it had the same keys or similar). For the most part though, weak typing is often seen as a negative to be avoided. For a long time, other languages have existed that compile to JavaScript, and as mentioned earlier in this chapter, there are JavaScript transpilers that take new JavaScript and make it backwards-compatible with old browsers. To this end, Microsoft has developed a language called TypeScript that looks and feels like JavaScript, but includes type annotations that are then checked in the transpilation process. An alternative approach has been taken by Facebook with their Flow type checker. Instead of using a new language that's derived from JavaScript, Flow allows you to add annotations to existing JavaScript code, which are then stripped out during the transpilation process. A separate type checker runs over the code to check that all the types are as expected.

```
function fetchTransactionValue(id: string): Promise<number> {
    ...
}
```

The preceding code is an example of a type annotation in Flow, indicating that the function takes a single parameter of type string and then returns a promise, which resolves to a number (often, the return type is inferred, so does not need to be explicitly specified).

TypeScript and Flow are popular methods for helping development teams write JavaScript and avoid bugs, and at the time of writing, it appears that adoption of these tools will only increase.

Object-Oriented Programming

Object-oriented programming has become the predominant methodology in software engineering over the last few decades, replacing structural programming. Although JavaScript supports object-orientation, it doesn't do so in the way most people are used to. Most programmers are trained on object-orientation in the classical sense (here, classical means "pertaining to classes," rather than "traditional"), where objects are instantiations of classes, and classes can have hierarchy. Until ES6, JavaScript differed in that JavaScript classes were prototypical. Rather than an object being an instance of a class, it's an instance of a prototype. As such, it is missing many features that a Java or PHP developer may take for granted, such as interfaces, inheritance, or even method visibility and defined fields.

ES6 has changed all that by introducing classes into JavaScript, which are much more familiar to those coming from other languages. Under the hood, objects are still prototype-based, but you can now treat them the way you would otherwise treat classes. Libraries also exist for older variants of JavaScript to make prototypes feel more like classes, but they never became a core part of the language. Other techniques give support for private fields, such as keeping the private fields in a different scope and enforcing access through getters/setters, but these often have a performance or memory overhead.

JavaScript isn't the only language to not have private methods/fields. Python also doesn't, taking a "gentleman's agreement" approach. "Private" methods and fields are prefixed with an underscore and not documented, and although this does not prevent them from being accessed directly, they indicate to a developer that they are doing something wrong and should not be relied upon. For many JavaScript applications, this approach is also sufficient, even if you're distributing a library for wider consumption.

Prototypical objects in JavaScript start by defining a constructor as a normal function, and then adding functions to an object of that function called `prototype`. It looks a bit like this:

```
function ShoppingBasket() {
    this._items = [];
}
```

```
ShoppingBasket.prototype.addItem = function(item) {
    this._items.push(item);
}
```

Running new `ShoppingBasket()` will create a new object from the prototype, set `this` to be that object, and then run the constructor.

ES6 classes simplify this syntax to make it look more familiar to developers coming from other languages, meaning you could instead specify the above in a more familiar sense:

```
class ShoppingBasket {
    constructor() {
        this._items = [];
    }

    addItem(item) {
        this._items.push(item);
    }
}
```

Now, recall that in our first example, `ShoppingBasket` is just a function. That means that if we call `ShoppingBasket()`, forgetting to add `new` at the start, then the code will execute, but will do the wrong thing. A new object will not be created, so `this` will be the `window` object, and nothing will be returned from it. JavaScript has a mode called strict mode to help prevent this from occurring. Strict mode can be enabled by adding `"use strict";` to the top of a file or function, and is designed to make common mistakes actually throw errors, rather than be silently ignored. In this case, it stops unknown variables from being set on `this` unless they are actual objects.

To avoid this, there is a pattern that prefers not to use `new` at all, but instead use functions for everything. For example, the previous code could be expressed as:

```
function ShoppingBasket() {
    const items = [];
    return {
        addItems(item) {
            items.push(item);
        },
    };
}
```

This code is a function that returns an object with functions. It also makes `items` private by not actually putting it onto an object that is returned. This has the downside of increasing memory, as each method on the object is a new instance rather than a shared prototype. However, for modern JavaScript, ES6 classes are far and away the preferred way of expressing classes, with the other approaches common only in older code. There are also various libraries that can help create different types of JS classes, but these mostly predate ES6 classes.

One of the biggest benefits of ES6 classes is that they make class inheritance behave as many would expect it to. Take for example:

```
class Animal {
    ...
}

class Dog extends Animal {
    constructor() {
        super();
        this.kennel = null;
    }
}
```

In this, the class `Dog` extends `Animal`, so when `new Dog()` is called, it has both the methods of `Dog` and the methods of `Animal` (assuming that `Dog` has not overridden them). The keyword `super` is also made available, and can call methods on the parent (or further away, if the inheritance chain is several layers deep). When using ES6 classes, this hides a lot of the complexity required to specify prototypes directly (this is why there were several helpers in JavaScript to do inheritance prior to ES6).

The best way to understand how inheritance works in JavaScript is to know about prototype chains. An instance of a JavaScript class is an object that has a prototype. However, this prototype is itself just an object, so it can itself have a prototype. This is called the prototype chain, and when you access a JavaScript object, the prototype chain is followed until the first thing with the name you're asking for is found. Ultimately, the last object you define in a chain will have a prototype of JavaScript's built-in `Object`, which itself has a prototype of `null`, indicating the end of the chain.

This shows that there's never actually a thing called a class in JavaScript—just objects and prototypes—but this implementation detail is mostly irrelevant for most common day-to-day uses of JavaScript.

A final word of warning regarding objects in JavaScript, involving the keyword this. For developers coming from almost any other object-oriented language, this always refers to the instance of the object that the method belongs to. In JavaScript, it refers to the context the function is operating in. For example, when a function is added as a click event handler, when it is executed, this will be the element that fired the event, as that is the context the callback is executed in. JavaScript doesn't differentiate between methods and functions, so passing a method to a click callback will divorce it from the object to which it otherwise belongs.

A common way of getting around this was to create a variable called that or _this or similar, and create a function that had that in scope (this is called a closure—more on that in the Functional Programming section), which gave it access to the object. In ES6, there are two alternative mechanisms in use: using .bind(this), which creates a new function with the this variable correctly referencing this (the same "this" that is passed in as an argument to bind), or using the arrow shorthand for defining a function (*()* => { ... }), which does that automatically.

Functional Programming

Functional programming isn't new —it predates the rise of object-oriented programming—but has seen a resurgence, and some of JavaScript's early design decisions have made it suitable for applying these functional programming techniques, even though it does not enforce pure functional programming.

One advantage of JavaScript in this context is that it allows you to switch between class-based, procedural and functional styles with ease, and even use them in combination with one another. Some consider pure functional programming unsuitable for certain kinds of tasks, and certainly for many developers it requires a change in thinking about how to structure programs. This has held back the rise of functional programming for a long time.

In essence, functional programming has risen from the world of mathematics. It can sometimes be intimidating to a newcomer, as many of the terms (functor, monad, etc.) are very unfamiliar, and the concepts are often not easily described without relying on a base knowledge of category theory. But you can use functional programming techniques without developing any deep knowledge. At the core of functional programming is the idea of a function. A function is something that, for a given input, always returns the same output. Contrast this to an object-oriented approach, such as this date object:

```
class Date {
  ...

  addDays(daysToAdd) {
    this.timestamp += daysToAdd * 24 * 60 * 60;
  }
}
```

if we run addDays multiple times, the result we get is different each time. We could write a similar function that performs the same each time, but the function stores no state. It returns a new result, and doesn't change the original one.

```
function addDays(date, daysToAdd) {
  return {
    timestamp: date.timestamp + (daysToAdd * 24 * 60 * 60),
    timezone: date.timezone,
  };
}
```

This is very powerful, as it eliminates a whole series of bugs, and it also allows us to chain together methods in new and interesting ways. Of course, it is possible to code a method this way too, such that it returns a new instance rather than modifying this one.

If you have worked extensively with JavaScript, there's a good chance you're using functional techniques already, without knowing it. Prior to .bind becoming a feature of the language, you may have seen this common technique:

```
Widget.prototype.setupEventListeners = function() {
    var that = this;
    foo.addEventListener('click', function(ev) {
        that.handleClick(ev);
    });
}
```

This employs two techniques that are core to functional programming: closures and functions as first-class objects.

A closure is simply a function that has access to the scope of where it is defined. In the setupEventListeners function, we declare a variable that, and the click callback handler. Even though the callback handler is a different function, and will potentially run long after setupEventListeners() has finished executing, it still can use that, as it has visibility to the scope (and also any nested scopes where it was declared).

WHAT IS SCOPE?

Scope determines which functions can "see" a particular variable or function. Take the example:

```
function getCircleArea(radius) {
    const PI = 3.1415926535;
    return PI * radius * radius;
}
```

(in reality you would use Math.PI)

The variable PI is in scope within this function, but no other functions or areas of code can access it. Because JavaScript allows us to nest functions and blocks, scopes can also be nested within each other to create different levels of scope. Many module-loading frameworks will also create a scope at a file level, so you can't arbitrarily use a variable in another file unless it's declared as an export, and you import it. Other languages also employ the idea of "global" scope, where something is automatically available without having to be imported. JavaScript does not quite use the same concept, but instead has a global object (window in browser-based environments) that you can add things to.

Prior to ES6, the only way to declare variables was with the keywords var or function (for functions), but these were subject to something known as variable hoisting. In variable hoisting, all variables are defined before any code runs. For example, in strict mode, you would expect this to fail, as a is declared when it is set:

```
a = 6;
var a = 5;
console.log(a);
```

Because of variable hoisting of var a, when a = 6 runs, var has been declared. a = 5 overrides the value, as the initial values are not hoisted, just the definition. This can be useful for recursive functions; for example:

```
function recurseDeep(items) {
    return [].concat(recurseWide(items[0]), recurseWide(items.splice(1)));
}

function recurseWide(items) {
    if (items[0].length > 1) {
        return recurseDeep(items);
    } else {
        return [].concat([items[0][0]], recurseWide(items.splice(1)));
    }
}
```

You want recurseWide to be in scope for recurseDeep, despite it having been declared before.

ES6 has introduced two new keywords that can help protect you from errors that can be accidentally introduced by var. These are let and const, and they are what is known as block-scoped. Instead of automatically being declared at the top of the function that contains the definition, they are declared at the point they are actually used, and are only in scope within the block (set of braces) where that definition occurs.

let is used for variables that can be reassigned, whereas const is for variables that are not reassigned. const is not necessarily constant; for example, a list or object defined as const can have new things added to or removed from it, because it is always pointing to the same list. The best practice is to always use const, unless you need to reassign, in which case you should instead use let.

A slightly contrived example of using let and const is:

```
function calculate(a, b, callback) {
  let wrappedCallback;
  if (callback === null) {
    wrappedCallback = () => {
      console.log('done');
    };
```

```
  } else {
    wrappedCallback = (result) => {
      callback(result);
      console.log('done');
    };
  }

  if (a > b) {
    const result = a + b;
    wrappedCallback(result);
  }

  wrappedCallback(null);
}
```

In this example (which calls back the result of adding a and b if a is greater than b, and then null to indicate the calculation is finished), `wrappedCallback` must be `let` because the value is assigned to it after the fact, whereas `result` is `const` because it is never reassigned. In the final line of the function, we would not be able to access `result` (it would give an error as an undeclared variable) because the scope of result is limited to the body of the `if` function where it is declared.

Functions as first-class objects simply means that functions are objects that can be passed around like any other object, such as a string or a number. One important concept this enables is that functions can be passed to other functions as callbacks. Contrast this to languages like Java and PHP, where a technique known as reflection is needed in order to access these functions, which gives a large amount of overhead for passing around things like callbacks.

This allows JavaScript to have many asynchronous features, compared to languages like PHP, which must wait for a function to execute (known as blocking) before continuing on to the next line of code, or Java, which uses threads to avoid blocking, although an individual thread can still block.

There are several techniques that functional programming makes use of that are not common in predominantly object-oriented approaches. One such technique is that of a partial function. A partial function is a version of another function that has some of its arguments "pre-filled." Take, for example, the following snippet:

```
function foo(a, b, c, d) { ... }

function makePartialFoo(a, b) {
    return function(c, d) { foo(a, b, c, d); };
}
```

This `makePartialFoo` is given the arguments a and b and returns a function that only needs c and d passed to run. Every time that new function is called, a and b are already supplied. This can be useful if a function takes some dependencies (through dependency injection) or other state into its first few arguments and then uses those as common arguments for a number of invocations.

`bind()` allows us to make partial functions much easier. We could instead make a partial version of the function foo above by calling: `foo.bind(this, a, b)` instead of needing to have a function to make the partial of foo (which can get unwieldy if you want multiple versions of foo). In pure functional languages, all functions can be made partial just by calling it with a subset of its arguments, a process known as currying.

In functional programming, functions should not hold some state. Instead, state is represented in a data structure that is passed to or returned from the function. Similarly, a pure function should not manipulate what it has been given. For example, if you had a function that added money to an account, and it was called as `addMoneyToAccount(account, money)`, then it should return a new account object with the money added to it, and the previous instance of the account object remains in the previous state. This is called immutability, in that once an object or thing is created, it should never change as a side effect or something else. Instead, a new object is created as the result of the operation.

This is useful because it allows you to chain together operations by calling another function on the result. In JavaScript this can get quite unwieldy—imagine `baz(bar(foo(thing)))`, but potentially even deeper. The code can be hard to follow, as the order of operations is backwards (i.e., foo executes first, then bar and finally baz). As a result, functional programming languages offer different ways of chaining functions like this (in Haskell, the syntax would be `foo . bar . baz thing`), and many functional programming frameworks in JavaScript offer ways to mimic this chaining. It may look unfamiliar, but remember that they are still function calls.

As a language that is neither purely object oriented nor functional, but allows you to mix both styles, it is hard to determine what is idiomatic JavaScript. When should classes be used, and when should functions be used? Often, it comes down to what you prefer, what already exists in a codebase, or the style used by any external libraries or frameworks you are building on top of. It is common to mix and match styles within a codebase, depending on the task at hand.

A reasonable rule of thumb is to use a functional style when you want to make more generic functions, which act on more generic data structures such as lists or dictionaries, and there are many ways you might want to manipulate that data. Classes are useful if you are working with data and want the methods of operating on it to be very tightly bound. Dates and times are good examples of things that can be classes, as the logic for manipulating them is tightly connected to the nature of the data. In this case, you might want to consider making these kinds of classes immutable, so the methods actually return new instances of the class rather than modify the one in place, to avoid some of the issues that come with classes and shared state. Other times classes might be useful is when you need wrappers around a particular resource, and multiple operations can operate on the same resource. An example might be an HTTP client that takes some configuration options, or a database connection. It is possible to use these functionally, but this can often be painful, as it requires passing around configuration or handles in many places (partial functions can help, but can also require a large number of functions to be passed around, whereas a class can simplify the process). In this case, state is often not modified once the class is constructed, and it acts simply as a collection of functions over some shared configuration or connection. Classes in this case can also correctly handle logic, such as connection pooling, reconnection, or circuit breakers, while presenting a simple interface to the user.

Communicating Between Components

Early JavaScript often had very simple requirements, and didn't require much code to be written. A single JavaScript file with little nesting or modularization, and global variables, may have sufficed for those needs, but as JavaScript applications have become larger and more complex, that is no longer the case. Instead, we structure JavaScript as modules, but those modules need to interact with one another. Coupling is the term used to describe the interaction between two modules, and how closely bound the modules are with each other.

It is usually desirable to have each module loosely coupled—that is, to minimize the amount of interaction between the two—through well-defined interfaces. By contrast, strong coupling would mean that two modules were highly linked together, interacting with each other very frequently in many different ways. Strong coupling can mean that the two modules become hard to separate and use independently. The concept of loose coupling is prevalent in object-oriented design, but applies to functional programming too.

The loosest coupling is one where there is no interaction whatsoever, but components often have to at least communicate state or changes to each other. One way to do that is to call methods directly on any component that needs to know when an event change happens. This, however, introduces a flaw in your component design—a component has to know every possible other component that could change based on that state, which can introduce a large amount of coupling. An alternate way to solve the problem of communicating state changes is by solving the problem the other way around. Rather than something that can generate a state change sending messages to those that need to respond to that change, you could set up the components that depend on that to register a callback when an event happens. However, this introduces a different form of coupling, as now these components have to know exactly which other components can generate those state changes.

A common way of getting around this is to use an event bus. In this scenario, things that cause state changes send messages to the event bus when an event occurs, and then others subscribe with callbacks to know when that has happened. In JavaScript, events are the predominant way the DOM indicates changes to interested code, but custom events can also be fired on the global `window` object, which allows a straightforward event bus to be created, where events get fired in the same way as DOM and subscribers can subscribe to that as needed.

There are many different architectural patterns that can be used with event buses. One pattern is known as a hexagonal architecture. In a hexagonal architecture, your app is split up into different layers (similar to model-view-controller). For example, at the very core is usually where domain models live, then this is surrounded by a layer that implements business logic, and eventually a layer that implements interaction with the outside world—not just UI, but also database and other persistence stores. Each layer communicates with the one above it through ports and adapters. A port is essentially an interface into a layer, and an adapter is what a layer implements to communicate with a particular port to transition from one layer to another. This hexagonal architecture often works well with another design pattern known as CQRS: command query responsibility segregation. In CQRS, the methods and data structures you use to interact with data and those you use to read data are different, with one corresponding to the adapters and the other to the ports.

This particular architecture can get very complicated when your application is closer to a CRUD (create-read-update-delete) use case. In CRUD, you are normally just editing underlying data structures, but CQRS is better for triggering particular events where the UI action is not directly linked to the underlying data structure changes.

For CRUD apps, a particular UI component may only be directly interested in one part of the state (or data model), so can set up event handlers on that data model directly, without necessarily using an event bus. The component in question can update the data model, and then set up events as needed. This is known as two-way binding, as communication happens in two ways. For apps that are more complicated and task-based, then separating the concerns through an event bus is often easier to manage, and instead a one-way binding to a data model is then used. In a one-way binding, a UI component fires an event into an event bus, and then receives a new/updated data model based on the changes. This separation means you do not need to know the detail of the whole structure of the underlying data model or how it needs to be manipulated—that can be left to a business logic layer. You only need to couple to the bits that give you the information you need to read, rather than what you need to change. With one-way binding, your application is closer to the CQRS application pattern, even if it is still performing CRUD-like applications.

Most event bus systems in JavaScript do not directly fire events through the DOM, but instead have their own event system outside of the DOM, which allows intermediate layers such as business logic to be better inserted.

One common JavaScript library for managing events with one-way flow is Redux. In Redux, events are triggered by dispatching an action. Redux provides a function called dispatch, which is bound to a particular instance of an event bus, and actions are defined by the developer as a particular thing that can be triggered. These are often linked to UI actions, but can be linked to other asynchronous events. Actions have a type, but can also carry other data. For example, you might have an action called SEND_MESSAGE that has the body of some text as an argument. A UI component dispatches this action when the user clicks "enter" in a chat window. For asynchronous actions, you may have a timer that triggers the background refresh of a user's state, which may then fire an event called

REQUEST_USER_STATUS to update away indicators of a friend's list. Then, the action causes the business logic to fire a request to get a new list, and then, once it completes, calls another action, UPDATE_USER_STATUS, with the response of the request.

Dispatching an action causes an event to be created, which is then passed to the business logic. In Redux, these bits of business logic are called reducers, but they essentially take a current state and the event, and then return a new system state that has been manipulated according to the needs of that action. The components are then notified of a change of state, and Redux provides mapping functions that allow a component to only be bound to the parts of the state that it actually needs to give us the loose coupling we desire. This is what is meant by uni-directional flow; the state changes may be started by an action being dispatched in a component, but the actual state changes only happen in one direction, rather than a component changing the state or data model directly, as happens in a two-way binding system.

Redux works especially well with React. React is a JavaScript library developed by Facebook that re-renders UI components when the data model they are bound to changes, which can greatly simplify logic. The full details of React are outside the scope of this book, but essentially, React allows you to define UI components, often using a language known as JSX, which allows you to express these UI components in an HTML-like way. React then takes a tree of these components and renders them out to HTML. Each component can maintain its own state, and is passed properties (props) that can be used to determine how a particular component behaves. A component cannot directly change the props of its parent—only its direct children. If any part of the state of a system changes, which results in changes to the props, React re-evaluates the components where the props have changed to see if they have resulted in any change to the resulting HTML. If it did, React makes only the changes it needs. This can be more performant than potentially re-rendering the entire DOM, or making a series of incremental updates as the state changes. With React and Redux, the coupling for a component becomes the actions it needs to dispatch into the store, and the specific parts of the state it needs to read out, which are done by mapping actions and state to props of a component using connect. The business logic is completely decoupled from logic, allowing React to figure out how the state maps to the attributes the UI needs, while Redux handles events.

Using this kind of event bus system also allows us to implement state machines to capture the particular state of a system, instead of simply mapping directly to values of particular data models. A state machine is used to map flow through a system—often, a higher-level component organizes other components based on the state, and then the actions that the other components can trigger may cause transitions into other states. Figure 8-1 demonstrates one way of depicting a state machine, where the circles represent the states and the arrows are annotated with the actions that can cause a transition between those states.

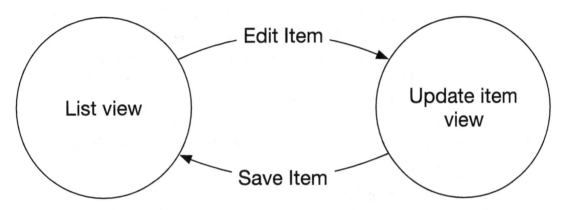

Figure 8-1. *A state machine for editing and saving an item*

In the above state machine, we can see a process for editing an item in a web app. We start in the state of "List View", and selecting "Edit Item" will cause the state to transition to "Update item view", with the item that is being edited set to the state. In the "Update item view state" pressing the save item causes the state to transition back to the list view (normally with a side-effect of saving the changes back to a database), but you may also have a "cancel" transition that also transitions back to "List View", but without the side-effect. Most systems will have a state machine somewhere, and although this can often be determined through the value of particular parts of the data model, it can be useful to directly model the current state as part of your data store, rather than trying to derive it from the values of the models in the data store, and being explicit in your business logic of the transitions, rather than leaving them implicit.

In state machines, though, some transitions are invalid, so care must be taken to only trigger an action that is valid from a particular state by a component. This is often done by making components that can cause a transition inactive during particular states.

Connecting Components Together

Although it's possible to reduce the coupling between components, there will often still be cases where you will need access to another component or library in your code, and there are two ways of doing this.

The first is to simply import the components or libraries that you depend on directly, and the second is a technique known as dependency injection, where a component is given specific objects that it depends on, rather than importing them itself. Considering the event bus approach with Redux discussed previously, this case also includes functions such as the dispatcher, which can be used to dispatch actions, and the bound values from the store, in addition to other utilities that might be needed.

For utility libraries, which are not configurable, the first approach often makes sense. Let's say we need to generate unique identifiers for something in our code. We might want to do the following:

```
const uuid = require('uuid');

function buildCommentModel(commentText, threadId) {
  if (commentText.length === 0) {
    throw new Error('Comment is empty');
  }

  return {
    id: uuid.v4(),
    body: commentText,
    thread: threadId,
  };
}
```

Often, the libraries and functions you import this way will be functional—they will not have any state, just things you can configure after importing. Similarly, importing a class from a file, the state will live in the instance, not the class.

This approach of pulling in dependencies can be thought of as a module asking for what it needs, rather than being given it. However, there are many cases when importing things in this way is not helpful—for example, if the module needs access to a shared resource, or an external library takes some configuration, but you want to configure it once, rather than every time it's used.

A tempting solution might be to create a module that exports an instance of your class, or an already-configured set of options for your functions. For example, many times in NodeJS we need to talk to other back-end services, and we import an HTTP client. However, especially in enterprise environments, it is not unusual for machines to live behind a proxy, or to require specific configuration—perhaps we want detailed logging in the development environment, but not in production. If every time we made an HTTP request we had to configure that HTTP client in every piece of code that imports the class, it would generate a lot of repeated code and require many changes every time we needed to change its behavior. A similar approach could be connections to databases—it'd be much more convenient for modules to simply get an active database connection than to create a new one from the raw classes or functions. It is tempting just to import an instance of an HTTP client that's configured.

However, this breaks the rule of coupling. That module is now specifically linked to that particular instance in that module. This may seem fine, but when it comes to unit testing your code, you may not want to use a real HTTP client, as this can result in very slow tests, and makes setting up test data much harder. We want to replace that HTTP client with a mock, but when a module asks for a dependency, there's no easy way to actually give it a different dependency than the one it asks for. There are tools, such as proxyquire, that replace the CommonJS `require()` with one that can return alternate options for the purposes of unit testing, but this can lead to non-obvious issues and spaghetti code, especially if, at a later time, we want to change which HTTP client we use in production (perhaps development and production environments use different proxies, or different TLS certificate authorities).

Furthermore, this approach actually reduces the flexibility of the component (a side effect of increasing the coupling). If we needed an HTTP client that was configured in a different way, then we'd have to create a new module that configures it differently, causing duplication.

A better solution is that of "dependency injection," where a module is instead given what it is needed to do the job, rather than importing them directly. For libraries and components that need configuration to be useful, this is a much better approach that can lead to cleaner code. For a developer coming from a Java background, dependency injection instantly evokes ideas of large frameworks for managing these, but this does not need to be the case, and many JavaScript apps do not need a framework to manage these for you. Often, having a "main" function that sets up all your dependencies and then wires it up is sufficient.

For classes, it is typical to set these dependencies through the constructor, and then reference them as fields when needed:

```
class ProductCatalogueApi {
  constructor(httpClient, catalogueApiUrl) {
    this._httpClient = httpClient;
    this._catalogueApiUrl = catalogueApiUrl
  }

  fetchCatalogueItem(id) {
    return this._httpClient
      .get(`${this._catalogueApiUrl}/product/${id}`)
      .json();
  }
}
```

In the example above, the ProductCatalogueApi class could then be instantiated in the main function and passed through to any controllers that need access to the product catalogue, again using dependency injection.

For modules that aim to be more functional, a closure can be used instead, where the module exports a function that takes in the dependencies and then returns the function that does the work of that module, which now has access to those dependencies in the scope of the closure.

```
function fetchCatalogueItemFactory(httpClient, catalogueApiUrl) {
  function fetchCatalogueItem(id) {
    return this._httpClient
      .get(`${this._catalogueApiUrl}/product/${id}`)
      .json();
  }
  return fetchCatalogueItem;
}
```

With this approach, when getting testing your class or function, you can set them up in the same way as your main application's code, but pass in compatible stubs with dummy data as the dependencies.

Testing

There are many options for running tests in JavaScript, with the most popular ones supporting the arrange-act-assert mechanism discussed in the Testing chapter. Specific styles tend to vary, with libraries like Jasmine allowing you to write the tests, and tools like Karma allowing you to run them from the command line and reporting on their success.

Earlier unit testing tools, like QUnit, run by opening a browser and visualizing the result. JSTestDriver was another popular early testing tool for JavaScript. Written in Java, it allows you to write tests very similar to the JUnit style, and manages reporting and execution in browsers too. These tools are rarely used for new projects, although you may come across them. The rise of headless browsers like PhantomJS, and then server-side runtimes like NodeJS, have simplified JavaScript test running. I would recommend Jest as the best tool for test running; it is an all-in-one test running and specification library that is compatible with Jasmine.

In Jasmine and Jest, you define a test by calling the function it, then passing a human-readable name of the test and the function to be run when the tests are run.

```
const ShoppingBasket = require('../lib/shopping-basket');
const Product = require('../lib/product');

describe('shopping basket', () => {
  it('can be added to', () => {
    const shoppingBasket = new ShoppingBasket();
    shoppingBasket.addItem(new Product('t-shirt'));
    expect(shoppingBasket.items).toBe(1);
  });
});
```

The describe() method allows for grouping, and a block of tests inside a describe() can also include another describe() nested inside of it. The method names and descriptions are supposed to encourage you to write natural language–inspired names, because when the test runs, the description of all the describes together, and that of the test itself, is used as the overall test name in the output. In the example above, this would be "shopping basket can be added to."

When writing many tests for a module, it is common to execute the same setup for each test, perhaps having to construct an instance of a class, or tear it down at the end. Most tools allow you to specify a common bit of code to run before and after each test (regardless of whether or not it passed) to avoid this repetition. In Jest/Jasmine, this is done by invoking beforeEach() and afterEach() with a callback

```
describe('shopping basket', () => {
  let shoppingBasket;

  beforeEach(() => {
    shoppingBasket = new ShoppingBasket();
  });

  it('can be added to', () => {
    shoppingBasket.addItem(new Product('t-shirt'));
    expect(shoppingBasket.items).toBe(1);
  });

  afterEach(() => {
    shoppingBasket.empty();
  });
});
```

By default, each test will be executed synchronously. If you are testing asynchronous code (for example, if the method you're testing returns a promise), then you need to have some way of telling the test that it should wait for all the asynchronous code to have completed. In Jest, you can return a promise to do this, and then the test will pass if the promise resolves, or fail if the promise rejects. Let's assume adding an item to the shopping basket is now an asynchronous operation that returns a promise:

```
describe('shopping basket', () => {
  let shoppingBasket;

  beforeEach(() => {
    shoppingBasket = new ShoppingBasket();
  });
```

```
  it('can be added to', () => {
    return shoppingBasket.addItem(new Product('t-shirt'))
      .then(() => expect(shoppingBasket.items).toBe(1));
  });

  afterEach(() => {
    shoppingBasket.empty();
  });
});
```

Another way of doing this is by taking in a single argument—normally called done—to your test function. You then call done() at the end of your tests, and done.fail() if you need to fail the tests.

```
describe('shopping basket', () => {
  let shoppingBasket;

  beforeEach(() => {
    shoppingBasket = new ShoppingBasket();
  });

  it('can be added to', (done) => {
    shoppingBasket.addItem(new Product('t-shirt'))
      .then(() => {
        expect(shoppingBasket.items).toBe(1);
        done();
      });
  });

  afterEach(() => {
    shoppingBasket.empty();
  });
});
```

If there is a bug in your asynchronous code such that the callback or promise never gets called, Jest/Jasmine will time out waiting for a test to complete (although the error messages might not be useful!)

Testing simple logic with JavaScript tests can be easy, as the output depends purely on the input, sometimes with some side effects on other members of a class or other dependencies that can be passed in and replaced with stubs or mocks (fake versions that simplify the external system's behavior—you can read more about these later in the chapter). JavaScript components that operate on the DOM can be hard to test. The JavaScript might assume that the DOM is in a particular shape when instantiated (for example, provided by the HTML), and the DOM is a form of global state. One test might leave it to be manipulated in a way that can cause the next test to fail, even if that test would otherwise be fine.

Using virtual DOM libraries like React can make this easier, as the virtual DOM can be replaced by a mocked-out version, and assertions can be made on that. There are libraries (such as Enzyme for React) that can help with this. For traditional "vanilla" JavaScript, a popular technique is to pass in the DOM element that the component operates on in as a dependency, rather than to let it find it in the global DOM. For example, when using a function to add a click handler to something, instead of the function using `document.querySelector`, it would instead be passed an argument that is the `HTMLElement` object to add the click handler to. This is an application of dependency injection.

With this approach, a new layer is needed above the individual components that does all the lookups from the real `document` and passes them through, but this allows for greater reuse of an individual component if need be. This is sometimes called the wiring, as it connects the individual components together. When we want to test a component, then our testing code can take on the role of this wiring layer. We can then construct fake snippets of the DOM in the test, perhaps by loading in a "fixture" file (an HTML file that contains a small snippet of the site that is needed to test this component), and then pass this constructed element through, without actually attaching it to the global document. This allows us to isolate each test from each other, although there is still a risk of leaks to global states, especially if things such as timers are set up. You will often end up writing ways of clearing any manipulation of global state up—for example, having a "destroy()" method on a class that uses `clearTimeout()`, or using lifecycle hooks such as `componentWillUnmount` in React, even if the destroy code never needs to be run in the running application. The test code will need to call these, and it can also be a good habit for writing real code, as it can help you avoid performance issues. Even if at first on the real page only one instance of a component will ever be created, this may not always be true, and the habit will help you there.

The kinds of tests written in this way are normally called unit tests. You can read more about these later in the Testing chapter, but in general they allow you to test one bit of your code in isolation, in many different configurations (including ones where it should error). There are many benefits of unit testing. In addition to regression suites and ensuring that your code is functionally correct, unit testing helps with the design of the interface of your modules. Applying test-driven development can help focus the role and responsibility of the module, but your module now automatically has two things that use it: the test code and the production code. If your code is hard to test, the design of the interface may not be optimal, or it may be too heavily coupled to another module. This may not cause you immediate pain, but can down the road, as code that has these characteristics is often hard to change, and being able to react quickly to changing business needs is one of the real benefits of agile software development. The chapter on testing has a full introduction to applying test-driven development.

Once you have written your tests, you will need a way to run them. Although server-side tests can be run as code in NodeJS, tests for client-side code must run in an environment similar to a browser in order for the code under test to behave appropriately. When JQuery was prominent, it came with a unit testing framework known as QUnit. With QUnit, it was common to run your tests manually in a browser window for each browser you needed to target, as a browser is, of course, the most browser-like environment out there.

This integrated poorly into continuous integration workflows, and also added maintenance overhead. It wasn't long before automation tools such as Karma came about, which ran tests programmatically by booting and remotely controlling browsers. Still, this caused problems for automated test running on a CI server, which ran in a headless mode or on Linux systems rather than the OS the browsers needed. Opening a browser to run the tests was slow, especially compared to the workflow of server-side code with frameworks like JUnit, which could run tests in milliseconds from within an editor. PhantomJS was a "headless" browser, based on WebKit, that worked in a cross-platform way without a UI and became a popular way to run unit tests, as it significantly sped up the load time for the browser, and therefore the tests themselves.

More recent developments have allowed server-side and client-side code to merge. Instead of trying to force a browser to run programmatically, libraries such as JSDOM instead make the NodeJS runtime behave like a browser. Although it might seem dangerous not to test the code in the actual environment it will be running in, the risks are actually minimal, and the benefits of quick test runs outweigh them. In modern browsers, most bugs are a result of logic errors in your code, rather than browser incompatibilities.

There are options for those who want to run their code in actual browsers, though. End-to-end tests, as opposed to unit tests, are commonly run in real browsers. There tend to be fewer end-to-end tests than unit tests, but each test will touch more parts of the system and can give you a higher degree of confidence in your system than a single unit test. End-to-end tests are also slower to run, and combined with the overhead of starting up browsers, this can make these tests especially slow to run. Running these tests also tends to happen in a different way than your unit tests—instead of your test code running in the same browser context as the code it tests, it instead spins up a different browser and remotely controls that browser (or possibly multiple browsers in parallel). This means you can actually write your integration tests in other languages (Java and Ruby are two common ones), although JavaScript itself is still common.

A library is used to support this, and by far the most mature library is known as Selenium. Selenium is a Java library, but defines an API known as WebDriver, which runs in the browsers. Other languages then have Selenium-like libraries, which interact with the WebDriver API to control the browsers remotely to run tests. With WebDriver, you can create tests within your normal testing framework, but these tests then use that library to control a browser remotely and make expectations/assertions through that library as per usual.

```
describe('shopping basket', () => {
  it('increases the number of items shown on the page', () => {
    browser.url('http://localhost:3000/catalogue/t-shirt');
    expect(browser.getText('#cart_size')).toEqual("Empty");
    browser.click('#add_to_cart');
    expect(browser.getText('#cart_size')).toEqual("1 item");
  });
});
```

The main difference between Selenium and mocking tools such as JSDOM is that you need to get a real browser instance to run on. When running these tests on a desktop, it's not unusual to see copies of browsers start up and physically watch the remotely controlled interactions occur. In CI environments, a GUI environment must be provisioned to allow this to happen. This is not always straightforward, and maintaining a suite of different OS's and browsers to provide full coverage can be a considerable overhead for an organization. Several SaaS providers offer pay-as-you-go, "cloud-based" browsers on infrastructure they control, which can be helpful in some circumstances (but not others—for example, if you want to check an intranet or lock your development environments down to specific IPs).

A common issue with end-to-end test suites is reliability, especially across browsers. In browsers, almost all actions should be treated as asynchronous, which can make writing tests tricky. A common way around this, especially in languages that do not have as much support for asynchronous functions as JS, is to add delays to the test. Say, for example, opening a dialogue box has a 200ms animation; it is common to see code such as:

```
describe('control panel', () => {
  it('opens when clicked', (done) => {
    browser.url('http://localhost:3000/')
    browser.click('#open_control_panel')
    setTimeout(() => {
      expect(browser.isVisible('#control_panel')).toBeTruthy();
      done();
    }, 250);
  });
});
```

The wait above is actually for 250ms, not 200, to allow for some overhead or variance in the browser's rendering engine. Where this approach really falls down is for actions where the delay is not exactly determined, such as for AJAX calls. Often, a delay is a number based on the worst-case scenario, which might still not be 100% reliable, and may introduce slowness if the call does complete more quickly. An alternative approach is known as "waiting," where you periodically check whether an action has completed, and then continue as soon as it has. Otherwise, once a timeout has been reached, the action fails.

```
describe('control panel', () => {
  it('opens when clicked', (done) => {
    browser.url('http://localhost:3000/')
    browser.click('#open_control_panel')
    browser.waitForVisible('#control_panel');
    expect(browser.isVisible('#control_panel')).toBeTruthy();
  });
});
```

This allows you to write faster and more resilient tests, and also helps decouple your code from the implementation. For example, if your animation speed becomes slightly slower, you would not necessarily need to update your test code, which you would have to do if you had used a sleep with a hard-coded interval.

Another approach to decoupling your test code from the specific implementation details even further is known as the page object model. Selenium uses CSS classes (or IDs) to find items on a page, but sometimes those classes need to change (if a major restyle is underway), but the actual behavior and structure of the components stays the same. Instead of writing several tests that refer to the same component by class name, you can instead encapsulate all the logic inside a helper class, and then make assertions about that class. If any information about an object on the page changes, then the definition in the class gets updated and all the classes use it. This is a good application of the DRY (don't repeat yourself) pattern.

When running your integration tests, you also have to consider how to control the state of the application under the hood. In unit tests, techniques like mocking can be used, but with these kind of tests, you are often running your app as a standalone server, which you do not have access to at runtime (although starting an instance of the server within the test code is also a possibility, and does allow you to directly manipulate the state of the server-side code). One way to solve this is to point your app at a fake database or API that you can control, rather than a real one, which makes it easier to integration test your app in several ways. Another interesting approach is to actually run these tests against your real web site. Some people prefer this because it offers a high degree of confidence in the version of the web site your audience will actually see, but it is not always appropriate. For example, making a real order on an e-commerce web site can be hard to test. Sometimes a pre-staging web site is used instead. Normally, the real web site must be provisioned with some test data that can cause confusion if a real user stumbles across it (see YouTube's "Webdriver Torso" tests), or depends on the existence of specific bits of content that, if changed, can break your tests.

Build Tools

As mentioned previously, it is rare to write JavaScript that is then executed by a browser with no interim transformation. Even when you do, it's still good to have some automated tooling that can help you execute tests or apply other quality checks to your codebase.

At the time of writing, there is no standard build tool for JavaScript, with several popular frameworks for doing so. However, most build toolchains have commonalities, and tend to help out in three ways: managing dependencies, checking code quality, and producing the end product (a "bundle"), which the browsers execute. It is common to put together different tools to fulfill all of these functions in a toolchain, although some do more than others. When different tools need to be combined a coordination layer is needed. This can be as simple as a shell script that runs different commands in sequence, or something more advanced (such as Gulp or Grunt) that supports parallelization and more complex chains, as well as watching for changes and rerunning builds during development.

The usual purposes of a build tool are to bundle multiple JavaScript files together into one, run any transpilation needed, and resolve dependencies from imported code—either other modules in the same system or third-party code installed from a repository. A single file can then be delivered to the browser in one request, which can offer some performance enhancements (although HTTP/2 offers alternative ways of negating the performance impact of making multiple requests from a browser). This file is often also minified, especially in production, meaning that any human niceties, such as white space, are stripped out and the variable made smaller to further reduce the size of the file. The downside of this is that it can make debugging harder, as the browser only sees the minified code. Source maps were invented to counteract this, and they provide a way for browser developer tools to relate the minified, transpiled code back to the original. It is common for build tools to have separate "development" and "production" modes for this process, as source maps can significantly increase the size of a file, so they are only included on local development builds.

Although often not part of the build tool itself, the test runner, dependency manager, and code quality checker and often bundled together into the same toolchain. Early JavaScript projects would either simply save any dependencies in the code repository alongside the code for this application (a process known as "vendoring," as the common location for these files was in a "vendor" subdirectory), or sometimes used features like SVN externals or Git submodules. It was also common (and remains so today) to include a remotely hosted version of common libraries such as JQuery as a script tag on your page and assume those dependencies were there.

In 2012, Twitter introduced a tool known as "Bower," which added tooling over the population of the vendor directory, by specifying which dependencies and versions you required in a config file and automatically downloading them. As NodeJS became popular, a tool known as Node Package Manager (NPM) became popular alongside it, which managed JavaScript dependencies for server-side code. It wasn't long before this became the most common way to distribute JavaScript code intended for execution in a browser too. NPM (and related tools, such as Yarn) is now considered the standard way to include dependencies into your JavaScript. The common build tools will understand how to resolve dependencies that have been installed using NPM, either using ES6 `import` or the CommonJS `require` syntax.

Code style and quality checkers have been long established as a powerful friend in writing maintainable code. The first style checker, called "lint," was created for the C language, and a "linter" is now the term used to refer to the same tools in other languages. There are several linters for JavaScript, with ESLint being one of the more modern and common. Over time, linters became responsible for more than just checking for style consistency, but also for potential mistakes in logic (such as using a variable that could have possibly not had a value assigned to it). Type checking tools such as Flow, as discussed previously, are also often integrated into a build toolchain here.

Code style is also the source of many heated debates within a development team, which can be reflected in the vast array of configuration options available for linting tools. For many other languages, the body responsible for publishing that language will also publish recommended style guides, such as PHP's PSR-2, or Python's PEP-8. For JavaScript, there is no one standard, but several popular styles. I would recommend just picking one of those styles and stick with it, as a simpler approach than defining your own internal style. Doing so will save many heated, and often unnecessary, discussions among your team members over personal preferences!

Some of this will seem similar to the roles of the build tools used for other parts of the front end, and in these case they are often merged into one tool or task runner that handles both.

Summary

Despite originating as a language to manipulate web pages, JavaScript is now often used server-side as well. For now, JavaScript remains the dominant language of the Web for client-side code, so must be a sharpened tool for any full stack web developer.

JavaScript is a rapidly evolving language. Following a long period of stagnation, with some browsers adding incompatible extensions that became ad-hoc parts of the language, 2015 saw the introduction of the sixth edition of the language specification, called ES6, and also a shift to a yearly model (so ES6 is ES2015), with smaller iterations constantly being added. Beyond being used for simple enhancements to a page, JavaScript can now be used for extremely rich and complex web applications.

As a language, JavaScript has some distinct features. One of those is its asynchronous nature. JavaScript runtimes run the code in a single thread, with I/O operations happening in the background, and functions registered as event handlers or callbacks that occur when a UI event or background I/O process happens. JavaScript has several features to help simplify the use of callbacks, and especially chained callbacks: promises and, more recently, the `async` and `await` keywords.

In the browser, JavaScript interacts with the UI using the Document Object Model (DOM) API. As JavaScript code is run by a potentially wide range and age of browsers, this can limit you to a lowest common denominator of the language, but there are tools that work around this by either making new language features available in older browsers (polyfills), or by transforming newer syntax into a backwards-compatible form (transpilation). Some libraries, such as JQuery, have also historically been used to provide a common API over multiple incompatible implementations of the same functionality.

On the server, the NodeJS runtime is used to run code, but with a different standard library, and particularly no DOM. NodeJS also has a technique that allows for JavaScript modules to be included to manage dependencies, using a technique known as CommonJS. On the browser, asynchronous module definitions (AMDs) were common for defining and loading other modules and namespaces, but CommonJS code can be transpiled into a form compatible with modern browsers. Becoming available is a native JavaScript module type, which is usable without any additional tool support.

JavaScript supports a small set of basic types, with more complex functionality developed by combining those. A common "gotcha" with JavaScript is the equality operator (==), which will coerce the two sides into a similar type to compare them, yielding surprising results. You will almost always want to use the identity operator (===), which behaves in a way that is less surprising. JavaScript's object-orientation approach differs from other languages too, using prototype-based, rather than class-based, inheritance, although ES6 allows you to work in a more familiar syntax. JavaScript also supports some basic primitives for functional programming—most importantly, anonymous functions that can be passed as first-class objects. JavaScript's scoping rules are often surprising too, where variables defined using var are subject to "hoisting," which happens when the definitions are evaluated before the code. The modern alternatives of let and const are preferred for newer code.

The other biggest pitfall of JavaScript is the this keyword. In other object-oriented languages, this refers to the object that the method exists on, but in JavaScript it refers to the context in which the method was called (potentially as a method, but also perhaps as an event callback). Closures or binding can be used to ensure that you have access to the this keyword or an equivalent when adding event handlers or callbacks. Event handlers and callbacks are a common way to communicate between components, and there are many libraries and frameworks to help structure event processing frameworks, as well as binding between models and UI code.

As a language, JavaScript has good tool support for writing and running automated tests. These include unit tests, which test a distinct part of an application, and integration tests, which run in the full browser environment. JavaScript unit testing frameworks borrow extensively from the common principles of unit testing, although they are often structured using describe and it statements, rather than as methods on classes. This way of structuring tests reflects JavaScript's nature as neither a pure OO, procedural nor functional language.

Although it is possible to write JavaScript directly for execution by a browser, it is more common to use tools to translate JavaScript into a backwards-compatible and optimized form for use in a web browser. These build tools also work with dependency management tools such as NPM, where third-party JavaScript libraries can be utilized and bundled into your final app.

JavaScript is an often imperfect language. But JavaScript is the language of the web, and as a web developer, having a good understanding of how to develop software in JavaScript will see you most of the way to satisfying the technical requirements of being a full stack developer.

CHAPTER 9

Accessibility

Accessibility seems mysterious to many, but the basic concept behind it is the same as usability—someone who visits a web page should be able to read its content easily, and those who open a web app should be able to use it. An accessible web site is one that is also usable to everyone who may try to access it. In fact, many accessibility features are used optionally by able-bodied people—keyboard navigation can be quicker than a mouse for filling in forms, and subtitles in video can be useful even if you're not hard of hearing.

Accessibility covers a large range of topics, and like much of software development, it rarely exists in a vacuum. Accessibility is often used to talk about assistive technologies (AT), like screen readers; or larger font size; or considerations specifically for people who have disabilities; but it's more than that. Compare building a web site to constructing a building, for example—all new buildings must be accessible. A particularly visible aspect of this may be ramps for wheelchair users, but it goes beyond that. Signs may have braille alternatives, and may have large, high-contrast text for those who have trouble seeing. Elevators will announce their floors audibly, and there won't be any strobes or flickering lights that may "look good" but risk triggering epilepsy. Many of these small details aren't just details added at the end by an accessibility specialist. Can you imagine a situation where a building was designed and built, and then before opening a specialist came in and demanded the installation of ramps and replacing all the signs in the building? When web sites are built that way, it's easy to see how accessibility can be dismissed as an additional cost and get dropped in a budget-constrained project. This is especially true if there are unidentified fundamental issues with the accessibility of your site; leaving it to the end can either result in only patching superficial issues, or a large amount of rework.

Designing and building a web site to be accessible from the start takes surprisingly little extra effort compared to adding it later. Accessibility can be thought of as a cross-functional requirement, in that it's something that should be built into every feature

© Chris Northwood 2018
C. Northwood, *The Full Stack Developer*, https://doi.org/10.1007/978-1-4842-4152-3_9

or story that you build, rather than a standalone feature to be added in at the end of a project. Indeed, as a software engineer, you have an ethical and legal obligation not to exclude classes of people from your application based on factors they cannot control.

Fortunately, accessibility is not a magic dust that is applied, but actually a fairly small set of principles supported by good APIs that are available to all web developers. By default, all pages are accessible—we build in complexity by adding styles and rich scripting that can introduce inaccessibility. There are guidelines for checking accessibility of pages, but like many automated tools, these are general and may miss the context of your specific application. Being compliant with the guidelines is good, but not enough to ensure your site is actually accessible.

Accessible from the Start

Accessibility starts with the design of a web site. If the text is too small, or if there is poor color contrast (for example, a light gray on white), then it can be hard for able-bodied people in full health to use, let alone those who may have sight difficulties. Building these kinds of design elements to be accessible has the benefit of helping everyone. Even those with perfect sight who may be fine with something that a partially sighted person struggles with can benefit if a design is reworked to be readable to all audience.

This type of accessibility is more than just helping out those with specific disabilities. It is natural for eyesight to deteriorate with age, and even a person with normal sight who is older may struggle with something a younger person finds acceptable. This problem is often confounded by the fact that development teams are often relatively young, as we remain a young industry in general, so these issues are often missed.

Going further, the lines of accessibility, usability, and user experience can start to blur. For example, people who have dyslexia or learning difficulties can find dense text hard to follow. The appropriate use of headings, which should serve to suggest the hierarchy of information, can make a page usable by these audiences, as well as benefiting other users by making it easy to scan a page to find specific content.

This kind of accessible development is done in the design stage, often before a developer is involved. However, the end result of a development process is always everyone's responsibility, and catching accessibility issues early can make them much easier to correct. When working with a designer to produce a wireframe or specification to implement, a critical eye looking for accessibility issues can be very helpful.

Working with Assistive Technologies

When the implementation of a new feature or story starts, the developer's role often revolves around ensuring web pages remain compatible with assistive technologies, which could explain why AT and accessibility are often conflated. However, facilitating this compatibility is not purely the job of the developer. Especially when implementing web apps, particularly complex UX patterns may need specific alternative implementations and interaction methods, which could require further collaboration with an interaction designer to define how those interactions work in these constrained environments. But like addressing other accessibility issues, this can benefit all users too.

When British law was changed to mandate dropped curbs at pedestrian crossings, this was mostly done to benefit wheelchair users. However, it was appreciated by other unintended users too, such as parents with prams, or skateboarders, where the change in level between the road and the pavement was previously a challenge to overcome. Adding keyboard shortcuts to a web app that relies largely on clicking buttons and mouse movement can benefit power users, where the shortcuts can be learned to speed up common tasks.

You won't be surprised to learn that progressive enhancement is an effective way of making web pages work well with assistive technologies. By starting with the base of a simple page and then layering on additional enhancements, you always maintain that accessible base, and all you then need to do is ensure that you don't break the accessibility of the base with these enhancements. The other benefit to HTML being accessible by default is that if you use HTML in the way it was designed to be used, then those enhancements you bring in will also be accessible with little extra work.

The main thing to be aware of if you're building highly customized interaction mechanisms (and this is often the case when you're building a web app) is that you need to use some way of indicating to assistive technology what the underlying meaning of those elements are. A technology called ARIA can be used to do this, and ARIA is used by adding attributes to HTML to indicate what the roles of these custom elements are.

The reason tools like ARIA are useful is that many assistive technologies, especially those that support non-sighted users, work by evaluating the structure of a page. By default, these tools will understand what the default elements of HTML mean.

From a purely visual perspective, it can be tempting to make everything a `<div>` and apply styles appropriately. This can resolve issues with browser default styling clashing with a button or a heading tag, for example, but is actually an anti-pattern known as div soup (or tag soup), as all the information is now completely unstructured and hard for a tool to discern.

Semantic HTML is the name given to the technique of using HTML as it was intended to be used—headings should be marked up as h1, h2, h3, etc., and paragraphs as p tags. This should be common sense, but can be tricky to get right. For example, if you have something that visually looks like a button, and takes you to another page, it might be tempting to use a `<button>` tag to get the visual style of a button. This can cause issues, as people who navigate links with a keyboard (as well as search engines that might follow them) will now not be able to see a `<button>` as a link. This works both ways. If you have something that looks like inline text that triggers an action when pressed (but doesn't actually navigate to a full page), that should actually be a `<button>` styled to look like a link. This is especially true when progressive enhancement is being applied, so that the `<a>` tag will correctly do a full page reload, even if it may be progressively enhanced to use AJAX to bring in a partial update.

There's another type of tool that analyzes the structure rather than the visual rendering of a page: search bots. An accessible web site is often also "search engine optimized" (SEO). Although there are SEO techniques that involve more than just using semantic HTML, Google in particular will reward well-structured HTML pages.

However, a warning must be applied here. Unlike web browsers, AT tools are often proprietary and paid for, meaning there's little incentive to upgrade, which would involve spending more money. For this reason, the understanding of brand new tags and semantics lags far behind the technology will support. For example, the defined semantics of a `<section>` were to reset any heading levels thus far, but support of this in screen readers is patchy at best. Although having a `<h1>` at the top of each `<section>` may appear to be fully compliant with the spec, it's not backwards compatible with HTML4, and some screen reading software will interpret it incorrectly. This kind of use is now officially discouraged, but be wary when dealing with these kinds of structural elements, especially new ones that pop up.

There are also cases where a plain HTML element (even when styled) is unsuitable. Perhaps there is none that fully satisfies what you're trying to do, so you're building a component from scratch using buttons and divs. The Web Accessibility Initiative's Accessible Rich Internet Applications specification (usually referred to as WAI-ARIA or just ARIA) can be a useful tool in this regard.

ARIA allows you to add hints that indicate what the semantics and structure of these elements are. Take, for example, a tabbed view on a web page. It is common to implement this with a list followed by a series of divs that are selectively made visible based on which list item is selected. By itself, this structure doesn't give enough information in the HTML to do the right thing, and CSS is often used to style this to look like the familiar tab structure a user might expect. Similar to the way we use CSS to style the list to look like tabs so that the user knows they're tabs, ARIA allows us to give the list a "role" so non-visual users also know their tabs. In the case of tabs, the list would be given a role of `tablist` by adding an HTML5 attribute of `role`, e.g., `<ul class="tabs-list" role="tablist">`. You would also give the link to each tab a role of `tab` and the divs containing the actual content a role of `tabpanel`.

The final missing piece is to describe the relationship between the divs and the appropriate item in the list. `aria-describedby` is another attribute that can be helpful here, and is used by adding to the content divs to reference the list item that describes this content. The downside here is that it refers to the other element by ID, and using the `id` attribute in HTML is often frowned upon (as it can limit reusability and cause issues with specificity in CSS), but careful choice of IDs for accessibility purposes can avoid any reusability issues and maintain manageable.

It's worth noting that overusing ARIA can sometimes introduce more problems than it can solve. You can make an element perfectly accessible and sensible without having to give everything ARIA attributes. ARIA is most helpful when used to fill the gaps and add additional hinting when standard HTML structure fails.

There are many types of ARIA attributes that can be used to add semantic meaning and structure—many more than can be described here. Fortunately, there is a dedicated group of accessibility experts within the web development community who have published many guides and documentation on these. The most important thing to do is including testing with AT as you develop your web site, and then try to find an appropriate pattern to use to correct any accessibility issues you find.

Dealing with Interactive UI

Although ARIA and semantic HTML will go a long way for content-style web sites, web apps are characterized by having a much richer type of interactivity. For assistive technologies, this can present a problem, as it's no longer a case of simply analyzing the structure of the page and then navigating through it, because the structure is dynamic and changes.

The situation is not as bad as it sounds—AT tools do interrogate the DOM dynamically, so any changes are reflected in them. The main issues are around notifying users when an action or other important event has happened (this is often done visually, such as with a validation error below a form field), making sure that you can trigger all the interactions you need to using tools such as a keyboard, and ensuring that if the content of the DOM changes, the user doesn't lose their place.

To deal with dynamic changes to content, we can add additional attributes to our content to indicate which elements are dynamic and give context to screen readers to help users navigate them. There are two attributes here that are of use: the `role` attribute and `aria-live`. `role` is preferred, sometimes along with `aria-live` for compatibility reasons, as it gives a better idea of context: `aria-live` simply says "this element will update," whereas the role says what type of information is being presented.

The following roles are useful to indicate content areas which can change:

- `role="alert"`
- `role="status"`
- `role="log"`
- `role="timer"`
- `role="progressbar"`

`alert` is probably the most common role, and is read immediately when the page loads, an element that contains it is added to the DOM, or the attribute is added to an existing element (for example, highlighting instructions that may have been missed while completing a form). Its most common use is for error messages—for example, during form validation, or after being logged out due to inactivity.

Many screen readers allow users to check the current status of a page, so `role="status"` may be appropriate for loading indicators, or perhaps features like Google Docs' "Saving... / Saved" indicator. For a loading bar, the `progressbar` role might be more appropriate. This role by itself is not enough, and should be combined with more descriptive attributes `aria-valuemin`, `aria-valuemax,` and `aria-valuenow`. `aria-valuetext` is also available for giving more detailed information about what is happening at each stage in a multi-step process.

The `log` role is used for streaming content, such as chat rooms (or even logs in a developer tool), where any added content is read out at an appropriate time.

The final role to discuss is `timer`. Most screen readers will not read content annotated with this role when it changes unless explicitly asked to, as it is assumed it will change fairly frequently and, as its name suggests, this is most appropriate for things like displaying the current time, timers, or countdowns.

`aria-live` has three possible values: `off`, `polite`, and `assertive`. `off` indicates that the region is not a live one, whereas `polite` means the screen reader will announce the updates when it next pauses. `assertive` will interrupt what is currently being read out to the user, so should be used sparingly. `aria-live` can be combined with the attributes `aria-atomic` and `aria-relevant` to control whether or not the whole element is re-spoken on change, or which parts of it are the most relevant.

All of these should be combined with the `aria-describedby` and other roles described previously to give an adequate level of coverage for these dynamic elements should screen readers fail to understand them by themselves.

Some HTML elements have an implicit ARIA role assigned to them—for example, the `<progress>` element will behave as if it has `role="progressbar"` set without anything further being done, as well as the other `aria` attributes that can be derived from the regular HTML attributes.

A common interaction mechanism for moving through web pages is to use the tab key to access elements such as form fields and buttons. There's a good chance you use this while filling in form fields yourself. When an element has been tabbed to, it is said to have focus. This can be thought of analogous to hovering over an element with a mouse, and it allows AT tools to indicate where a user is on a page. If you're using standard HTML components, then most interactive ones can be tabbed to and interacted with directly without any further work. However, if you're using elements such as divs, then you can use the `tabindex` attribute to indicate that the element should be able to be selected with the tab key.

The `tabindex` attribute is given a numeric value to indicate where it should appear when the document is being tabbed through. You should always set this to 0 to make an element be able to be tabbed to, which simply means that the order should be as it would naturally appear in the document (conversely, you can hide an element that is normally accessible by setting the `tabindex` to -1). Other numbers are possible, but this can introduce subtle bugs and dependencies with other fields (for example, if you add an element at the top of the page, you'd have to increase the `tabindex` of everything that comes after it, as they must be sequential). It is thought of as an anti-pattern if explicit `tabindexes` (i.e., not 0) are needed, as this often means that your page structure does not match the visual flow, and AT tools can get very confused if this is the case. There should be a strong link between the structure of your HTML and the visual flow of the page and the information.

You should also ensure that you listen to the appropriate events in JavaScript. Most important are the `focus` and `blur` events, which you should use if at any point you're responding to mouse events like `onmouseover`. By listening to these events, you're ensuring that, for users who navigate with a keyboard, the components respond in the same way as those who navigate with a mouse. This type of keyboard focus has equivalent pseudo-selectors in CSS too, like `:hover` and `:focus`. Of course, with the rise of touchscreen devices, relying on mouse hover and similar events is decreasing in popularity. Instead, listening for explicit touch or click events is now a common interaction mode, but fortunately selecting an item with the keyboard still fires the `click` event, which can simplify the logic.

The final aspect to consider, especially for screen readers, is making sure it is clear what a button does. Links such as "click here" give very little indication to the user what the link actually does without the visual context of what surrounds it. "Submit" is not a very good name either, so it is often useful to make a form's submit button explicitly name the action it will complete (such as "Add Product"). This is especially true when there are multiple buttons with the same name on the page, perhaps for different forms, because a screen reader may not have a sense of location on the page, so it can be unclear which form the button is referring to.

Icons are popular to use in buttons, but even for users who browse without AT, these can be confusing without context. As a result, it is very common to have an icon and a textual description of the action side by side for all users, which then makes the icon a decorative element that is not read out for screen readers. A common way of making it a purely decorative element is to use a CSS pseudo-element with a `background-image` element to bring the logo in, or an `img` tag with an empty `alt` tag to denote that it is purely decorative.

In the event that you decide an icon by itself is enough, then you must make a textual alternative available. Be careful when you do this! A lot of research has been done into icons and has found that, with the exception of a few very common ones used in a familiar context, icons can be confusing to users. Take, for example, the cross symbol. If this appears in the top right corner of a popup, then this is commonly taken to mean close the popup. But using the same cross icon as a button in the list item might feasibly mean "delete this item from the list," or perhaps "disable," or "discard changes," so even the subset of universally recognized icons are only identifyable in an appropriate context.

HAVING TEXT ONLY FOR SCREEN READERS

There might be other use cases where you want to make a textual alternative available for screen readers only. For example, sometimes you want the contents of a h1 tag to be the logo or name of your site, but using an img tag can have negative consequences for SEO, as often the alt tag will be ignored, making it look like you have an empty h1. A common technique to avoid this is to specify your h1 like normal, but with a nested span inside:

```
<h1 class="site-title">
  <span class="site-title__inner">My Site</span>
</h1>
```

CSS is then used to hide the inner span and a background-image used on the h1 to insert the logo image. However, the way in which you go around hiding the text can result in it being hidden from screen readers too, if care is not taken. A naive approach might be to give the inner span a display: none;, but this also hides the element from AT tools and CSS-aware search engines (which include Google). The traditional approach is to give the h1 element a CSS attribute of text-indent: -9999px; which will push the text out of the viewport, but still show iton the screen, so screen readers (and bots) will still find it. Note that if the inner span bothers you, you can achieve the same result using CSS pseudo-elements.

The text-indent method is not without its flaws. The first is an impact on performance, as it causes the browser to render the text off-page, increasing the area the browser has to render. Some people also jokingly refer to the "10,000px-pocalypse," where once the average screen size is over 10,000px, the hidden text will start to reappear. More realistically, if your site has any horizontally scrolling components (for example, a slideshow/carousel), then this technique can fail.

Instead of the `text-indent` method, a more modern alternative has sprung up, which instead uses a clipping rectangle and resizes the container to hide the text from view while keeping it in its present location in the DOM, avoiding the performance hit. This can be implemented using the following snippet of CSS:

```css
.sr-only {
    clip: rect(0, 0, 0, 0);
    clip-path: inset(50%);
    height: 1px;
    overflow: hidden;
    padding: 0;
    position: absolute;
    white-space: nowrap;
    width: 1px;
}
```

Unless you need to support very old browsers, this is a better method to use, and many CSS frameworks will provide this as a utility class (often called `.sr-only` for "screen-reader only.")

If both the 1px box and the `text-indent` methods feel like hacks to you, that's because they are, so overuse of these methods can be indicative of accessibility issues in your site. Be mindful when using them.

Screen readers and other AT tools use the concept of focus to keep track of the current position of a user who is navigating a page. Focus can be thought of as analogous to scrolling through a long web page, where the current position in the scroll indicates where a user currently is.

It is common for interactive elements to make changes to the DOM in response to user events, such as adding a new item to a list, or opening/collapsing trays. The techniques used to notify users of messages and contents will work in that case, but less well when the change is not actually an announcement or message.

For users of these tools, doing an action such as toggling open a list or drawer seems the same as clicking a button where the effect happens offscreen—it is not immediately obvious to the user what has just happened. Fortunately, we can manipulate focus using JavaScript to move users to the modified area of the page, so their flow is not broken. The `focus()` method on an `HTMLElement` allows us to change the focus.

We also need to consider cases where the opposite has happened—an item has disappeared from the page. Often, there is little to do here beyond a success announcement to ensure that the user knows an action has been successful, but there are cases where it is not so simple. When the element that is currently in focus is removed or hidden from the DOM, then the browser is said to have lost focus, and resets it to the start of the page. This can be a very jarring experience for screen readers.

Take, for example a drawer that has a "close" button inside. When close is selected, then the drawer is hidden from the DOM, including the close button that was inside it. This causes the focus to be lost. The same technique of deliberately setting focus can be used here to avoid that jar. For example, you may want to set focus back to the open button, or instead to the next element in the list, depending on what you're trying to achieve.

The final thing to consider is something known as a keyboard trap. A keyboard trap occurs when a user cannot leave an element using the keyboard and gets "stuck." This can be both a blessing and a curse. One way this could happen is if you re-map the tab button to some other purpose, or if your app has a bug that constantly resets focus to the same element. This is very frustrating for the user, as it keeps them from fully exploring the page. Conversely, a keyboard trap can be useful if you have a modal dialog, as you can trap the keyboard user into that dialog, similar to the way you might block UI interaction with the page.

Most controls will behave in an accessible way by default, but if you want to implement your own custom behavior, the above gives an overview of how to start considering accessibility. However, it is far from comprehensive; there are many guides online that provide the patterns you should subscribe to, with ARIA specifications considered the most definitive and widely respected versions.

Testing for Accessibility

Of course, compliance with the ARIA spec is not enough to make a web page accessible. You should also test how your web site actually works and performs with AT tools.

Testing for accessibility is similar to testing a web site normally. Instead of simply using a browser to navigate the site, a screen reader or similar tool should also be used, so interactions are executed in the same way a real user would. And, as a developer would always do a sanity check of a feature on their machine before handing it over to a QA, it is your responsibility to do sanity checks for screen readers too. Like normal web browsers, AT tools have varying levels of support for standards, as well as per-tool quirks and bugs. These will often require workarounds and shims in order to give the user an acceptable experience.

As a web developer, you should learn how to use a screen reader to complete basic actions to navigate your web pages or app. Fortunately, there are many introductory articles on how to do this. If you are using macOS, then this is a built-in feature of the operating system known as VoiceOver. Pressing ⌘ + F5 will toggle this feature on and off, and you can then use a keyboard to move around your web browser. On Windows, the applications NVDA and JAWS are popular.

Once you are familiar with a screen reader, you can then do some ad hoc sanity testing on accessibility/usability before a QA might do a fuller test. The simplest thing to do is run through and make sure your page makes sense when read out loud; that if you use your keyboard to navigate to an action, it's obvious what that action will do; and that performing an action ensures the screen reader matches any actions that a user of a regular browser will see.

Once you are sure that your content is readable and actions are properly marked up to behave correctly, the final step is to check for "traps" when navigating with a keyboard. Especially if you are manipulating focus, or showing/hiding things on keyboard focus, it can be possible to get into a loop with keyboard focus where you cannot escape or go any further to access other parts of the document.

Beyond these sanity checks, there are specific sets of guidelines for testing accessibility. These guidelines by themselves are not sufficient to ensure a web site is accessible. Web Content Accessibility Guidelines (WCAG) is the most common one, and there are automated tools that can check compliance with these guidelines. However, like usability testing in general, these tools have not evolved to the point where they can replace a human, as they do not understand the context of your application. These checkers will almost certainly miss some issues and misdiagnose others, so cannot be used as an alternative to manual checking.

A standards checker can tell you that your web site has well-formed HTML, but it won't tell you if your design intent will correctly render in all the user's browsers. Accessibility tools have the same problem. What they can do is check that any programmatic hooks are in place, but you should use these alongside actually doing testing using accessibility tools like screen readers to ensure full compliance. Pally, released by *Nature*, is one such tool you can run to get a report on how compliant you are with various specifications.

One good side effect of building an accessible web site, with good programmatic hooks for screen readers, is that it actually makes the general automated testing of your web site or web app much easier. Automation tools like Selenium can control a browser in a very similar way as browser accessibility tools (they often go above and beyond this too, such as with JavaScript hooks), but if you have a component that is hard to hook into for tests with Selenium, there's a good chance that the component is also not compatible with AT either.

Avoiding Common Mistakes

It can sometimes be surprisingly easy to accidentally break accessibility. The final section in this chapter looks at some of those common mistakes and how to avoid them.

Hover and Focus Styling

When using the CSS pseudo-selector `:hover` to style an element while a mouse is hovering over it, you should almost always use the `:focus` pseudo-selector as well, so that keyboard users get the same behavior to indicate when something is highlighted.

outline: 0

Quite often, a bug will be reported along the lines of "an ugly ring appears outside the element when it is clicked on." This is the outline ring that indicates which element has keyboard focus, and `outline: 0` will hide it, sometimes making for more pleasing aesthetics. However, this can make a site completely unusable for a keyboard user, as they cannot see where the site has focus. The "ugly ring" appears on many different web sites, so users are often used to seeing it. Getting rid of it in the name of aesthetics is often unnecessary! If you absolutely must get rid of the outline, then make sure that some other way of indicating focus is included, but bear in mind that users are familiar with the outline ring, so another way of indicating focus may not be as effective the default outline ring.

The Order of Headings

It is easy to fall into the trap of making the structure of your HTML match the visual structure, but headings are an important navigational aid. In particular, heading levels should be used in order, rather than skipping or re-using levels to match a visual style. Going straight to a h4 when the previous heading element was a h2 can confuse screen reader navigation. Another common anti-pattern is when a card starts with an image:

```
<div class="card">
  <img src="/contents.jpg" alt="Photograph of John">
  <h3>John</h3>
  <p>John is the marketing director of FooBar Inc.</p>
</div>
```

From the heading structure alone, it is not obvious that the image actually belongs under the heading of "John." Instead, the <h3> should be the first thing in the div and the image below that. A padding-top in CSS can then be used to make space for the image, with the image being absolutely positioned at the top of the card to make the visual style correct. This might seem counterintuitive, but for users of AT who navigate using heading levels, it's the only way to correctly indicate the structure of the document.

Multiple h1s

The HTML5 spec previously specified that using some of the new semantic elements, like <section>, reset the meaning of the heading hierarchy, but screen readers have been slow to adopt these semantics. For consistency it's best to ignore this and assume a global hierarchy for the heading structure. In particular, there should only be one h1 per page, as this is often used to jump to the main body of a page.

Skip Links

One common problem with web page design is that the first elements on the page can be navigation bars, logos, etc., which is a lot of cruft for an AT tool user to navigate through to get to the actual content. Although skipping to an h1 can be a way to get around this, another way is to use a pattern known as a "skip link." A skip link is an anchor link that appears close to the top of a page and allows a user to skip to the main content of the page. Quite often, you will want to make this anchor invisible to non-keyboard users for aesthetic reasons, and a common pattern to solve this is only use a `:focus` pseudo-selector in the CSS to hide it off screen until it has keyboard focus.

Buttons vs. Anchors

When creating dynamic elements, it can be tempting to use `<a>` tags and add click event handlers to it in JavaScript. This can be jarring for users of AT tools, as the usual semantics of an `<a>` tag take you somewhere else (a different part of the same document, or another document altogether), as opposed to a `<button>`, which is used to trigger an action.

When implementing actions, using the right HTML element can help screen readers interpret the page as well as suggesting the correct semantics, although styling a `button` can seem like more work than styling an `a` tag. The use of `<a href="#">` is an anti-pattern to be avoided, as the `href` indicates that a link goes nowhere, which suggests that the link is actually an action, and should be a button.

The Correct Use of an `alt` Attribute

The use of `alt` attributes on images is a rare accessibility requirement that is hard-coded into the HTML spec, and that a standard validator will check for. Despite this (or because of this), inappropriate use of the `alt` attribute is common.

`alt` attributes should only be used when an image adds content (not just aesthetics) to a page, and as the name suggests, it should be a *textual alternative*, not simply a description of the image. If an image exists only to add some styling information to a page, then it is often best to actually include it as a background image in CSS, rather than as an `<img>` tag. Although `alt` attributes are compulsory, it is okay to leave them empty to indicate that the image is purely for styling reasons. It is particularly egregious when an `alt` attribute simply repeats a heading, as all this does is cause duplicate text to be read out in a screen reader.

Icon Fonts

A common optimization for icons is to deliver a set of icons to the browser as an icon font, using Unicode or other characters to indicate custom characters, which are then typed into the document. However, a screen reader does not know how to "read" these characters, and may cause them to read nonsense when interpreting a document. Instead of using icon fonts, CSS sprites or other techniques are a better way of including an icon, either with the use of hidden text for screen readers to give textual meaning to the icon or, better yet, using a text label alongside the image.

Color Contrast

The final common mistake to look out for is color contrast. Although this is often considered to live in the realm of visual design, the way colors are implemented can make a big difference to the accessibility of a page. It can be easy to assume that when text is on top of an appropriate background image, that the color contrast is fine, but in the case of an image failing, or being slow to load, a `background-color` attribute should also be set, alongside the `background-image`, that should give sufficient contrast to the text on top of it.

Often, when white text is used on a dark background image, and the default background color of the page is white, then at first white text will render on top of the white background until the image loads, which makes for a less-than-optimal loading experience. Similarly, the use of color alone as an indicator of something is not reliable, as color blindness is fairly common. When color is used, then another way of indicating what the color means is also needed (for example, text or an icon).

Summary

As a professional, you have an obligation to build your products in a way that doesn't discriminate against those who use assistive technology. Fortunately, the Web and browsers have been built in a way that reduces the level of friction needed to support accessibility tools beyond what native apps can offer. Bending web standards, or implementing completely custom components out of generic HTML elements, can lead to breaking compatibility with assistive technologies, potentially alienating a sizeable portion of your user base.

There are many different types of accessibility to consider, some of which use tools such as screen readers to deliver experiences, and others that are solely implemented in browsers and designs. It's important to treat these AT tools similar to other web browsers, and correct bugs that are found in them, as well as testing your site using interaction mechanisms beyond the standard mouse or touchscreen.

Like many cross-functional requirements, accessibility should be built in from the start of a project, and there are several techniques to address this, both for structuring a document using semantic HTML and setting up JavaScript event handlers for particular event types and considering other flows of engaging with interactive elements. In particular, HTML can be augmented with ARIA attributes to provide hints to AT tools when non-standard HTML is used, and JavaScript should handle focus in the same way that it considers click- or touch-based interaction methods.

If you remember one thing from this chapter, it should be to test your site in the way that many of your users will be interacting with it, either with a screen reader or with keyboard shortcuts, as this will identify the biggest issues preventing your site or app from being accessible.

CHAPTER 10

APIs

Every application has an API of some sort, whether it's an external API that's designed to be used by applications other than yours, or an internal API that allows modules within your application to talk to each other. Designing the first kind of API is much harder than building the second kind, as it can become very hard to make changes that do not break those other applications. In the second kind of API, the code that defines the API and the code that uses it often move together, so refactoring is much simpler.

In the early days of computing, external APIs were shared libraries that you could link your application against, accessing the functions and classes in that library using normal function calls. In web development, the environment you're running in will provide a set of APIs for you to use, as well as any libraries or frameworks you might install, such as from NPM. However, the types of APIs we're going to discuss here are ones that are available over a network, and will often be on a different machine than the one your code is running on.

In the early days of the Web, a mechanism known as RPC (remote procedure calls) was very popular. It was a single URL you could hit with parameters, where the function would get executed and a response given to you. However, this wasn't in keeping with the structure of the Web as having documents and resources at distinct URLs, and RPC at a single URL became difficult to handle where browser caching and scaling became involved.

Simple Object Access Protocol (SOAP) is the most common example of this in the web world. SOAP grew out of other ad-hoc mechanisms for communicating over the Web, using patterns known as AJAX and XML-RPC, but was designed to work over protocols other than HTTP (such as message queues or e-mail). SOAP is implemented by having a schema that defines which types of messages are available, and the structure of the requests and responses as XML, and then a single URL where HTTP POSTs are

© Chris Northwood 2018
C. Northwood, *The Full Stack Developer*, https://doi.org/10.1007/978-1-4842-4152-3_10

sent. The body of the POST specifies the request (perhaps to get data, or to do some other action) and then the server responds in an expected format. The strength of SOAP is in its schemas. These schemas can simplify interacting with an API, as well as be self-documenting about the type of procedure calls that are available, but this is also its main pain point. Dedicated tools and libraries were needed to support these schemas and effectively use the endpoint, which complicated debugging and added other development overheads.

Much of the complexity that SOAP tried to solve was complexity that the protocol itself introduced. Although it was in use before, Roy Fielding codified an alternative structure for building APIs, which he called Representational State Transfer (REST).[1] This kind of API deals with resources on the service, reusing existing HTTP mechanisms that deal with these resources similar to the way a web browser treats documents. This simplified the implementations and ways of interacting with APIs by making existing web tools, such as security and caching layers, work naturally. These approaches were already in use in ad-hoc ways before Fielding published his dissertation, but his description has set the best standard practices to follow.

At its core, REST may appear to be about using the appropriate HTTP methods (sometimes called verbs) and an appropriate URL structure, but the most important parts of it are the design constraints underlying these APIs: separation of concerns between client and server, statelessness, cachability, a layered system, and a uniform interface. REST can be used to describe any system that has these constraints, but the "uniform interface" is usually interpreted as meaning HTTP, so it becomes a set of web interfaces.

The biggest difference between SOAP and REST is in terms of how easy it is to use. SOAP usually requires a special library to help deal with making requests in the right form and handling the responses, as well as matters such as authentication, but REST can re-use standard mechanisms for making HTTP requests. In web browsers, this technique is known as AJAX, which uses an API called XMLHttpRequest (XHR) to make standard requests to a server (in ES6, a new API called Fetch replaces XHR, and simplifies the way requests are made).

---

[1]Roy Thomas Fielding, "Architectural Styles and the Design of Network-Based Software Architectures," 2000.

API Responsibilities

A common mistake for people who build APIs is to try to build one API to satisfy every situation in which it may be called. For example, a product API might be designed to be accessible from a JavaScript app running in a browser and from automated batch import processes. This can cause issues where the API ends up having to implement functionality that it doesn't necessarily need, or a lot of browser-specific features. It is common for server-to-server communication to use API keys, but for users of your application to have some common login. If your API is handling both server-to-server authentication and this typical user authentication, it can cause complexity, and complexity leads to bugs.

Instead, what we could do is introduce layering to APIs. One such set of layers is a rich backend API, and an API that allows front-end UIs to communicate back to a server. This layer is a concept called "backends for frontends." In this, our product API is locked down, so it's only available for server-to-server communication (this can be done by requiring an API key or some other secret that isn't exposed to users, or by implementing a firewall at a network level). We then have a "backend-for-frontend" API layer, which is often the same application that serves the original HTML for the page. This API simply exposes a set of AJAX endpoints that the front end can use to query the back end. Figure 10-1 demonstrates this.

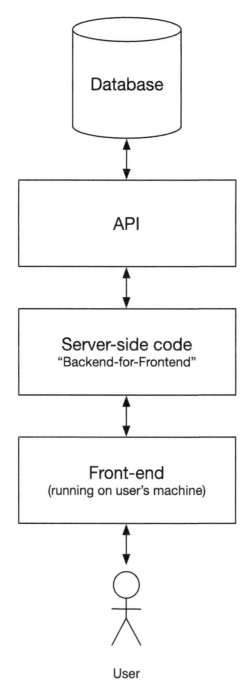

Figure 10-1. *The layers of the "backends-for-frontends" pattern*

This layer often acts as a translation layer, as it can simplify the API that your front end needs to interact with and map it onto the concepts of your back-end API (which can be more abstract or complex than the front end needs to care about). This also becomes an excellent place to put strong validation and authentication checks, which means your back-end API does not necessarily need to have as complex validation rules or authorization structure, which simplifies it and reduces the chance of bugs. The back-end API can be then heavily locked down so only other components directly under your control can access it directly, and it can trust that the edges of the system provide additional security for the information and interactions that happen with it. The backends-for-frontends pattern is especially powerful when multiple front ends or systems want to communicate with the same back-end API.

Designing a REST API

Designing an API is similar to designing a graphical user interface in that you need to think of the needs of the end user (perhaps yourself, another developer on your team, or an external team that uses your API), the actions they might take, and what the underlying structure and consistency of your data is. However, a perfectly designed API is not always achievable, as it can be constrained by the performance of the underlying databases.

The first part of an API to consider when designing it is the URL structure. Technically, REST includes the concept of Hypermedia As the Engine of Application State (HATEOAS), which establishes that an API should have a simple fixed-entry point, and you should navigate the described links from that entry point to find the resource and action you want to undertake. For example, a response from a paginated API may look like this:

```
{
    "items": [ ... ],
    "_links": {
        "self": "https://api.example.com/blogposts/2",
        "first": " https://api.example.com/blogposts/1",
        "prev": " https://api.example.com/blogposts/1",
        "next": " https://api.example.com/blogposts/3"
    }
}
```

This is often not implemented for a whole API for performance's sake. If a client has to navigate an API to find the action it wants to undertake, this can cause many requests and slow things down. Many APIs still implement this feature, but it becomes more of a help to developers of the service, rather than used by servers that utilize that API. Instead, knowledge of how URLs are structured are used to interact directly with the desired resource.

However, it can become quite easy to fall back on knowledge of how URLs are structured, when in many situations, relying on HATEOAS can actually simplify your code. For example, in a product catalogue, you may want to show some related products alongside an item you have selected. This could result in multiple API calls, and one approach might be to include the IDs of the other catalogue items to look up, and then a front end will need to know how to look up those IDs in order to fetch the metadata. A way to do it that is more in keeping with HATEOAS would be to include the full URIs, to avoid having to know how to look up an ID.

You must be careful when working with external APIs to not follow URLs blindly, because if that API is untrusted, it can lead you to a place that you may not want to load.

When it comes to building your API, it can be tempting to apply all the HTTP best practices, and in particular content negotiation, to support many different types of clients. However, unless you have a specific need for this, it can simply overcomplicate your application without bringing much in the way of benefit. For example, giving a single product in your product API a URL such as "`https://api.example.com/products/533-4499`" and then having the user-facing URL be "`https://www.example.com/products/533-4499`" is considered not to be best practice, as you have two different URLs that refer to the same thing. However, this is a common occurrence and can especially help when it comes to applying security and caching (you can lock down the whole api.example.com domain name while keeping `www.example.com` visible). Furthermore, many APIs make it easy to give different representations of the same resource. In the example above, api.example.com/products/533-4499 could give a JSON version of your product data when requested with the header "Accept: application/json," and an XML version when requested with the header "Accept: application/xml." This can seem tempting, especially if you get it for "free" with your framework, but the concepts behind XML and JSON are different enough that trying to automatically translate between the two will result in a representation that is idiomatically neither and would be hard to work with. Additionally, when it comes to caching, you now need to include a

"Vary: Accept" header in your response for caches to handle this appropriately. This can mean that cache servers could have different cached copies of the same URL depending on the Accept header sent by clients, which minimizes the benefit caching gives you.

The KISS ("keep it simple, stupid") principle works very well here, even though it can be tempting to follow the theoretical best practices of HTTP and REST. Simply always giving back JSON (or XML) and serving your API from a different set of URLs to your front-end can vastly simplify your implementation. HTTP best practices also suggest using "vendor" MIME types for your JSON responses to make it conform to a schema, but doing so will potentially make it harder for clients to use it (they need to know a specific MIME type is now parseable as JSON, which many can automatically infer if the "Content-Type" header is application/json). This may seem to break the constraint of REST that messages are self-describing, but many it as a weaker version of it than originally intended for ease of implementation (i.e., you can still parse the syntax of the message as JSON, but the message does not necessarily self-define the semantics of how that response should be handled).

The most important thing to consider about RESTful APIs is that they should not hold any state about the clients that are using it. A single request from a client should be considered in isolation to any other. Your API should not expect a user to have to make multiple requests to change to a resource before that change actually occurs. This gives you the freedom to scale the implementation of your API by allowing it to run on many different servers, with only the underlying database shared.

This implementation constraint allows us to make use of a property called idempotence for our end points. Idempotence means that making the same request should always have the same result.

HTTP defines several "methods" that can be called on a particular URL. They are GET, HEAD, POST, PUT, DELETE, PATCH, OPTIONS, and CONNECT. Of these, CONNECT is only used by HTTP proxy servers to start TLS connection to the remote server, so can generally be ignored, and HEAD and OPTIONS are often implemented by the web server or framework for you, unless you're doing a very low-level implementation. HEAD is defined as performing a GET request without actually returning the body, just the headers of the response. OPTIONS is similar, but for the requests that change state: POST, PUT, PATCH, and DELETE). OPTIONS doesn't actually change the state, but will tell you what methods can be used on a resource. It is also used by browsers in a technique known as CORS preflight, where the returned headers are checked for the cross-origin policy to determine whether or not the actual request should be allowed.

The request to a web server consists of some headers, and optionally a body. The headers specify at least the URL and the method, but also some key value pairs that can add additional information to the request. Some common fields include User-Agent, which indicates the type of program being used to make the request, and the Host, which indicates the hostname of the web site being requested (to allow one server to serve multiple different hostnames). Others are used to indicate things about the response, such as Accept-Language, which dictates which (human) languages the page should be returned in (for example, to support internationalization), or Referer,* which indicates which page linked to this one.

---

*No, I didn't make a spelling mistake; the original HTTP specification misspelled "referer" as "referer" (apparently, neither word was in the dictionary of the UNIX spellchecker the editors were using). The typo "referer" is now the accepted spelling when discussing HTTP, as the standard has never corrected it and it has been implemented that way by both servers and browsers.

There is much to be said about the methods and correct use of HTTP methods by an API. GET is essentially a request to read some content. GET requests can be cached, so should never be used to change content or perform an action (as you'll be unsure if the request actually reached the server or was just served by a cache). As a result, we can consider a GET request to be one that is idempotent: making the same request should always return the same information (unless, for example, the state of the underlying resource has changed through some other means).

PUT is used to replace the contents of a URL with some new contents. A PUT always replaces the description of that resource in its entirety, or could create a brand new resource where something does not exist. For example, if you have a product catalogue and want to update a field within it, you may perform a GET on that URL, modify the field you want to change, and then PUT the whole description back to that URL. PUT is also sometimes used to create a whole resource from scratch, by doing a PUT to a URL that previously did not exist to create it. A more common way to create something, though, is to make a POST request to an endpoint that dedicates itself to creating new resources and that will generate a new URL and ID for you.

One issue with PUT is that if you want to update a resource, you first have to GET it, change the fields, and then PUT the whole thing back. There will inevitably be a gap, however small, between the GET and a PUT. If another user or application makes an unrelated change on the same resource in that time, then you would override your changes on your PUT. One method to avoid this is called PATCH (discussed later), but mechanisms also exist alongside a PUT to handle this case.

On a GET, it is common to add a header to the response known as an "ETag," or entity tag. This tag is used to uniquely identify that version of the resource (perhaps being an actual version number, or a hash of the response). When the client receives a response, it should make a note of that ETag, and then when a PUT request is made, the header If-Match is sent with the value of the ETag. The If-Match header indicates that the action should only be taken if the value of that header matches the ETag of the resource, so if the resource has changed in the meantime, an error will be received and you can retry.

Like with request headers, there are many other types of response headers. For example, instead of ETag and If-Match, you could instead use Last-Modified and If-Not-Modified-Since. Others are used for other reasons to express metadata, but there are too many to cover here.

DELETE works as you would expect. If you make an HTTP request with the DELETE method on a URL, then that resource will be removed from the database.

Unlike GET, PUT, and DELETE, PATCH and POST are not idempotent, and repeating the request may have unexpected side effects. POST is used to trigger an action on the server. As mentioned in the section on PUT, sometimes this action is to create a new thing in your database, but POST started out as a more general term to describe processing the submission of an HTML form. POST is not idempotent, as submitting the same request several times will cause that action to be triggered that same number of times. For example, imagine you have an endpoint to add something to a catalogue. If you POST that twice, then two items will be created, but if PUT was used instead, the second would just replace the newly created item with an identical description. POST is useful for triggering items like background actions (for example, a video transcode) or other actions that have side effects, like sending an e-mail.

PATCH is often used in collaboration with PUT. With a PUT, you must send the entire description of the resource because it replaces it in its entirety, but PATCH allows you to update a single field or a subset of the resource. Like PUT, there is a chance for race conditions with PATCH if two conflicting diffs are applied in near succession, but the impact can be minimized, or avoided entirely. The exact body of a PATCH to describe a change also varies between implementations of PATCH.

Once you have picked the correct HTTP verb for each type of request you make to a URL that you have defined in your API, you can start thinking about how you should structure your response to the person who made the request. An HTTP response, like a request, is split into two parts: the headers and the body. The headers of the response are similar to the request in that they describe additional metadata about the response and the server that sent it that may not exist in the body (such as the ETag, as discussed previously, or the cross-origin policy of that resource for OPTIONS responses). Where the response structure differs is that instead of an HTTP method, there is a status code that indicates what type of response it is. Status codes are split into five main categories, and within each category there are many variations. Only the most common ones will be covered here.

Status codes are three-digit numbers, and the first digit indicates the category. Codes starting with 1 are classed as informational, 2 as success, 3 as redirection, 4 as client errors, and 5 as server errors.

You will rarely come across 1xx codes during development, with the exception of "101 Switching Protocols," which you may see in a dev console if you use WebSockets (WebSockets are technically a different protocol than HTTP, but they start off as HTTP and then switch to the WebSockets protocol to allow for two-way communication).

"200 OK" is widely considered to be the normal response for the Web, and most frameworks will send a 200 response by default, unless you explicitly override it. 200 indicates that whatever request was made was a valid one, and the response is what you would expect. Another 2xx code of interest is "201 Created," which you can send along with a Location header after a request to make a new resource to indicate where that has been made. For example, if your API to register a new article in a CMS is a POST to /articles/, then you may want to respond with "201 Created" and a Location header with the URL of the newly created article (for example, indicating the ID that has been auto generated for it).

The 3xx status codes are used for redirection, but mistakes made by early browsers meant that 301 and 302 were implemented incorrectly, so there appear to be many similar codes. 3xx responses are usually combined with the Location header, which contains the new URL that the client should go to. After browsers implemented 301 and 302 in a way that differed from the spec, servers then matched what the browsers wanted rather than what the standards indicated. In order to allow the original semantics, and to avoid confusion, new codes were created to force browsers to behave correctly, and the old codes were redefined to match the browser semantics, although using the new codes is recommended.

301 and 308 both indicate permanent changes to a URL. For GET requests, both behave the same, but for other types of requests, most browsers will GET the target URL for 301 requests, even if it was a POST or similar, but for 308 requests the original method must stay the same.

302 was originally used to indicate a temporary change, but its use is even less clear, with some browsers changing a POST to a GET (like 301), and others remaining the same. 303 was created to explicitly say that a POST should change to a GET, and 307 to say that the request method should stay the same.

The main difference between permanent and temporary redirects are that permanent ones are cached, whereas temporary ones are not. They also have an impact on SEO. If you are restructuring your site and delete or consolidate some pages together, or just change the URLs, then you should use permanent 301 redirects. Temporary redirects are useful if the redirect ever has to change. For example, some conference web sites may redirect their home page to a year for the current event (for example, `https://www.example.com/conference/` to `https://www.example.com/conference/2019/`), but then update that redirect the following year. In this case, a 302 (or 307) redirect can be used, and you can give the same URL to people year after year, but not break bookmarks people have to previous years when you launch a new event. 303 is mostly useful for dealing with form submissions. If a user submits a form to a site, you can process it and then redirect them to a results page using 303.

4xx codes are used for reporting when the user of the API or the browser has made some sort of error. The most well-known 4xx code is "404 Not Found," which indicates that a URL has been mistyped or a non-existing resource requested. Technically, if a page used to exist there, but has since been deleted, another code, "410 Gone," should be used, but many people do not implement this functionality. Other popular 4xx codes are "401 Unauthorized" and "403 Forbidden," with the former indicating that the user needs to send some valid credentials with the request, and the latter indicating that your credentials are valid, but you do not have permission to access that URL. For example, if you have an API where some users are administrative but others are non-privileged, then for an administrative endpoint, you would send 401 if no (or invalid) credentials are sent, and 403 if the credentials are valid, but they are for a non-administrative user.

The final 4xx code I will cover is "400 Bad Request." This code indicates that there was something wrong with the request, and can be very useful for APIs. For example, if the body of a POST or PUT request fails to parse as JSON, or fails some other sort of validation check (perhaps missing fields), then 400 would be an appropriate status code to return.

The 4xx endpoints should return an error message to the user. For non-API servers, these are often HTML pages, but for APIs, it can be useful to return a JSON (or similar) message that the API users can parse. For example, in a 400 response, sending back a structured list of any validation errors that occurred can be useful for the API client to build a good error-message user experience for the client. RFC 7807 attempts to define a standard way of building these error messages, but many APIs also implement their own JSON structure for error messages.

HTTP 418

Looking at lists of HTTP status codes, you notice that one stands out: code 418. The Internet Engineering Task Force, which defines many Internet standards, has a long running tradition of "joke" standards on April Fool's Day, and in 1998, a joke standard called "Hypertext Coffee Pot Control Protocol" was introduced, including the error code 418 "I'm a teapot," indicating that you've asked a teapot to brew coffee.

As an Easter egg, many web server developers have adopted the 418 error code from the joke coffee standard into HTTP, although you can safely ignore it when implementing your application!

The last set of HTTP error codes are 5xx. "500 Internal Server Error" is one you will have come across before, and represents a "catch-all" error state, where some sort of error has occurred on the server (that's not the fault of the client).

Like 4xx codes, 5xx codes should also send a request body, but unlike 4xx codes, it's good to hide information here. Some frameworks have a debug mode where 500 requests will return stack traces, but this should be turned off in production, and error information should go into logs only (it can be a good idea to do this in development too). The main reason for this is that stack traces or other verbose error messages can accidentally leak sensitive data (such as reporting the database password if a database connection failed) that you will not want the outside world to know.

Once the metadata around your requests has been designed, you will also need to design what the body of your requests and response should look like. JSON is very popular, but is not the only format to consider. XML once held favor, but is less common nowadays, as it can be a very complex way of expressing information. Where XML succeeds over JSON is if you need your users to express additional metadata inline with text (for example, perhaps expressing formatting information in an e-mail submission), but for most simple key/value requests, JSON is effective. When the client of an API is a web browser, it can also be worth considering the format with the MIME type "application/x-www-form-urlencoded," which is the native format of an HTML form.

A historic advantage of XML over JSON is that XML has schema definitions that provide a good way to check the well-formedness of XML, and XML schemas are widely supported. There are tools that provide similar capabilities for JSON, although there is no universal support. JSON Schema is a popular format for documenting data structures, and is commonly combined with tools like RAML and Swagger to create API documentation and validation.

There are many other serialization formats to consider, and some frameworks will be format agnostic and convert it for you, allowing you to accept many in one request. However, this adds complexity and has been known to accidentally cause security issues. For example, YAML is a very powerful language that allows you to define functions in the code, which has led to hacks of popular sites such as GitHub and Equifax, where bugs or inappropriate deserialization has led to a request executing code on your system. Sticking to one serialization format is a reasonable thing to do and limits the complexity of your application. Even when you do so, care should be taken. For example, a famous XML exploit known as a "billion laughs" can make a relatively small document decompress to use several gigabytes in memory when parsed. Many parsers will often have a "safe" mode that treats the input as untrusted before parsing it to protect against these kinds of attacks, but when reserializing content from an untrusted source, you should ensure you fully understand the features of the library you are using to deserialize and build robust error handling.

The actual structure of your requests and responses will of course depend on your use cases. However, keeping parity between a response and a request can make life simpler. For example, if you GET a URL that supports updating, you should be able to PUT the body of the request right back without actually making any changes. However, sometimes a data structure will refer to other, linked resources, such as an article that may have links to other recommended articles. When you GET the resource, for performance reasons a client will not necessarily want to go and look up all the linked resources through making multiple requests in order to render the page, so a common thing to do is to allow ?expand=true flag, or something similar, to be specified on the GET request that adds additional data around the linked resources to minimize the amount of work the client needs to do. This expanded resource might not be capable of being PUT back as is.

Another thing to consider when designing the schemas for your API is that some degree of change should be inevitable. For example, you may want to add new fields in the future. You should be able to add a new field without having to update any clients (they should ignore anything extra that they do not recognize), but any major restructuring will require either some breakage, or for you to handle both the new and old data structures in parallel for some period of time while all the users of the API update. One common mistake is to use a JSON list as a top-level resource. For example, if you have an endpoint that returns search results, you might just have a list of objects. In the future though, you may decide to introduce pagination, which involves adding fields, such as the current page number. If the API instead returned an object instead of a list, you could add those fields, but by returning a list at the top level, it is now a breaking change. You should always use objects as the top-level resource.

One common technique is to include a version number in the URL of the API endpoint— for example, "`https://api.example.com/v1/products/`." Another school of thought says that if custom content MIME types are used, a version number could be encoded in that. Some prefer to eliminate versioning entirely, arguing that if an endpoint needs a complete rewrite, it should be a brand-new URL, or a brand-new service, rather than a new version of an existing API. Older versions can then run in parallel with newer ones until all users have migrated to the new system, at which point they can be decommissioned. However you decide to handle versioning and change, you should include it from the start to expect change, minimizing the risk of breaking any users of your APIs.

Securing Your API

APIs are often fairly powerful parts of your infrastructure, and you will often wish to restrict some, or all, of your APIs from the public Internet. There are a number of ways to achieve this, and a more general overview of security is discussed in the Security chapter.

It's important to understand the difference between authentication and authorization (sometimes abbreviated as "authn" and "authz"). Authentication deals with proving that someone is who they say they are, and authorization is proving that someone has access to the resources and actions they try to access.

A simple way to secure your API might just be to firewall it so that only the applications that need access to it have access to it. This is risky when used by itself, because if someone compromises a server that has access to that API, they suddenly have the keys to the kingdom. It also means that all applications have full access to all the API, rather than only a subset.

Going a step beyond this might involve introducing a level of authentication, but still granting access to all API calls to anyone who can authenticate ("being behind the firewall" might be seen as the simplest form of authentication). HTTP itself has built-in mechanisms for authentication in the form of request headers, and if you're using servers like Apache or nginx, you can configure simple username/password-based authentication fairly trivially. However, in larger setups, maintaining simple username/password files can be challenging, and some larger enterprises use a feature of HTTPS known as TLS client certificates to authenticate users of an API. Like normal HTTPS certificates on a server, which verify that a server is who it claims to be, a client certificate is sent to the server from the client to prove that who is making the request knows who they are too. Client certificates are powerful because they are harder to attack through brute-force and can be set to expire or manually revoked, which can centralize the handling of stolen credentials. They also can be integrated with OS logins on many desktops for users, which can minimize the number of usernames and passwords a user is required to memorize. However, setting up the tooling required to generate and manage client certificates (known as an X.509 public key infrastructure) is complex, so is only common in larger enterprises. Another common approach is to use an API key as a header or in a query string, which is then checked against a database.

You will often also want to introduce authorization to your APIs. For example, if you are distributing a mobile app that talks directly to an API, then someone could decompile your code to extract the API credentials. If simply having these credentials gives complete access to the system, this is clearly undesirable.

One way of implementing authorization may be to simply bake in to your application code that checking whoever the user has authenticated as has access to do whatever it is they have requested to do. This is often referred to as whitelisting, where a user has no access to do anything unless they are on a whitelist that includes their username, and the parts of the application that they have access to. Often the nature of these things depends on exactly what your business logic is, so it can be hard to be generic. Sometimes whitelists might be bundled into the application or as configuration, but this can be inflexible (for example, you may need to deploy a configuration change to remove someone from a whitelist), and it is also hard to see what a user has access to over an entire estate. Another common approach is to have a central authorization service that systems call out to in order to check whether or not a user is authorized.

Often, this authentication/authorization logic can end up deep in your code, causing a mixture of concerns in any controller logic. Some frameworks use methods like decorators to help with this, but another common approach is to use a service that provides an API gateway. These API gateways sit in front of your service and provide both authentication and authorization. Authentication is usually provided using HTTP credentials or by an API key, but checking the validity of these is centralized in the gateway service. Authorization is then usually checked against a whitelist dictating which URLs a service is allowed to hit, which can be an effective top-level check and can also simplify development. API gateways introduce their own risk, though—for example, if they are bypassed, or if the authorization needed is more fine-grained.

There are also authorization protocols that do not deal with authentication. The most famous of this is OAuth, but other standards such as JSON Web Tokens exist in this space too. With OAuth (and OAuth 2), an application that needs to access an API (for example, some front-end code or a mobile app) generates a request for certain permissions, and then gives a user that request and sends them to the API to log in using their credentials and generate an API key that has the specific capabilities the application needs. Once the application has that API key, it can then use it to access the endpoints it needs, but it does not know anything about who the user is. Often, one of the endpoints an application might provide is a "who am I?" function that allows authorized applications to access the authentication information, but this is not necessarily the case. It is not often used for server-to-server communications that do not involve a user.

JSON Web Tokens (JWT) are a simpler form of this. A JWT is simply a statement of something (perhaps who the user is, or what they have access to) that is then cryptographically signed by an issuer. Applications can then verify the signature to check that the statement is not fraudulent.

Going further than simply authenticating and authorizing a user, there are also techniques that can be used to further protect your API against rogue clients. A common technique is that of rate limiting, which means that no single user of your API can generate inappropriate load that may cause performance issues for other clients. This is particularly useful for APIs where the action can have a high cost or performance impact. Rate limiting is commonly implemented by allowing a client a maximum number of requests in a certain time period, and if they go over that limit, returning an error code rather than doing the action. Rate limiting can be implemented inside the application, but is a common feature of API gateways.

Event-Based APIs

Although the most popular type of API on the Web is the traditional RESTful API, there is a different API paradigm known as event-based APIs. RESTful APIs are useful when you want to discover or change the state of an external system, but sometimes your application needs to know when a change has occurred and behave appropriately.

For back-end applications, then it is common for them to be told when a change occurs. For example, a shipping label printing system might be instructed, through a request from a coordinating system, to print the label when an order is picked for fulfillment. Additionally, very complicated processes, where perhaps many systems need to be told when a change occurs, can put a lot of responsibility onto one component, perhaps with that logic being distributed if there are many different places the change can occur.

For front-end applications that need to be aware of a change, it's rare for a back-end system to have a way of communicating it, as they do not expose REST APIs themselves. For example, think of a web chat program, where a user will want to see if any other users in the chat room have said something new. The "quick" solution to this is to make several requests to the REST API and then check if the response changes. But this makes for a lot of work if a change is infrequent, or there are many elements that might change. It also adds delay—for example, if you check for changes once per second, it could take up to a second for you to see a new message. Instead, the client could open up a connection to the server, and when the state changes on the server, the server sends a message to all the clients via the connections they have left open. However, the original model of the Web did not support this interaction mode, so workarounds were used at first to enable it. In 2000, a technique known as Comet was introduced, where the server seemingly sends the content of a page very slowly, and this slow page is added as an IFrame. The server then wrote a `<script>` tag with some JavaScript that would call an appropriate function every time an event occurred.

Following the introduction of AJAX, Comet was extended to support "long polling." In an application that uses long polling, it is at first provided with all the data of the current state of the system, and then the length of time that data is valid for. An AJAX request covers all changes since that time, but if there are no changes, instead of returning an empty list, the server returns no response, leaving the connection open, until there is a change to notify the client of, and then sends the response. This response includes a new time, and the client repeats this process.

Introduced in 2011, WebSockets are an HTML5 feature that eliminate the need for techniques like Comet. WebSockets allow a browser to set up a connection to a server that allows for two-way conversations by sending messages to and from the server, rather than having to make a new connection for a request, which long polling forces you to do. For back-end systems, message queue technologies can be used to accomplish a similar goal.

The method I just described is based on the idea of sending the initial state and then subscribing to changes. This depends on an upstream system maintaining some initial state. Another approach is to simply receive all the events that have ever occurred within the system and then process those to have your application form its own view of the state of the system, rather than relying on an external system for some initial state.

Once your system is deployed, it can then read only new changes and process those, but this gives you advantages. For example, if you ever need to migrate your database to a new schema or rebuild it after data corruption, you can simply replay all events to build up your new state (although it is advisable to make a note of which events you've seen and processed to avoid triggering actions such as taking a payment twice). At some point, the number of events ever received in a system may be too large, so some early events that have been completely superseded are discarded (for example, in the case of an "update address" event, only the most recent one of these for an individual customer actually matters). This "only event" approach is advanced, but it is useful at scale in massively distributed systems where eliminating a single point of failure (the API that stores the state) is desirable (albeit at the expense of introducing your new event broker system as a new single point of failure).

Discovering APIs

Once you've deployed an API, then applications that want to use it will want to know what URL that the API is accessible at. For a very simple application, this could be hardcoded into the code that makes the request, but this practice isn't sustainable, especially if you're working in multiple environments. Code in your production environment will probably need to talk to the production version of the API, but in a development environment, there will often be different APIs.

There are many solutions to this problem, but the simplest one is to simply make the URL a configuration option (provided in a configuration file or as an environment variable, for example). When your API is deployed, it makes sense to give it a sensible name in DNS (for example, productapi.dev.example.com vs. productapi.prod.example.com), and if there are multiple servers running on an API in each environment, that URL could point to a load balancer that has the multiple servers behind it. This works when you need to migrate an API to a different server too.

This approach works well in many use cases, although there are some scenarios where it may be too simplistic. The main example is when you're looking for a specific instance of a resource, so abstracting it behind a load balancer or hard-coding a DNS name doesn't necessarily work. In some cases, wrapping up these concerns behind an API can help, so the service discovery becomes an internal concern of that component, rather than one that is exposed to the edge of the system. Another situation where specifying names of dependent services as configuration values may not be desirable is if you're frequently provisioning new environments, which requires new URLs to be specified. A bootstrap script that automatically generates these config files according to a template can alleviate this problem.

There are many tools and applications that can help with this problem of service discovery. The standard approach is to have a component register itself with a service discovery tool, and then use that to run queries to discover the hostnames of individual services. In this case, you only need to know how to find the service discovery tool itself in order to discover other tools.

Service discovery tools do become a critical dependency in your application, so you should only use them if you're completely sure you need them.

Using APIs

Once you have built an API, and the client has found the location of that API, it also needs to use the API. This can seem as simple as making an appropriate HTTP request (usually with some sort of credentials) and parsing the response, and in many cases, this is indeed all it takes. But for some APIs or types of interaction, you might need to take a more considered approach to how you use that API.

Interacting with an API means you are communicating with another part of your system, and that external system can suddenly start behaving unexpectedly or fail in unexpected ways. Error handling therefore becomes an important part of how you interact with APIs. With error handling, you must take into account both expected errors (such as a 404 Not Found error when checking if a particular resource exists), and unexpected errors (for example, 500 errors or responses that are indicated to be valid, but perhaps are unparseable). Understanding the failure modes of an API you are using is important because, oftentimes, a failure will need to be propagated through your system, perhaps a notification to the operations team or reflected in your user interface. It is common to wrap up your communications to external APIs with a module inside your client code, so all API handling happens in one place. This module should be able to indicate when an error occurs to the user of this module (perhaps by rejecting a promise or throwing an exception), but should do so by passing an error that makes sense to the caller, rather than just directly passing through the error from the remote API. If the error is directly passed through, it might not be obvious to the caller what's actually going on, or might lead to logic duplicated throughout your system as to whether it's an expected or unexpected error.

Error handling becomes more complex if an API call is one in a series. If one fails, then it could perhaps leave your system in an inappropriate state (for example, if a checkout front end calls a payment API that succeeds, but then raises a request with a shipping system, which fails). This kind of error handling is complex; in some circumstances, it might be appropriate to undo the actions that succeeded (although if the undo fails, you may be stuck) and indicate the failure to the user, but in others you may need to notify someone that manual intervention is needed. Alternatively, queueing the request for retry might be effective, but if these kind of requests in your system are common, then it might suggest your API designs need rethinking, or that moving to an event-based model would be more appropriate. The Designing for Failure section in the Systems chapter covers how to handle failures between modules in more detail, including the circuit breaker pattern, which can be used to help protect your user experience during outages.

Having a module in your application that deals with APIs that you need to interact with is a common pattern, as it leaves a single point of responsibility for any other things you may want to do when interacting with external systems. These concerns often include logging interactions with external systems (particularly failures), but also issues like monitoring. Measuring aspects like response times to external systems, as well as counting the number of successful and failed requests, allows you to set monitoring thresholds that can help with debugging any issues in a deployed system.

If the API you are using implements rate limits, you may also want to manage this in the client that uses the API. One approach may be to integrate with a circuit breaker, such that if you hit the rate limit, you trip the circuit breaker until the end of that rate limit period. Another approach is to queue up requests for retry, and retry them at rates below the limit.

Caching can be an effective approach for dealing with rate limits, and also has advantages to performance of your application. Caching is not without issues, however, and should be considered within the context of your whole application. There's not much point in adding a cache to your application if there is already a cache on the API, as this increases the risk of stale information and no performance gain. When implementing a cache in your application, the simplest thing to do is record a response in your cache (perhaps using a tool such as memcached, so it's shared across your whole application tier), and if a response exists in the cache, use that instead of making a request to the actual API. If it does not exist, then make the request and record the response in the cache. Often, only positive responses are cached, in order to avoid any errors persisting longer than they have to, but sometimes it may be desirable to cache any error responses, especially if it's an expected error (such as a 404). Some DoS attacks have been known to hit a 404 page repeatedly, as this goes through to the back end to check if the page exists every time. Caching in this case is called negative caching. Negative caching can be problematic, as a bug may cause an error state to be incorrectly cached.

This simple approach to caching can cause issues as well. Consider the fact that, when the cache expires, if there are multiple requests coming at once, there will be a period of time between the cache expiring and a successful response being added to the cache. During this time, the API may receive many identical requests at once, potentially causing errors. This is known as the "thundering herd problem," and is shown in Figure 10-2. Here, a number of requests are made, but between the cache expiring and the next response being delivered, an additional number of requests are made, which could flood the back-end service. After that response is received, further requests are once again served from the cache.

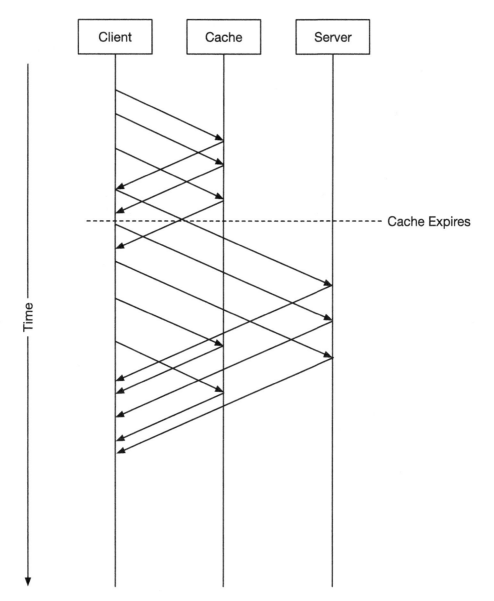

Figure 10-2. *A timeline of requests and responses between a client and a server through a caching layer, showing the thundering herd problem*

One common solution to this is to not remove an item from the cache at the moment it expires, but to instead mark it as stale. The first client to read from the cache after the item goes stale then acquires a lock and makes the request to refresh the cache. In the meantime, that client, and any other that sees the stale item in the cache once the lock has been acquired, serves the stale item to the client. This is known as "stale-while-revalidate."

Retaining stale items in the cache also allows you to use a related technique, known as "stale-on-error." If your API starts having issues or crashes, then the front end can still display information by using the stale information in the cache. Use of stale items is not always appropriate, though. If the user is relying on the timeliness of the information, showing an error indicating that up-to-date information cannot be shown is a better solution.

Summary

APIs exist for different parts of your system, and parts outside of it, to communicate. APIs can be thought of as the user experience for *other* applications, in that they must be designed to be usable and to ease integrations.

An API can also be hard to change, as it can require adjustments to many systems. Sometimes these changes are straightforward to coordinate, especially when you're working in a system you control all of the parts of, but for others, when third parties are integrating with it, those changes must be carefully managed. Versioning is often used to do this, but clients of an API must also be resilient to change—for example, if new fields in a response appear.

For web-based systems, the most popular form of an API is a REST API (Representational State Transfer). SOAP is a common alternative, especially in enterprise systems, but REST is more popular, as it grew out of the fundamental primitives of the web. REST uses HTTP verbs such as GET, PUT, or DELETE to manipulate resources, which are identified as URLs, and these operations must conform to several properties. Standard HTTP response codes are used to indicate success or failure of an operation. SOAP communicates with a single URL using requests and responses that conform to a published schema, whereas REST requests and responses aim to be self-describing according to a MIME type. Other APIs are event-based, where connections between systems are not just request-response, but where one listens to another and gets notified when events occur.

An API is a key part of your system when considering security. This includes both authentication and authorization, to ensure that not only is a person who they claim to be, but that they have permission to execute the operation in question, regardless of whether or not that operation has been exposed to them in a UI.

The use of APIs by a client is also something to be considered, as many servers depend on clients behaving reasonably when making requests to not cause performance issues, and others enforce this reasonableness using techniques such as rate limiting. Finding the right API is also something an important decision for a client, and there are many mechanisms to do this, from configuration values with particular URLs, to service discovery servers that a client uses to discover the needed API.

CHAPTER 11

Storing Data

For anything but the simplest web site, you will have to store data somewhere. Fortunately, data storage is a problem that has been worked on since the earliest computers were designed, and there have been many decades of research into the best ways of storing and retrieving data of all types, at scales ranging from small product catalogues to industrial systems tracking and storing millions of variables and events per second.

Your data is often the most valuable asset belonging to your organization, not only because it helps you meet your goals, but because of the potential cost to you if it is incorrectly protected or accidentally leaked. Although developers working in highly regulated industries like finance or healthcare might be used to legal compliance of their products, there are many developers working in industries that are not so heavily regulated, and legal implications on software engineering are not routinely considered. Data protection and privacy regulations are an exception to this rule, as they apply to almost all industries. Having a well-understood architecture for what data you're storing and where makes it easier to build protections in that ensure you are in compliance with the law. These requirements are not only legal, but ethical too. Exact data privacy and protection legislation varies between countries, but in most cases, there are organizations that offer advice on how to ensure you remain in compliance with these requirements, such as the UK's Information Commissioner's Office.

This chapter only scratches the surface of how you might structure your data and use databases, but as with many decisions, there is no one right answer. When choosing a strategy, the most important factors are what the data you're storing is (meaning its structure, and how important and sensitive it is), and how much of it there is—the average size of each item- and what the proportion of reads to writes is. Many databases, such as product catalogues, will be updated infrequently but read from much more frequently, while others, such as shopping carts, may have a more even balance. Still others (such as log analytics) might have many writes but infrequent reads for analysis.

The focus of this chapter is on the former of these types of data, which will often make up the most important bits of data in an organization.

© Chris Northwood 2018
C. Northwood, *The Full Stack Developer*, https://doi.org/10.1007/978-1-4842-4152-3_11

Types of Databases

For a long time, relational databases such as MySQL dominated the database scene, but an increasing number of applications now use "NoSQL" databases, such as MongoDB or Redis.

Relational databases are referred to as such because you can express relationships between the data in the schema. Relational databases are structured into tables, where an individual record in that database is called a row, and each field within that record is called a column, and all rows have the same columns with the same types. Relationships come into play because one of these columns could be a "foreign key," which is an identifier that relates to a record in another table. Usually, each record has a "primary key" that uniquely identifies it in that table. For example, a "posts" table could have a foreign key called "author" to a record in the "users" table that defines the author of a blog post. If the author then changes names, you simply need to update that author in the users table and all the blog posts they've written will inherit that change.

Relational databases are underpinned by an awful lot of theories, and the most popular databases have been around for decades, giving them time to mature into high-performance and reliable bits of software. They are not without limitation, though. The guarantees many relational databases make on data integrity can result in performance bottlenecks, and being forced to define a schema up front can make managing changes difficult. Alternatives to relational databases have become more popular and have been classified as "NoSQL" databases (SQL being the language used to work with most relational databases).

Although the conceptual model of all relational databases is similar, there are many different types of databases that are classified as NoSQL. The most common types are key-value stores and document stores, but you may also come across columnar and graph databases.

A key-value store can be thought of as similar to a hash or a dictionary in dynamic programming languages, in that the only way of addressing content is by using a key, and the actual data stored at that key is opaque. Many key-value stores do offer some abstractions over this; for example, Redis allows a key to refer to a set or a list, but the rule of finding a value using only a key still applies. The actual value stored at each key need not be alike, and could widely differ in structure between keys.

Document stores like MongoDB go a step further. In a document store, although a document will often have a unique ID like a key, it is often just a field inside a larger document. These "documents" tend to hold data structured as JSON or XML, and the key difference between these types of stores and key-value stores is that you can look up data based on the content of the document, not just the key.

There are also hybrids between key-value stores and document stores. DynamoDB, for example, behaves like a key-value store, but you can also add a schema to describe the type of data stored at a key that allows you to query on the value too. This schema is used to define an index. For performance, both relational and NoSQL databases allow you to specify an index on a table or collection, which can be used for fast lookups by looking up the data in an index, rather than searching all the raw data in response to a query.

Graph databases such as Neo4J represent data as a graph (that is, a collection of items with typed connections between them) and allow you to write queries by traversing the graph, while columnar databases such as Cassandra work by storing data by the column, rather than by the row, as in a traditional relational database. This is usually done for performance reasons when dealing with very large data sets.

One of the other most important characteristics of a database is the way it scales. Some databases simply scale by growing on one large machine, and others can be distributed over several machines, which can also offer resilience. The moment you want to distribute data, a theorem known as Brewer's CAP Theorem applies. This theorem states that a service can only ever have two of the following qualities: consistent, available and partition tolerant. It cannot be all three. Consistency here means that a system will always return the results of the most recent write to any read (or an error, if it knows it cannot be filled); availability means every request receives a non-error response (although there is no guarantee that it is consistent); and partition tolerant means that if communication is lost between different parts of the system, the system continues to operate.

The CAP theorem interacts with two prevailing philosophies that are usually aligned with the concepts of relational and NoSQL databases. Relational databases exemplify the philosophy that database transactions should be ACID, which means that consistency is chosen over availability, and NoSQL databases often determine that transactions should be *eventually consistent*, where availability is chosen over consistency.

ACID is an acronym for:

- *Atomic*: A write to a database that consists of multiple operations either complete as a whole where all operations have had their effect, or fail as a whole resulting in none applying.

- *Consistent*: Any transaction leaves the system in a state where all validation rules or constraints that are specified in the database are satisfied.

- *Isolated*: If multiple writes are applied to a database at the same time, or a read occurs while a transaction is in process due to parallel execution, the database will be left in the same state as if each transaction had been done one after the other (that is, multiple interactions at the same time do not interfere with one another).

- *Durable*: Once a write has been completed (the transaction committed), it will remain in that state if the server is shut down or restarted.

On the other hand, eventually consistent systems (sometimes called BASE in contrast to ACID: basically available, soft state, eventually consistent) can achieve high availability, but can mean that a write in a distributed system might not be able to be read back immediately, or reads might yield different results if given across different nodes. Eventually consistent systems can be high performance and highly available, but can make it harder to reason about the state in certain circumstances. Another risk with eventual consistency is that if transactions are applied in different orders on other parts of a distributed system, the nodes may end up in different states, which can be very dangerous. A modified form of eventual consistency, known as strong eventual consistency, adds an additional requirement that all nodes must be in exactly the same state, even if the transactions are applied in different orders. Most eventually consistent databases are strong.

To SQL, or NoSQL?

Many NoSQL databases are promoted based on the performance advantages they offer over relational databases, and the benefit of avoiding doing any schema design or migrations (changes to the schema that require the stored data to be updated to match the new schema), but they do have their downsides too.

Much of the power from relational databases comes from the fact that tables can be "joined" based on these relationships to get a result in a single query from multiple different tables. Most NoSQL databases do not allow this kind of joining, so can work out to be less performant for certain types of query. This is often worked around by repeating information inside documents (for example, author name, rather than linking to an author table), a process known as denormalization. A database that is normalized does not contain any repeated or redundant information. Although denormalized tables are not necessarily problematic, they do make it easier to introduce inconsistencies, and can make it harder to update data that appears in many places in the database.

Some relational databases are now adopting techniques from the NoSQL world. For example, PostgreSQL supports a JSON column type, rather than having to store all the data in a flat table. Whether or not to go relational or NoSQL depends on the type of data you have. Although NoSQL databases avoid the constraint of formally specifying a schema, you will often want to have some type of schema to keep a reasonable data structure, either to be read from in your application or to create indexes. NoSQL databases can also be faster to write to, so if you have many more writes than reads, this can be a better fit, but for most other types of data, a relational database will serve you well.

There are many exceptions to this rule of thumb, but one that's worth calling out is data that is often called "session data." This could include the contents of a shopping cart, or the ID of a user that is currently logged in. Sessions often expire, limiting any migrations to long-lived data, and are simply stored as one blob of data identified by an ID. Key-value stores such as Redis are perfect for this scenario. Some frameworks often support storing this kind of data in the memory of the application—this is especially common in Java—but it should be avoided. Restarting or deploying a service that uses in-memory session stores will often leave users logged out and missing data, and it can also cause problems with horizontal scale, which is an important attribute to design for when targeting cloud infrastructure.

Where to Store Your Data

Although there are many standalone databases, there are also databases that work by embedding themselves in your application, such as SQLite, or Neo4J (although this also has a standalone mode), but like in-memory storage of session data, this can have a negative effect on scalability, forcing you to run only a single instance of your application server. Separating your database out into a separate service (as servers like MySQL and MongoDB offer) allows you to scale your database and application tiers separately.

Some languages and frameworks make it easy to accidentally introduce a data store into your application tier. For example, in Java, a private field on a controller class may persist between requests and become an accidental place to store state. Languages like PHP or Perl (in a typical deployment) by contrast make this hard, as each execution of a script is tied to the request, and components cannot live between requests unless persisted elsewhere. Languages that support a functional or procedural programming paradigm (as long as you don't use global variables for state) can be long-running (so the same execution of your application serves multiple requests), but also force you away from holding state between requests in your application. Sometimes it is okay to hold state, perhaps as a fast in-memory cache, but you should never design so that the only place some data lives is in your application tier.

When designing and implementing an application, it is especially important to identify what types of data you need to persist, and where you will persist it. Having a strong understanding of these concepts allows you to reason through backups and security, which are discussed later in this chapter.

One naïve approach to breaking out the database from the application server might unfold as follows: if there are multiple application services that need to access that data, then they can connect to the database and access it directly. This approach can cause issues. If there are multiple applications accessing the same database, then this can make it easier to introduce bad data into a database, or make it hard to coordinate any changes to the database schema. Although many SQL databases support strong typing, stored procedures, and validation rules, this is less true of NoSQL databases. This often means that when multiple components need to access that database, then the same validation rules might need to be re-implemented multiple times, increasing a risk of bugs and a duplication of concepts in several places. Instead, it is better to encapsulate the actual data store behind a simple service that provides access to that layer. This service can then focus on implementing the validation rules and any other appropriate business logic pertaining to the data, as well as be a place where any performance optimizations can be focused. This service can then expose an API in a way that is consistent with any other services you may have (usually RESTful) and remain consistent even if you completely change the underlying data structure or storage engine. The Designing Systems chapter discusses this further.

In some circumstances, a single data store accessed through an API might not be appropriate. Some data is so important and fundamental that almost every service needs to touch it, which can introduce a single point of failure into your architecture. Another scenario might be when you have another service that has to be aware of any changes to that data—for example, a service that is responsible for sending out membership packs to new customers, or one that might cancel a credit card if a customer's account is marked as closed. In simple cases, adding message queues to your API to publish events can be useful. An alternative way of managing data can be used here, called "event sourcing."

With event-sourcing data models, there is no single point of truth within your system. Rather, event sourcing consists of a feed of events where every application that cares about the data can build their own view on it. Creating, updating, and deleting data still happens through a service that is responsible for publishing the events and any other validation and business logic around creation, but any business logic around reading the data is then devolved into individual services. As an application receives an event, it then updates its own database, often discarding any information it does not need.

In this model, there is still a need for a central store. For example, if an application realizes it needs to collect more data than it did before, a bug causes messages to be lost, or a new service is brought online. Then, the messages might need to be replayed, and the messages themselves must be recorded for that to happen. Event-sourcing frameworks like Apache Kafka support this functionality. Quite often, it is also possible to simplify the messages so that, instead of playing every single message, only messages needed to represent the current state of the system are played. So perhaps products that were added and then deleted are simply never sent, or only a single creation message needs to be generated, containing the latest values of all the fields, rather than a single creation message and a number of update messages.

This way of storing data as a series of events distributed across your app can introduce a large amount of complexity, and should only be considered when you have the specific scaling issues that such an architecture can solve. Often, each part of your app then has its own internal database that it builds based on those events.

Another place you might want to build a local database derived from some external data is if you need to cache some data, either as a result of an expensive query for performance reasons, or for resilience. Caching is discussed in more detail in the Systems chapter, but despite often being considered separately, caching is still a type of database. Caching is often implemented using a key-value store, with the key deriving from the query or resource that is being cached, and the value being the raw body of the item from an external system or query that's been cached.

Some key-value stores, such as Redis, support specifying expiry times on particular items to allow them to be used easier in a caching layer. Others, such as Memcached, are very focused on the caching use case and optimize for speed over reliability, as it will deliberately evict items from the cache before they expire if memory is running low—a feature you normally do not want from a data store!

Accessing Data from Your App

Once you have a database set up and an application server connected to it, you need a way to access the data. For relational databases, a language called Structured Query Language (or SQL, which is pronounced equally often as "sequel" and as just the individual initials) has become the de facto standard for writing queries and manipulating the database.

Unfortunately, as individual databases have become more complex, SQL has developed many different "dialects" to allow access to some more powerful features that some databases have adopted that the initial SQL language did not support. You will find that although simple SELECT, INSERT, and UPDATE queries may be transferrable between SQL servers, you will often come across cases where you need to write SQL that is specific to the particular database you have. Do not be scared by this. It can seem tempting to restrict yourself to generic SQL in order to maximize your ability to swap out a different database, but the actual circumstances under which you might actually want to change database software are rare enough that it makes more sense to write SQL for the specific server you are using. Furthermore, restricting yourself to generic SQL will often keep you from using powerful features of a database that can make your life a lot easier.

NoSQL databases, as the name suggests, do not use SQL for interacting with databases. Instead, each NoSQL database will often have its own distinct way of writing queries.

One downside of SQL and database interaction is that the data stored in a database does not necessarily have an implicit link to a data type or structure in your application code. Libraries known as "object-relational mappers," or ORMs, can deal with these, as they will translate between database queries and results, and the types and objects you use in your application code. Despite their name, there are ORM-type libraries for non-relational databases too.

Different ORM libraries provide different layers of abstraction between your code and the underlying libraries. Simple ones still expect you to write SQL and simply provide the results back as objects with the type you expect, whereas others might provide methods such as `create()`, `update()`, and `delete()` on your objects too, which then also handle the full life cycle of a particular record in your database. Accessing linked objects (in the case of relational databases) can be done too. The most full-featured ORMs often provide a series of methods and classes to deal with building queries to search a database, as well as managing any changes in the structure of your application data. These can be helpful in simple cases, but often cannot handle more complex scenarios, so will often include a fallback allowing you to write SQL directly.

The most full-featured ORMs can be quite restrictive, especially if you're building a complex app, so some prefer to avoid them. One common reason for doing so is that the way an ORM might build a query may result in a database query that is far from optimal and has performance issues. For simpler Create-Read-Update-Delete type applications, they can be a huge timesaver, so like many tools, their appropriateness depends on the context of your particular problem.

Although databases do a good job of abstracting a lot of the complexity of managing large sets of data away from you, they can't hide all the complexity. For large databases, performing a simple query to fetch data can be very slow if the database has to check every field to see if it's valid. Most databases support the concept of indexes that optimize against this. When an index exists, the database can search the index as opposed to the entire table to find the right data. Most databases have an index called the primary key, which is a way of looking up a single record by its primary ID quickly. Say, however, you wanted to filter your entire database by a field called "category"—then, if you did not have an index on the category field, when you apply that filter, the database would have to look at every record to check the value of the category field. However, if you had indexed the category field, then at first the (much smaller) index is looked at to get the list of records to be fetched, and then only those are fetched, which can be a significant time saver for larger databases.

For more complicated queries, getting indexes right can be hard to do. Fortunately, there are good tools available to help you run queries. SQL databases support commands like ANALYZE, and other databases have similar commands that tell you if a particular query is using the indexes or falling back to an unoptimized query, which can be slow.

It might seem prudent to simply add an index to everything, but this is counter-productive. Indexes make inserts and updates slow, as all the indexes also need to be updated for each operation, so only having indexes on a table that you actually use is important. A good rule of thumb is to look at the WHERE part of an SQL statement (or the equivalent for another database) and make sure that for each type of query you have, there are indexes on each of the combinations of columns you use.

It's important to realize that there are different types of indexes too. Detailing all of these is beyond the scope of this book, but if you are making queries beyond a simple equal to or comparison, then you might want to find out what kind of indexes exist in the database you are using. For example, geospatial indexes are common, allowing you to do fast searches based on geographic coordinates (e.g., show me all stores within 30km of the user's current location), as well as full-text search indexes (for queries like, show me all posts containing the words "Barack Obama").

Managing Your Data

Your database has one important difference from the rest of your application—it will often live with and evolve alongside your code for a long time. With regular code, all you need to do if you change it is deploy it, and your new code will be in use. But if you want to change the way your data is structured, that requires much more careful management.

It has for a long time been common practice to have a single large database, managed by a central team responsible for maintaining and optimizing it. Your application then connects to that database, and you discuss your requirements with the team who set it up and helped design your schemas. The name often used for this role is "database administrator," or "DBA," and the team often called the "DBA team" or similar. However, with microservices, there are now often lots of smaller databases throughout a system, and although teams responsible for particularly important databases may have a person with DBA skills on their team, this is by no means always the case.

Although the typical role of a DBA covers many bases (including advice in setting up schemas and appropriate indexes, as covered in the previous section, and backups and encryption, as covered in the next), one role a DBA may undertake is managing database performance. As discussed in the In Production chapter, application metrics can be used to set up alerts for your application, but for databases, there are many metrics relating to speed of queries too, and you should monitor them to identify any performance issues with your database.

There will come times when your data structures will need to change, either to correct issues with any existing structure, add new fields that need to be captured to support new features, or address performance issues. These kinds of structural changes can often be difficult, as you need to figure out how to translate any existing data into the new structure, especially if you're adding a new compulsory field. This can involve changes to your application code too, so if a new compulsory field is added, users may be prompted to update their profile before continuing, but leave some profile incomplete if they rarely log in.

In relational databases, the process of managing structural changes is called migration, and most languages have frameworks to help manage database migrations. The most efficient of these frameworks, which include standalone tools like Flyway as well as some integrated into frameworks like Django, will store these migrations as code alongside your main application, and can manage running these migrations as part of your application deployment.

In contrast to relational databases, one advantage of a NoSQL database is that you do not have to migrate all your data at once, and different bits of data can coexist in a single database with different structures, perhaps depending on when the record was originally created.

In NoSQL databases, you can write application code that upgrades a model to the latest version of the schema whenever it is accessed, rather than migrating all the records at once (which, for a large database, can involve downtime if there is a long processing time). Adding a version to a document in a NoSQL database can assist here.

The need for migrations can depend on the type of data you're storing. For example, in session stores, the data does not necessarily last long, and it might be fine to simply reset all the sessions and cut over to the latest version of a session schema. Alternatively, for simple cases like adding a new field, you can run the two schemas in parallel, and make your application code tolerant of the fact that some fields might be missing and assume that they are in a default state.

One downside to migrations is that they can make it hard to roll back a release of application code, and as a result it is common to also have a reverse (or "down") migration, which will revert the result of a migration to put things back into the previous structure. Applying migrations without causing downtime is also a challenge. A basic approach might see you make a new version of your code that uses the new schema, then, to deploy, put your application into a maintenance mode and shut down the existing code. Then, you would apply the database migration and bring up a new version of the application's code. For critical systems, this kind of downtime may be unacceptable, so it is often common to have an intermediate release of code that supports both the new and old schemas, and then do a second release that removes support for the old schema once the migration has been completed. In the case of changes that are simple, like adding a new field, this can be skipped entirely, as long as your application is tolerant to new fields in your database appearing, and just ignores any unexpected ones.

Regardless of whether or not you use a relational or NoSQL database, it's important to consider data and schema migrations alongside code deployments. In an earlier chapter, we looked at how techniques such as continuous integration, continuous delivery, and continuous deployment can be used to help minimize the time it takes to deliver a change to a live system. If your system has to manage data, you must consider incorporating your migrations into these deployment processes, either in a completely automated way, or perhaps with a level of manual intervention, depending on your circumstances.

Protecting Your Data

It should come as no surprise to learn that you should back up your database. However, executing the right kinds of backups can be tricky. The simplest types of backups protect against technical failure, such as a hard drive crash or corruption, but do not necessarily protect against other kinds of errors, such as operator errors or a bug causing data corruption.

A simple backup could involve executing a dump of your database on a timer (perhaps using a tool like `mysqldump` with a scheduler like cron) and copying the resulting file on another server. This, however, leaves a period of time after the most recent backup where some transactions would be lost in the event of a crash. Whether or not this is acceptable depends entirely on the type of data you're storing.

An alternative backup strategy involves setting up replication. When using replication, a second database server (historically known as a slave, but more recently as a replica) runs, having its own copy of the database and connecting to the first server (historically the master, but more recently referred to as a primary), and then makes any changes on its own copy that the primary server makes. This means that the replica is keeping up to date with the primary and is usually only a second or two behind the state of the primary. Often these replicas can then be switched to be a primary in the event of failure of the primary server, minimizing downtime for your system.

This kind of backup system does have the downside of any mistakes quickly being propagated to the replicas, so a bug, mistake, or even hack that may damage the database will not be easy to recover from once the change has been replicated.

The most effective backup regimes employ a combination of the above two strategies, using replication to provide recovery in the event of a technical failure, and then database dumps (which are stored for a set period of time) to cover other kinds of data destruction.

As the old adage goes, an untested backup is often as good as no backup at all. Regular testing of your backup regime, and making sure you can use your backups to bring your system back to a working state as expected, is just as important as getting your backup system set up in the first place. Fire drills (discussed further in the In Production chapter) are an effective way to test this. Often, a regular test of your backup system involves using your backups to populate a development environment if there is no sensitive data in it. Furthermore, setting up monitoring of your backups (for example, checking that the size of the file is in the expected range, or the date on the newest file is not too far away) can give you an additional level of protection.

Protecting your data does not necessarily mean only ensuring it's safe against being lost, but also that it's safe from being leaked and spread too far. Encryption is a well-understood practice, and many databases support it natively. When combining encryption with backups, you must also make sure your backups are appropriately encrypted and protected too, as stealing a backup is as good as stealing a copy of a live database, and has been the cause of many security incidents. For sensitive cases, this can mean the mechanism of testing your backups by recovering production data into your development environment is inappropriate, as your sensitive data should often be restricted to those who need access to it, which may not be the whole dev team.

There are two key types of encryption to use when considering data: encryption in transit, and encryption at rest. Encryption in transit refers to how your data moves between the application server and the database server, or any other server that may be involved in communication, and Transport Layer Security has become the dominant approach here, with most database servers supporting TLS connections. Encryption at rest refers to how your database is stored—if someone somehow gets access to the hard disk your data is stored on (perhaps by stealing it, or hacking in to the server the software is running on), could they simply read the data bypassing any security in your database software?

Some database software also supports the idea of encryption at rest, so that the files themselves are encrypted, and this can be effective for all but the most sensitive data. However, this does mean that anyone who can connect to a running instance of a database server (perhaps by using social engineering to steal an admin username and password) can run appropriate queries and see the plain data. You can go a step further and actually encrypt the data in your application, so the database never sees the unencrypted data. This means that access to the database is not enough—users will also need access to the encryption keys that the application uses. This might still be achievable for a determined hacker—though there does ultimately need to be some way to decrypt the data for the application to use it—but by increasing the layers of protection, you can prevent the most common security violations. One downside to database encryption is that some forms of indexing and querying on the encrypted fields are no longer possible.

Summary

Most web sites need to store data somewhere within a wider system, and databases are used to achieve this. Databases are difficult to manage, as they contain state, and may need to evolve in structure alongside your application, without using data along the way. The data in your database must be carefully managed too, as in many cases there are legal, financial, or ethical consequences to you and your organization if it leaks inappropriately.

Databases are often categorized as relational-such as MySQL, MariaDB and PostgreSQL-or NoSQL-such as Redis, MongoDB or CouchDB. Unlike relational, NoSQL is not a single type of database, and covers a number of different approaches for storing data, including key-value, document-based, graph, time-series, or columnar. One main difference is in the way you move between versions of the structure of your database. With relational, migrations are used to change the data and structure, and with NoSQL, this is often managed in code, with potentially multiple different versions of the structure being present at once, depending on which key is being looked at.

A systems architecture should identify where data is being stored in your app, and care should be taken not to accidentally introduce another store as part of your application, making sure all state lives in an appropriate database. Sometimes local databases can be used, perhaps as a caching tier or in an event-sourcing model, to build a local view of the data when that model is used.

Applications also need to access data. In relational databases, a language known as SQL is used, and some frameworks known as object-relational mappers (ORMs) can help build queries and map them to objects in your language of choice. NoSQL databases do not use SQL, and other mechanisms can be used to query them depending on the exact database. Indexes based on specific fields can be used to help speed up queries.

The data in your database should be protected, from accidental loss or damage, as well as from deliberate attack. Backups can be used to protect against the former, and techniques including encryption can help the latter. Remember that your backups should be protected using techniques like encryption too—otherwise you run the risk of negating that initial level of protection!

CHAPTER 12

Security

Building systems that are secure is a legal and ethical obligation for software developers, but the world of computer and information security can at first seem like an intimidating hurdle to a newbie, with the community often appearing cliquey and focused on hypotheticals. The reality is that the most secure system is one that is disconnected from the network and switched off, but this system is also unusable. Building a secure but usable system is a challenge that can only be met through compromise.

Like accessibility, security at first can seem like it may require specialized skills to address fully. However, for most applications out there, the special knowledge of a security expert is unnecessary, as you can use existing libraries and patterns for building a secure web application. In larger enterprises, a dedicated security team is common, but can be seen as a barrier to delivery. If you are able to talk confidently about the application and build simple, effective techniques in from the start, these barriers can be dropped and built in to your delivery process, yielding usable applications that are effectively secure.

Most of us aren't building *Mission Impossible*-style computer systems, and although there are pieces of critical infrastructure that require greater knowledge than a generalist will possess, most web developers will never come across them. Even for those developers building SCADA systems for nuclear reactors, these concepts are a good start. By learning a few key principles and identifying the limitations in your knowledge, you can build systems that satisfy your security requirements.

Trust and Secrets

During the build of your application, it's important to be able to spot when you're working with something that might be a security-sensitive component. As a generalist, if you find yourself working directly with credit card processing, passwords, or encrypting/decrypting systems, you're in the danger zone. Building these kinds of

© Chris Northwood 2018
C. Northwood, *The Full Stack Developer*, https://doi.org/10.1007/978-1-4842-4152-3_12

systems from scratch should not be approached lightly, and is often the wrong thing to do. There are many libraries and frameworks for these common tasks, so when you find yourself dealing with functionality such as this, using a reputable library (reputation can be determined by a number of factors, such as activity of a GitHub repository, or the number of StackOverflow questions about the framework, but this is far from a guarantee) will make your job a lot easier.

Security through obscurity means that you're relying on the fact that a potential attacker does not know some bit of information needed to access a secured part of your system. For example, having a hidden URL for an admin section is considered security through obscurity. Relying on security through obscurity is very dangerous, but there is a difference between obscurity and secrets. Something that is secret should be very hard to guess, whereas something that's obscure can be feasibly guessed or known. Most systems rely on some knowledge being hidden from a potential attacker—an API key, a password, or an SSH key—but this kind of knowledge can be considered a "secret" rather than just obscurity.

Secrets should be kept separate from your source code. In many organizations, access to the source code can be quite widespread—perhaps everyone has access to source control and can check out a read-only copy of your source code, or you invite a contractor in for a period of time to help out with some tricky functionality. Keeping secrets alongside the code could allow them to spread more widely than intended. This also means that it should not be the code itself that needs to be kept secret; if the information needed to circumvent security can be found in your code, then this is security by obscurity.

Secrets should be handled like nuclear waste—with care, and in a controlled manner. The people who have access to the secrets should be locked down on a need-to-know basis, and you should also change these secrets on a regular basis, particularly if someone leaves the organization (this is sometimes referred to as key rotation). There are many ways to manage secrets. Some deployment tools allow you to submit secret configuration values (so once the configuration has been set, it cannot be read by the user), which is sometimes appropriate, but other methods including having a separate config file containing the secrets, which is kept outside the main repository (such as only on the live server or in an encrypted shared drive), and can then be deployed from a trusted machine. Another option is to have a service that is responsible for managing secrets that other applications can connect to, and once authenticated, can load those secrets from that service.

Some secrets can be considered to be less secret than others. For example, a default password for a developer environment that can only be accessed over localhost may be safe to have in the codebase for speed of setting up new environments, as long as the database only contains dummy or test data.

Responding to Incidents

A security breach can be one of the highest-impact events to happen to an organization, but it's impossible to know what the impact of a breach is without a full investigation.

In the UK, and in many other countries, organizations have a legal responsibility to notify any affected users of a data breach, notwithstanding any internal policies and ethical obligations to fully identify a breach and its impact. As with many things in life, the best approach here is to hope for the best, but plan for the worst. It's important to make sure you have tools in place that will allow you to reconstruct as best you can any actions an attacker took, in order to understand the impact. For most systems, this means comprehensive audit logging.

It can at first be tempting to consider this type of logging to be similar to typical application logging, but it's useful to separate out audit logs into their own files, as these activities can clog up an application log when debugging typical errors. There are some tools that can assist with audit logging that provide tamper-proofing (so the logs cannot be edited after they have been written), which provides a high degree of confidence in your logs. It's usually a good idea to record an audit log off the infrastructure you are using, to make it harder for them to be deleted or tampered with.

The exact contents of audit logs will vary based on your application, but you will generally want to capture actions such as accessing or editing sensitive data. This can include the date/time, the user, their IP address, the action that was performed, and detailed information on what was changed. Logging when access was denied can also be useful, as this shows any unsuccessful attempts to infiltrate a system and gives you an idea of how far an attacker got. Full access logs from your web server can be used to identify any other suspicious activities an attacker performed.

Some breaches happen as a result of weak or stolen passwords from a privileged user. Often this occurs using social engineering, which can be hard to defend against, but there are technological countermeasures that can be put in place, such as enforcing long passwords and implementing two-factor authentication.

Many breaches happen through exploiting a bug in the application, and looking at the application log alongside the audit log could therefore be enlightening. Any odd or unexpected exceptions or errors from the database (for example, a malformed SQL query) can help pinpoint a vulnerability.

Once the investigation is complete, the most important thing to do is correct the flaw. This could involve suspending a compromised user account, or pushing a code fix to correct a bug. With the impact of the attack understood, the organization should be able to respond appropriately. Although it can be tempting to downplay an attack, honesty is one of the best mechanisms to maintain trust in an organization, rather than risk a slow release of detail, which show an increased impact from what was originally announced. Similarly, vagueness in any announcement can increase uncertainty. Honesty and specifics are the best policy here.

The Golden Rule

When building a web application, there is a golden rule to follow: validate on input, sanitize on output.

When receiving input from a user, or any external system, it is crucially important to make sure that the input is roughly what you expected it to be—this is validation. Generally, you should not try and clean up data a user has submitted except in very limited circumstances (such as stripping leading/trailing whitespace). This also makes for good UX. Most frameworks offer libraries that help you do this, and if you do get something that fails validation, you should abort immediately and show it back to the user as an error to correct rather than to try to cleverly sanitize it.

REGULAR EXPRESSIONS

Regular expressions (regexes) are a popular mechanism for writing validation rules, but you must take care! For example, if you specify that an ID must be lower-case alphanumeric, then you could be tempted to write a regex in the form `/[a-z0-9_]+/`. This has the unintended side effect of matching anywhere that sequence occurs in a string, not the whole string. If someone then sends through a string in the form `valid_slug But This Bit Is Invalid"`, the regex would match it, as it will match `valid_slug`, but that does not mean the whole string matches the regex.

Anchors can be used to ensure that the regex matches the whole string. ^ and $ are special characters that indicate the start and end of a string respectively, so you could write a regex in the form `/^[a-z0-9_]+$` to match the previous example. However, note that ^ and $ mean "start" and "end" of line, so it might mean that this would match against a string like `valid_slug\nBut This Bit Is Invalid`, as one line matches. Most regex engines will treat the entire input as one line, even if contains newlines, unless put into a multi-line mode, so it would work the way you would expect. Sadly, this is all implementation specific, so it's worth reading the documentation for your language before making your assumption. Some languages and libraries (notably Ruby) operate in multi-line mode by default, and the anchors `\A` and `\z` should be used instead of ^ and $ to indicate start-of-string and end-of-string, although they are not supported by all languages.

You should also do your validation in one place. This could be in the controller, or in a specific model class set up to handle user data. If you limit the area of your code responsible for handling user input to that one place, it is less likely that you will make a mistake (forgetting to validate one thing from the input will stick out in the code), and means that other areas of the code are insulated from direct user input and can either assume that the data it is handling is clean or, if full defensive programming is in use, reduce the impact of a missed validation at another point in the stack.

It is important to apply this validation in situations where any external system can submit data, rather than just the user. **Simply validating in JavaScript on the client and submitting it to a second service is not sufficient**—that service must also validate what it receives, because a malicious user can skip the JavaScript step and craft a request to the server directly. This is a commonly overlooked rule, as only the primary interaction path is considered, missing any other points where data could potentially be injected.

Sanitization, on the other hand, refers to ensuring that any data that is either shown to a user or submitted to another system does not corrupt the structure of the message.

| **PHREAKING** |

The need for sanitization is a result of mixing user data with "control" data in syntaxes such as JSON or HTML. If the control data and contents could be completely separated (for example, in different files), then sanitization would be unnecessary, and this would eliminate a whole class of errors (although it would make the data harder to deal with in other contexts). Mixing control and user data into one channel is what led to the earliest "hacks," where phone hackers (phreakers) discovered certain frequencies that, sent down a telephone line via a long-distance connection, would allow them to impersonate a telephone exchange, so the long-distance exchange would trust commands they gave as if they were another exchange. This was fixed by filtering the frequencies in those early telephone exchanges, and modern telephone exchanges do not mix users' voice data with the control data used between telephone exchanges.

When displaying content to a user that comes from an external source (for example, a message from another user), it is possible for that message to include HTML special characters, which could result in the page being corrupted with bad markup. In the simplest case, this could break the design; in the worst, it could allow JavaScript to steal your user's cookies. Fortunately, most templating libraries will convert any HTML in a variable into their safe equivalents by default (for example, `<strong>` will be converted to `&lt;strong&gt;`) which will execute the correct command—this process is called escaping. It can be tempting to simply remove any "special" characters from the output, but these special characters could be legitimately input by a user, and are sometimes easy to miss. This kind of conversion should always be done by a reputable library or framework; attempting to build your own is a high-risk strategy.

It's worth calling out cases where some HTML is valid—for example, you may want to allow your users to use limited markup in a forum or comments system. In these cases, special HTML sanitizer libraries can be used, which will permit some tags but remove or reject others. It is often helpful to run these when the user submits data too, as a validation step, to give them an appropriate error message and reject any invalid tags. As with other sanitizers, rolling your own is not recommended. Instead, you should trust a reliable library. Additionally, there are two types of approaches that can be taken by sanitizers: an allow list (sometimes called whitelisting), and blocking (sometimes called blacklisting). Allow-listing permits only certain HTML tags to be used, whereas blocking enforces a list of banned tags. It is preferable to use the allow-list mechanism, as evolutions to the HTML spec could introduce new tags that are undesirable, and would require a blocklist update to ban them. It is also easy to miss tags when taking a blocklisting approach.

As with validation, sanitization does not only apply when dealing with displaying information to the user. Any data that leaves the system should be sanitized. A common anti-pattern occurs when a request to an external system (such as a database, or a JSON request to another server) is made by concatenating strings together yourself. These kinds of requests should always be prepared by an appropriate library, such as a JSON serializer, or a SQL library, rather than directly passing strings in. These underlying libraries will handle sanitization for you and bypass this common class of errors.

The main exception to this is when calling a command line program, where often the commands are passed through a shell. Where possible, you should execute a program directly, rather than through a shell library (if you're using a single string, rather than a list of arguments, to call a program, it's likely going through a shell library). However, even in this case, it could be possible for invalid data to pass through. Therefore, careful validation is needed, in addition to sanitization.

There are cases when sanitization is not needed. If your data has been validated and can be trusted (for example, if it is guaranteed to be an integer, or is from a trusted set of strings), then sanitization may be unnecessary, but it's easier to include it and minimize the risk of a mistake than to exclude it and accidentally introduce a vulnerability.

As with validation, sanitization should always be performed at the edge of a system (for example, in the adapter, which makes a request to an external system, or in the view templates). Sticking to this rule simplifies the design, as there's only one place to check that sanitization has occurred, but it also avoids the risk of double sanitization (especially in HTML), which can show corrupt data to the user.

Threats

Applying secure programming practices will often get you far, but you will always have to make some security compromises as you build your system. This could be for practical implementation reasons, or for user experience reasons, but it's impossible to build a system that is perfectly secure. In many cases, this is actually okay! The key is to properly understand exactly what the important parts of your application are in order to appropriately protect them.

Information security is a bit like occupational health and safety. Done right, it keeps people safe with a minimum amount of fuss, but done wrong, it just gets in everyone's way, or worse, allows for serious accidents to occur. In health and safety, risk assessments are used as a way for organizations to develop appropriate protections. In information security, threat modelling is used.

In a risk assessment, you are supposed to identify anything that can cause harm (a risk; calculate the chance of that risk happening and the impact if it does; and then identify an appropriate way of mitigating against it based on that knowledge (a control). Threat modelling is similar, in that it starts with identifying theoretical security holes and threats in your application, then figuring out the chance of that happening and the impact of it if it does, and then strategizing appropriate mitigation—a way of preventing that thing from happening.

Sometimes, an appropriate mitigation might be to do nothing. If there's a theoretical risk that would have very little impact, and the chance of it happening is very small, or requires lots of unlikely things to happen, then it might be reasonable to identify the fact it's possible, and then not actually do anything about it, as the cost of fixing the hole may be unrealistically high. For example, if you are using two-factor authentication to log in to an admin system that is behind a firewall, then a risk exists where an administrator is blackmailed and forced to authenticate, but the risk of this is low and the cost of mitigation high (maybe requiring two people to take any action), so it's an accepted risk.

There are several frameworks that can be used for threat modelling, but they all follow a similar approach. The first is to break your system down into constituent parts, then identify all the threats towards a particular part of a system. Each threat is then evaluated to determine how important it is to deal with, and mitigations identified.

Microsoft's threat model is popular, and starts by identifying the exact security objectives of your application. For example, does it protect users' identities? Or would an attack have direct financial consequences? Availability is also considered a security feature, because if a security flaw can take your web site offline, even if no information is lost, this can have financial impact if you provide service-layer agreements to customers, or if that system powers another that is needed for you to do your business.

Threat modelling also requires a good understanding of your systems' architecture. Designing a system architecture is discussed further in the Systems chapter, but the architecture should show the boundaries of your system, and be able to be annotated where trust between components exists. Understanding how data flows through your systems (using data flow diagrams) is also useful in understanding which parts of your system may be vulnerable. For working with other components of a distributed system, interface contracts can also provide this knowledge. With this understanding, you can now try to identify the threats that could affect each part of the system. When threat modelling against a running system, you should approach this assuming you have no existing mitigations in place, to check that any assumptions you have made previously are valid. Although taking an unstructured approach to this can result in some threats being identified, there are more effective approaches you can use and combine here. The first is to think about it the way you think about your users, and consider the different types of attackers you may face: script kiddies (who try a bunch of common exploits automatically), disgruntled ex-employees (who have inside knowledge of your system design), normal users (who may stumble across something by accident and decide to explore), or determined attackers (including organized criminals or state actors who may have significant resources).

You can also consider different types of attacks. Microsoft introduced the mnemonic STRIDE to remember some common types:

- *Spoofing identity*: where a user can somehow impersonate another user or log in as another user to take on their characteristics.

- *Tampering with data*: where a user can manipulate data that they should not have access to (often caused by validation failures).

- *Repudiation*: where an action cannot be reliably traced back to a user—for example, in an e-commerce app, a user may claim they placed an order and paid more than they actually did.

- *Information disclosure*: when information that should be private is revealed to someone who should not have access to that data.

- *Denial of service*: when the application is flooded with requests, or run to capacity, stopping other users from accessing it. Oftentimes, limiting how much of a system a particular user can access, or limiting long-running searches, and the like, can mitigate these.

- *Elevation of privilege*: if different users have different layers of privilege (for example, administrator and non-administrator roles), then the application should ensure that a logged-in user cannot get access to any more functionality than they should have access to, by doing authorization checks, for example.

Once these aspects have been considered and a comprehensive list of threats identified, then you will need to rate them to determine if they need addressing, or if your existing controls are suitable. A simple way of doing this is for each threat to be categorized according to the chance of it happening—low, medium or high—and the level of impact it would have—again, low, medium or high. This is the approach outlined by the NIST guideline 800-30, on IT risk management. You can then assign each threat an overall risk and determine the priority of addressing each one. Figure 12-1 shows a common way of doing this using a matrix, and then using the overall score to determine overall risk, shown by how red that part of the matrix is.

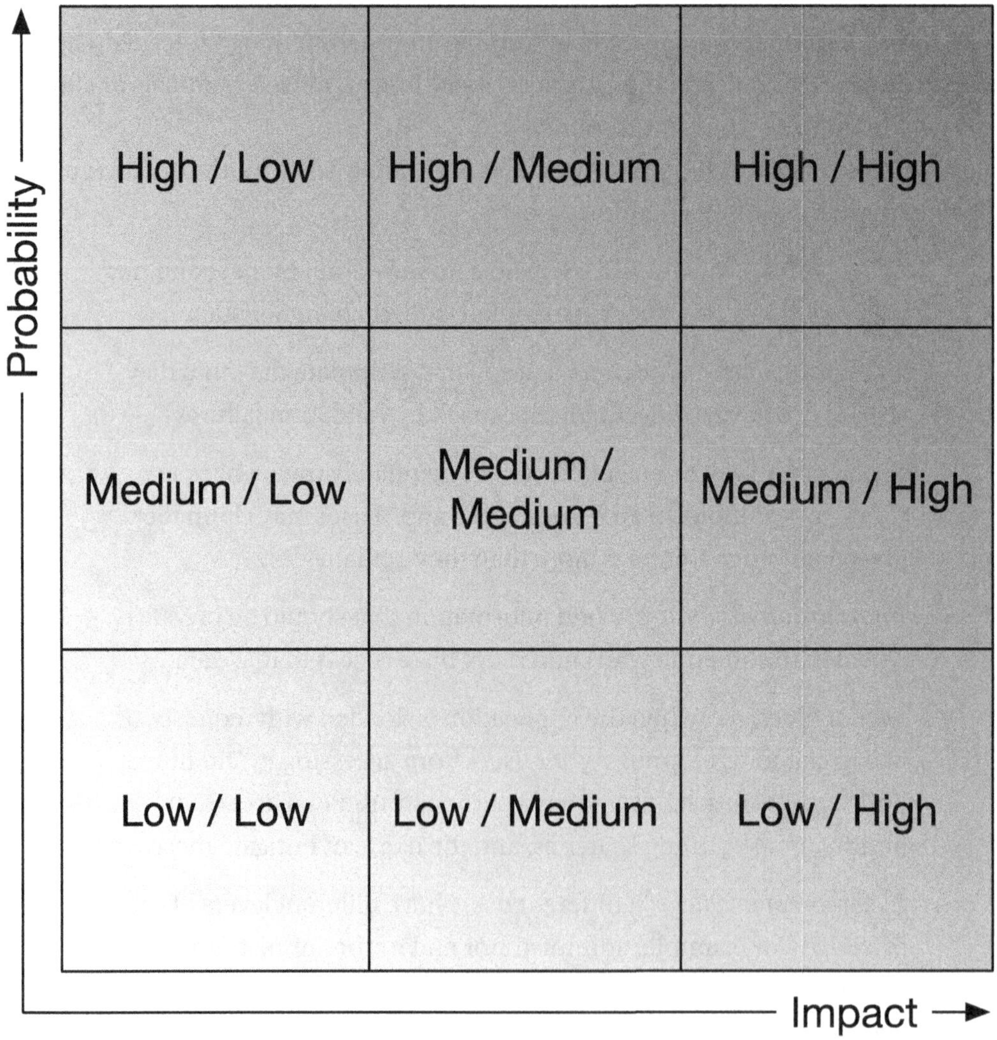

Probability ↑	High / Low	High / Medium	High / High
	Medium / Low	Medium / Medium	Medium / High
	Low / Low	Low / Medium	Low / High

Impact →

Figure 12-1. *Probability vs. Impact matrix*

Another common mnemonic used here is DREAD, where five different attributes are considered and then a score assigned. Often, a score of zero to ten is used, although any scale, as long as the same is used for all attributes, will work. The five attributes are:

- *Damage*: What will the negative impact of an attack be? Zero is often "none," and ten may be something like the business going bankrupt.

- *Reproducibility*: How consistently can the attack be executed, or does it require a number of constraints outside the control of the attacker to be right before it will work? Zero indicates that no one, not even the developers, can reproduce this attack against a running system (so it is theoretical), and ten that the attack will work every time.

- *Exploitability*: How hard is it to actually do the attack? Zero means that no one possesses the knowledge or skills to be able to execute the attack, and ten means that a layperson would be able to stumble upon the attack during normal system use.

- *Affected users*: How many users will this attack affect? Zero is none, and ten is all.

- *Discoverability*: How easy is it for an attacker to find out about this threat? Zero indicates it's impossible to determine in a running system, and that only reading the source will reveal the threat; and ten that it is obvious to even a casual attacker or by the use of automated tools.

The "discoverability" aspect is often the cause of some controversy, as it is felt that relying on something being hidden is not suitable, and as a result some threat modelling practitioners will set discoverability to ten (or the highest level), or discount it completely. The overall score for a threat is the sum of these attributes (or sometimes an average), which allows the highest-priority issues to be identified first.

Once you have identified each threat, you can then design mitigation for them. Some of these mitigations are a part of good code cleanliness, such as validation, and will often not require any extra work, but others may require further effort.

In many safety-critical systems, there's a saying: it's not the first mistake that kills you, but the second. Of course, ideally a system should never kill you, but making two mistakes in a row is rarer than making one, so ensuring that a mistake that removes one layer of safety is in itself not lethal is good enough. The same is true in security—relying on just a single layer can be dangerous, and you should always behave as if an individual layer is capable of being exploited.

This is known as defense-in-depth, where multiple layers of security are used. For example, instead of your API servers relying on only being accessed from a private network, perhaps enforced by firewall rules, you should also consider using API keys or another mechanism. This gives you an additional layer of protection in case a firewall ends up incorrectly configured, or a vulnerability in another server gives an attacker access to your private network. Threat modelling is a great way to identify where additional layers will be of most use. When you model threats, it can also be useful to identify scenarios where there's been a partial compromise of a system you rely upon, and then identify where additional layers could be of most use.

Security Checklists

Checklists are a powerful tool to help verify consistency and remind you, and new developers to the team, of all the risks involved in software, especially if they're not obvious.

In Kanban, checklists form the entry/exit criteria for a column, and in Scrum, the definition of done. For code reviews, a checklist (often automated) is useful for the consistency of a discussion. Security checklists are the same, as they force you to think, even if only briefly, and confirm that you have addressed any relevant security issues. Security professionals have produced "Top N" lists for common types of security vulnerabilities, and simply familiarizing yourself with these lists and iterating over them will address the most common types of errors.

The two most popular lists are the OWASP (Open Web Application Security Project) Top 10, which is focused mostly on web development, and the CWE (Common Weakness Enumeration) Top 25, which is more general for all types of software. Like threat modelling, each risk identified should have an appropriate control placed against it to ensure that the risk is either mitigated or irrelevant. For example, the CWE Top 25 includes CWE-120: Buffer Copy Without Checking Size of Input ("Classic Buffer Overflow"). In many modern web languages, this isn't relevant, as you never have to manage buffers by hand, so the mitigation/control is that it's handled for you by a trusted lower library.

In the sections below, the OWASP Top 10 risks are discussed, with a brief overview of what each flaw means to you, and how to protect against them.

Injection

Injection attacks are the single most important type of security flaw that can be introduced into an application. They make the very top of the OWASP Top 10 and are the top two of the CWE Top 25 for a reason. Injection attacks occur when untrusted data gets mixed with trusted data—for example, including search terms in a SQL query that can be interpreted as part of the structure of the SQL statement. By following the "golden rule" discussed previously in this chapter, and using appropriate libraries and techniques to construct these requests, you can avoid this class of error.

Injection attacks can cause many types of damage—for example, they can be used to execute a SQL query that will return results for another user, or even cause data loss as the result of a malformed UPDATE or DELETE query.

Broken Authentication and Session Management

Badly implemented login and session management features can cause a lot of damage. A badly implemented login feature might simply check a username and password on login and then set a cookie "Logged_In_User: chris." The rest of the application blindly trusts that this cookie was set by the application, but an attacker could set it by hand without knowing the password, and gain access to someone else's account. Similarly, cookies that indicate a level of access should be avoided.

You should instead use an authentication library or framework that can reduce the risk of writing your own. These normally follow a recommended approach of having a session hash or token, which references a database (that only the application can control) containing that important information. This means that a stolen cookie could be used to impersonate a user, but stealing a cookie is generally considered to be difficult enough to successfully mitigate this risk. However, some other common vulnerabilities, if successfully attacked, could be used to steal a cookie, so it is not foolproof.

An alternate approach is to make a cookie that has a cryptographic signature signed by a private key only the server knows, so the server can verify that it was the one that set that cookie. These tokens should either expire or be updated regularly in order to minimize the impact of a token being stolen. Sometimes tokens can be made into session cookies, which means they only live as long as the browser is open—otherwise, the user has to explicitly log out. A common way of avoiding a user having to log in too frequently is to require a session cookie for any sensitive functionality (like making a payment) but have a longer-lasting cookie for general browsing, to allow things like personalization to occur.

Regardless, most languages have many libraries that implement this functionality, and for most sites, there is not much of a reason to implement it yourself rather than use an existing solution. Implementing your own should be considered an advanced activity.

Another way you can accidentally introduce this vulnerability is to include a session token or unique identifier in a URL as a query parameter. This could mean that copying or sharing a URL could accidentally allow a user to let their friend log in as them, or for corporate proxies to accidentally log the URL. Session tokens are generally considered sensitive information, so should only be served on an encrypted web site.

Password reset mechanisms should be carefully designed too, in order to stop people from using them as a way to bypass a login process, with the login process itself having defenses against brute-force attacks (for example, limiting the rate at which users can make requests, or locking accounts after a certain number of bad requests).

Cross-Site Scripting (XSS)

Cross-site scripting is a form of injection into the structure of the page that can cause arbitrary scripts to run in your user's browser. Like injection, the golden rule applies here in order to address this concern.

Web browsers have a security model known as the same-origin policy. The core of this policy is that JavaScript code only has access to web pages that are in the same domain (e.g., `www.example.com`) as the one that loaded the JavaScript. For example, you cannot read or set cookies for a different domain, which can stop credentials from being stolen, nor can you load an iframe for another site and then execute code on that page. With XSS, this means that an attacker can make code run on your domain, and therefore get access to credentials they shouldn't, and perform activities the same-origin policy would normally block.

The three attacks above can be combined to cause even more damage. For example, injecting malformed content into a database can result in an XSS attack on users visiting the web site. XSS can be used to steal authentication tokens, or cause fake actions to occur, if it is allowed to occur on an administration screen where a high-level user is logged in.

Insecure Direct Object References

Insecure direct object references are a type of error that occurs when an "object"—for example, an HTML page or an image—does not properly check whether or not that user is allowed to access it.

This can often occur with things like user uploaded content, or generated PDFs. For example, if you are building an invoice system that generates PDFs, then it may seem sensible to upload these PDFs to a place where the user can download it and give a link to the PDF in the page. There is a basic mistake to make here: if your URL is, for example, `https://invoice-downloads.example.com/invoice0042.pdf`, then the user might be able to guess that other invoices perhaps exist at `https://invoice-downloads.example.com/invoice0041.pdf` and get access to another user's information simply by changing the URL.

The importance of protecting these kinds of objects depends on the type of application you have. For low-risk applications, then simply having random URLs might work well enough, or some object stores allow generating URLs which are signed with a time-limited hash that offers a greater level of protection. Often the simplest thing to do is set your assets to be served by your application and use the same type of authentication and authorization you use for your regular application code.

The pages that make up your web site should also be considered objects. For example, in 2011, the bank CitiGroup allowed people to see other people's accounts by changing the account number in the URL once they had logged in.[1]

If something has a URL, that means it is accessible, so when implementing your security, you should consider what authentication and authorization for that URL (and any query parameters it might take) will need.

Security Misconfiguration

Security misconfiguration can occur when you are using a tool or library that has been incorrectly configured and can leave yourself open to vulnerability. For example, an off-the-shelf password may have a default password which must be changed, then forgetting to do so would introduce a vulnerability. Issues such as incorrect firewall configurations would be classified as this kind of vulnerability too.

---

[1]Dan Goodin, "Citigroup Hack Exploited Easy-to-Detect Web Flaw," `http://www.theregister.co.uk/2011/06/14/citigroup_website_hack_simple/`, June 14, 2011.

Another common issue relates to debug modes in frameworks. Often, with these turned on, when an error occurs, you will get a stack trace or some other debug-type information. Often, this debug detail can give away information that is helpful to attackers, such as the source code or usernames and passwords for databases.

Sensitive Data Exposure

Sensitive data exposure vulnerabilities relate to how you manage any data that can be considered sensitive. It is important to define which data is considered sensitive, and then determine a way to protect that data. Data can be considered to be "in-transit" (moving between systems), or "at rest" (stored on disk).

For example, if you are using session cookies in order to manage login, then those cookies should be considered sensitive, because if someone got ahold of them, they could impersonate that user. At rest, the session token is stored as a cookie on the user's machine, and in your database. Appropriate access controls on the database may be sufficient to protect the token (if the database is leaked, encrypting the session token is no help, as the user's information has already been exposed), and it may be sufficient to assume that the user's browser and cookie store is already sufficiently protected. The session token is also sent in transit as part of a cookie on the HTTP request, where it is more vulnerable. Coffee shop wi-fi is often "open" wi-fi, which means that anyone on the same network can see what other users are sending. If your cookies are sent over plain HTTP, then that leaves them exposed in transit. Using HTTPS encryption and marking your cookie as secure will avoid this use case and will protect your cookie in transit.

In another example, a user database is often the store for lots of sensitive data. Passwords are one example of this, and the safe storage of passwords is discussed later in the chapter. The law often defines "personally identifiable" information to be sensitive, and care must be taken with this data especially. This includes things like National Insurance/Social Security numbers and dates of birth. The simplest way to handle this information is to simply never store it, but if you do, you should make sure it is handled appropriately.

Again, data may be in transit in many directions—between your web server and your database, or to a backup server—and these should be encrypted. Most database servers also support encryption at rest, and it is important to make sure that this applies to any backups too. It is especially important with backups to make sure that you don't store the decryption keys next to the database!

Missing Function Level Access Control

Function level access control refers to checking permissions at a fine-grain level within an application. For example, it is not sufficient for someone to need to be logged in to access all features, and if a user does not have access to something, it is considered good practice to hide it in the UI. However, restricting someone from doing an action in your front end is not enough; you also need to do a check on the server side, too.

Missing function level access control occurs when someone who is logged in performs an action they shouldn't be able to do because the server does not appropriately check that they have the right to do so. That is, the user is authenticated (we know who they are), but not authorized (we do not know what they can do). For example, a feature for creating a new product in a catalogue may only appear for users who are logged in as an admin, but if the AJAX endpoint didn't also do that check on the server side, then any user could make an AJAX request to that endpoint directly, skipping any front-end checks.

There are many libraries to help manage authentication and authorization, and these kinds of errors often creep in when you simply forget to do a check. Test-driven development around authentication, and code review, can help protect you against these kinds of errors. If your libraries and frameworks support it, it is a sensible practice to default your endpoints to reject use until a specific check is in place.

Cross-Site Request Forgery (CSRF)

Cross-site request forgery occurs as a result of the same-origin policy that web browsers use for security. In a CSRF attack, the user visits a malicious web site that makes a request to your web site, for example, by tricking them into clicking on a form, or loading it via an <img> tag. Although the malicious web site can't get access to your user's cookies, when it triggers a request, the browser does send cookies along with it, so if your user is logged in to your web site, then it appears they've made a valid request, and that action is triggered.

The simplest solution to this is to check that the Origin or Referer header exists and is set to a domain or page that that type of request is expected to come from.

A more comprehensive solution is also available. In a good RESTful design of your API, any potentially damaging/malicious action should be hidden behind a POST request, rather than a GET request, so only POST requests (form submissions) need to be checked. A hidden field can be included in the form, which is sent to the user including a unique token. The server can then check that the token it gets back matches the one that was sent to the user (so it is known that the expected form generated the request), and this token can be either stored in the session or in a cookie that is also sent to the user.

Using Known Vulnerable Components

This kind of vulnerability occurs when a dependency you are using is not kept up to date. Managing dependencies, making sure they're up to date, and being aware of any security issues remains a challenge due to the fragmented nature of development: there isn't a universal standard for reporting these, nor a central database or set of tooling for becoming aware of a vulnerability in your dependencies. There do exist tools that are focused on particular domains, and including them in your build chain and having an approach is valuable. The Indirect Attacks section below goes into more detail about how to protect against this kind of attack.

Unvalidated Redirects and Forwards

Sometimes your web site may need to redirect the user to another page on your site—for example, a success page after a form submission. Some of these redirects may use user input to build part of the URL, and these are vulnerable to a type of injection attack. Unvalidated redirects are dangerous because the user can click on a link that appears to be valid (as it's a URL on your site), but ultimately can end up elsewhere due to injection. Again, applying the golden rule will resolve these kinds of issues.

A similar issue is when parts of your application take a whole URL as a parameter to redirect back to. Login pages are a common place where these vulnerabilities can be introduced. For example, if I visited `https://www.example.com/my-account` as a user that is not logged in, I may get redirected to `https://www.example.com/login?returnto=https://www.example.com/my-account`. This redirect is fine, as none of the values are directly designated by the user, but after logging in, the login page may simply redirect to the returnto parameter without validating it. If a malicious user tricked another user into following a link to `https://www.example.com/login?returnto=https://www.mybadsite.com/`, perhaps in a phishing attack, a user may be lulled into a false sense of confidence because the link is your site—but they end up elsewhere. This is another example where the golden rule can be applied—the returnto parameter should be checked to make sure the URL it is redirecting to exists on a domain you control.

Passwords

When it comes to identifying users, there are two main approaches you can take: asking them for some information that only they know, or asking them to prove that they have something that only they can have. Passwords are one way of doing this, as they are information that, in theory, only the user knows. However, passwords have become one of the worst security patterns in widespread use.

One issue with passwords is that the only way to check whether or not someone knows a particular secret is if you yourself also know the secret. In order to do this, we need to store the password so we can check that the password the user gives us is correct. This is risky, as it means that anyone who has access to the database (either legitimately, or through a hack) now has the passwords for every user and can impersonate them. In order to deal with this, we can hash the passwords that we store. Hashing is a process similar to computing a checksum, where you take your data and run it through some mathematical functions to generate a hash (normally a very large number expressed in hexadecimal). Because hashes involve throwing away information, it is impossible (for an unbroken hash function) to go back from the hash to the original password. Your application now needs to take the hash of the password the user gives you and compare that to your hash, without having to store the password.

Simply hashing is not good enough to protect against database leaks, though. Although it's impossible to reverse a hash, an attacker could take advantage of the fact that most passwords are dictionary words, and instead simply compute the hash of every word in the dictionary and then check if any hashes match. Furthermore, as the same word will always hash to the same value, if several people share the same password, they will have the same hash, which can give information away. We can work around this by salting the hash. Salting works by taking the result of hashing the password, adding salt to the end of it, and then hashing it again. Salt is a randomly generated string that is stored alongside the password and is unique for every password in the system, rendering this kind of dictionary attack more difficult, as an attacker would have to try generating different hashes for each salt, rather than trying all the hashes in a database at once. Peppering is a similar concept, except the additional value is a secret and is the same for every user, but not stored in the database (usually it is hard coded into the application, or applied as a run-time configuration option). Using salt and pepper together is common.

The final thing to consider is which hash function to choose. Hash functions have been in use for a long time to check that file transfers are correct (if you send the file and the hash, then if the hash of the file doesn't match the expected one, then some corruption has occurred). For these use cases, speed is important, as you could be hashing many megabytes of data. For passwords, though, the opposite is true. As passwords are short, even if passwords are salted, they can still be cracked by trying many words until a matching hash is found. If your hashing algorithm is slow, this can slow down this process significantly, so choosing a slow hash is more secure. Of course, there is a performance trade-off, so your hash function shouldn't take seconds to complete, but perhaps 100ms. The type of hashing functions that satisfy these criteria are called key-stretching algorithms, and include algorithms such as bcrypt and scrypt.

There are other ways of protecting your database against dictionary attacks, but they are flawed. One common way is to require your users to complicate their password by including numbers, capital letters, or special characters, but this comes at a significantly increased user overhead of having to remember the variety. Conversely, sometimes web sites put maximum length restrictions on passwords in order to ensure users pick something easy to remember. You will want to include a maximum length, because password hashing algorithms take longer on long passwords, so an attacker can try using passwords that are several megabytes in size which could take minutes to hash and cause your site to crash—but make the maximum length very long. You should also ensure that your user can use any character in a password—even emojis should be valid in a password!

The most effective restriction to put on a password is minimum length. Long passwords are much more secure than short ones, without necessarily putting an undue burden on your users. An alternative name for passwords is passphrases—using this word encourages users to use multiple words or even a whole sentence as a password.

Even if you appropriately secure your database against leaks, there is a much bigger risk with passwords. It is very common for users to use the same password across multiple sites in order to reduce the burden of remembering them. This means that if another web site, unrelated to yours, gets hacked, and your user used the same username and password, then a hacker can now log in to your web site, even though your code remains secure. This is the fundamental issue with passwords, but there is no perfect alternative; just a number of alternatives and solutions that each have their own tradeoffs.

There are many ways to avoid this problem though. One is to avoid using passwords entirely on your site, and instead ask users to log in using an account they have on another site. This can be very effective for an organization's internal tools, where you can link into a central logon system for that organization, but essentially moves the problem around. It often offers a better user experience too, as users only need to sign in to one site and many others can piggyback off that, rather than having to enter your username and password multiple times. For public-facing web sites, social media web sites can provide this functionality, but not all of your users will necessarily have an account on those sites, so a traditional username/password fallback (as well as supporting multiple sites) is also needed. Some sites use a novel alternative to this, by e-mailing you a link containing a token that allows you to log in. This has issues though, as the e-mail account becomes a single point of failure, and if you lose access to it or the e-mail account is hacked, then your user loses the ability to log in to that web site. The process also isn't always smooth, as users have to navigate to their e-mail to log in.

The other alternative to passwords is to instead use something that the user has in order to validate their identity. This can be a virtual or physical token. TLS client certificates are useful here too, as a virtual option, and are common in large enterprises. Users may be more familiar with devices that display a code that changes over time. These devices are synchronized with the server when they are first issued and then pseudo-randomly generate a new number using an initial "seed" (computers cannot generate a truly random number, but instead generate a "pseudo-random" number by applying mathematical functions to a known seed, or start state. These pseudo-random numbers should be impossible to predict without knowing the start state). The number is then entered as a second factor. These tokens are common in online banking and remote access or VPN connections for larger enterprises. However, having to have a physical token for each site is also very unwieldy. Instead, a common algorithm known as TOTP (time-based one-time passwords) has become widely used, and allows for multiple sites to use different seeds but have the same process for generating a valid password for "now." Multiple sites are then added to an app, which generates the current valid number for each site. There are also physical tokens, such as Yubikey, that work in a similar way but do not require the user to enter the number themselves, as it communicates directly with the site. One of the biggest constraints in this system is that the time on all the devices must be correct (or within a few seconds). Otherwise, the generated and expected numbers will not match.

However, the issue with using something a user has is that if it is lost, the user is locked out of their account, and if it is stolen, then the thief can use it to log in. Instead of solely relying on this method, it is increasingly common to combine this approach with passwords. This approach is known as "two-factor authentication," where the user has to give their password as well as prove they have the physical token. These two factors combined cancel out the negatives of the other factor, but have the downside that forgetting the password, or losing the second factor, can result in your being locked out of your account. The login process is also slightly longer and more inconvenient, resulting in a usability trade-off. Two-factor authentication is more commonly used to protect especially sensitive systems, such as bank accounts.

If using passwords is unavoidable, you will also have to deal with the inevitability of users forgetting them. Some mechanism is therefore needed to reset a user's password. For small teams, this could be as simple as having a developer's override and the user approaching you directly, but this does not scale, especially when members of the public use your application, so a common solution is implementing a way to let users reset their own password. Care must be taken when designing a solution for this, though. There have been some famous hacks of individuals resulting from a vulnerable password reset mechanism. A system is only as strong as its weakest link, so even if your normal password scheme is very strong, a weak password reset mechanism will leave your users vulnerable to being hacked by that approach.

A common example of a password reset mechanism is to ask users to register "secret questions" from a common list—such as their mother's maiden name, or anniversary dates—during sign-up, the idea being that these are relatively easy to remember. When a user forgets a password, they then need to answer these questions to prove who they are, but the problem is that the answer to these questions can often be guessed or figured out based on someone's public record. These essentially become very weak versions of a password. Another approach is to use an alternative means of getting in touch with the user, such as sending them an e-mail, calling them, or posting them a letter to verify their identity before allowing them to reset their password. This can be slower, and have a cost implication, especially for sending a letter, but is more secure than using the questions alone. It is not infallible, though. Like the "login-via-a-link-to-your-mail" alternative to passwords above, if someone has control of your e-mail address, then they can also take control of any account that is linked to it. In targeted cases, it can be possible to "steal" a mobile phone number too. This also assumes, of course, that the user has kept their contact details up to date.

Password resets get even more complicated when using TOTP second-factor-authentication-like solutions. If resetting a password allows you to bypass the second factor, then that will ultimately weaken the whole system. A common solution is to provide users with a set of "backup codes" that can be used as an alternative to a TOTP code in case the main device is lost. This requires the user to keep these safe, though.

When building password login systems, the final thing to take into consideration is "brute-forcing." Brute-forcing is a mechanism attackers use to try to hack a site. In a brute force attack, an attacker will constantly try many different passwords for a user, until one eventually works. You should build in protections against brute forcing. One way to do this is to prevent a user from attempting to log in after a number of attempts, either for a set period of time, or until manually reset by an administrator, but this can be inconvenient for a user too. Another mechanism might be to temporarily ban an IP address after a number of unsuccessful logins. (for example, only let an IP try to log in five times every 60 seconds). Another type of brute-forcing attempt involves trying to figure out if a user has an account on a service, or which e-mail address they're using. When building a password reset mechanism, it can be helpful to the user to know if an e-mail address or username they've entered was invalid or not. However, this can give an attacker useful information that can help target an attack, so usability and security must be carefully balanced, depending on how valuable an individual user's account is.

While passwords are far from perfect, they are ultimately unavoidable. There will be times when you will have to manage passwords during the development process for parts of your development systems. For this, using a password database is a modern best practice. As the name suggests, a password database manages passwords, allowing you to keep a unique password for each site, and they can be long and complex, as they do not need to be memorized. The databases are encrypted, and there are two main types of apps for this: ones that manage files, where you either keep the file locally, and ones that manage synchronization between devices. The first is ultimately more secure, but at the expense of convenience. When working on a development team, you will often need to store some shared passwords, perhaps for root accounts. Day-to-day use of shared passwords should be avoided, as it's hard to keep track of who does what action, and if someone leaves the team, you will need to change the password to ensure it is secure. Wherever possible, you should have an individual account per user, but often some sort of "root" password is needed. A password database for your team becomes a useful way of sharing these secrets.

Indirect Attacks

Although direct attacks on your infrastructure may seem like the most obvious to protect against, they aren't the only ones. Many attacks on software you write will be by automated tools and scanners that try common techniques to detect SQL injection, XSS vulnerabilities, etc., or by scanners that detect known vulnerabilities in popular software and libraries.

Following the best practices above will protect you against common types of security error, but it is incredibly rare (and also a bad idea) to write your software from scratch without using any libraries or frameworks. Every web site out there relies on some code written by someone else, whether that's a useful library, framework, or programming language, or tools like Apache HTTPD Server, Varnish, or even OS-level utilities like network drivers or an OS kernel. For every dependency you introduce, you need to consider its security impact. This gets even more nightmarish when you're doing modern JavaScript development, as it has become common for many transitive and nested dependencies to be introduced, and it becomes unrealistic to effectively audit them all.

When introducing a new dependency or library, you should take the time to think about how you know you're not accidentally introducing a vulnerability. Gut feelings can be useful here—does the project look like it's maintained and has an active community around it (or, if you're purchasing it, do the vendor seem aware of security)? The idiom "many eyes make all bugs shallow" is popular, but when a vulnerability in a large open-source software occurs, it is often higher profile, so carries a higher risk. On the flip side, a smaller project may not have had as much scrutiny applied to it from a security perspective, so could potentially have undetected vulnerabilities. The potential trade-offs often depend on the context too. A front-end library for animations is much less likely to have vulnerabilities as compared to a library that is responsible for validating form inputs.

You should also think about how you will stay aware of security vulnerabilities. High-profile vulnerabilities often make it into the specialist tech news sites and communities, so you may hear about them by osmosis, but smaller ones do not. Frequently checking for out-of-date dependencies (e.g., using `npm outdated`) and updating them to the latest patch releases can be effective, and there are specialist services that will check your dependencies to see if you are relying on known vulnerable versions. Many OS vendors have a security feed or tool you can use to see if any packages with known issues are installed. Automating these once as part of your deployment pipeline can make your life a lot easier in the future and, if you're working within a large enterprise, can often quickly help you make friends with a central infosec team.

Although the advice above will protect you from most types of attacks, there also exists a rarer, but scarier, risk, which is a targeted attack. Although an attack can be targeted directly at your application and the infrastructure in production, a well-written and well-configured application will stand a good chance against such an attack. Even though lower-impact vulnerabilities may still be found, there is a way to get the highest level of access to your application and data, which is the ability to alter the code running on your server directly. Tools like your Git repository, your CI server, or deployment tools are very attractive targets, because if someone can take control of those, they have complete control over your infrastructure.

There have been a number of high-profile attacks caused by outdated or inappropriately secured Jenkins servers, as well as a number of lower-profile but very damaging attacks undertaken by disgruntled former employees. Similar to a "fire drill" used to discover the failure modes for your application for operations purposes, you should run exercises to figure out all the ways someone malicious could push code into production. Common vulnerabilities include a Jenkins server without proper authentication on a "hidden" URL, a shared SSH account for deployment where the passwords aren't changed when people leave the team, or leaving people on a GitHub repository after they have left the organization.

Securing the way code is put into production is as important as securing the code itself, and you should take care when managing access to code repositories and control of your deployment tools. Managing backups becomes a security issue, too; if you are accidentally backing up database credentials, or allow your backups to be overwritten when they are created, you can give an attacker the ability to create unrecoverable damage using vectors you can't even think of.

The "disgruntled employee" can be one of the worst threats to an organization. It's relatively common, and employees are given a large amount of access without a lot of trust. Sometimes, these employees also have the ability to cover their trail. Audit logs are important so you can trace actions undertaken by a user, and should be protected so they cannot be deleted. Another risk is for users who use Git. Git allows you to alter history or fake the names of committers, as they are just metadata. If you are using Git around a site like GitHub, then you can enable GPG signing-of commits to verify that the author is correct.

Even if you secure your build pipeline and minimize the damage a single disgruntled employee can do, and then apply best practices in building your software to minimize the risk of a drive-by scan or even a targeted attack finding a vulnerability, your dependencies can still introduce a vulnerability. Fortunately, in addition to being rare, this is easy to mitigate against, so it makes a lot of sense to do it. If you have a dependency with a less-protected build chain, then it may be feasible for a particularly determined attacker to push a malicious build of that dependency, and for your build server to download that and bundle it into your code. For many commercial or organization-run package repositories (like the Ubuntu or Red Hat repositories), only trusted users can push builds in, and they have very secure build chains. However, for community-run repositories, like NPM or PyPI, the provenance of a package is less clear. If a developer's credentials are compromised, then the attacker can push a new version up immediately. Often, semantic versioning ("semver") is used to allow your build tooling to automatically pick up patch releases of a dependency without input from you, but this leaves you open to this kind of issue (it's also worth noting that it can leave you open to accidentally introducing bugs—semver is a nice idea, but is still fallible!). Most package managers support version locking (for example, PHP's Composer with composer.lock, JavaScript's NPM with shrinkwrapping, Python's Pipenv with Pipfile. lock, and Ruby's RubyGem with Gemfile.lock), and most of the community package repositories do not allow you to republish something with the same version as existed before. For those that do, you may want to put a local cache of packages between the build server and the upstream repository. This is a normally a good idea to do anyway, as you can guarantee a known "good" version will not suddenly become bad, and it will make your builds resilient against downtime of the remote package server.

Summary

The Web is becoming an increasingly hostile place, with more and more attacks—some targeted and others more scattergun—becoming a real challenge for many organizations. Building public-facing web sites and apps presents a potential weak point for attackers to break in. You have an obligation as a full stack developer to build appropriately secure applications, and building security in at a foundational level is the best way to achieve that.

Security not only covers bugs that can inadvertently give an attacker access to information or systems that they should not, but also intervenes in the design phase to determine where trust lives in a system, and how to execute careful management of secrets such as passwords or user data. This trust also includes third parties—for example, if you use dependencies from public repositories, or include JavaScript on your site directly from another domain, are you sure that domain cannot be compromised?

You should also plan for the worse case, so in the event a security incident does occur, you have processes in place to handle and minimize the impact. Analyzing your system and designs for security issues is also an effective way to build secure systems, and there are systems that help do this. When dealing with theoretical risks, a likelihood/ impact analysis can determine which risks are worth fixing.

A system is only as secure as its weakest point. Security by obscurity is often maligned, but this means that security can not *only* be through obscurity, and in fact obscurity can be part of a layered approach that is effective. This means you should not rely on only a single layer of security, unless, for example, databases could be protected by firewalls as well as passwords. This includes your infrastructure and development environments, as this can often be a way in for attackers if not appropriately secured.

When it comes to secure coding, the golden rule is to validate on input to avoid corrupt data coming into the system, and to sanitize on output to avoid showing any damaging data that can inadvertently corrupt your UI. Checking new features against security checklists is also a good way to ensure you've thought through possible issues.

Building a system that uses passwords also takes special consideration, as passwords are a weak point in many security systems, especially password reset mechanisms. There are alternatives, but a common approach is to combine a password with a second factor (combining something someone has with something someone knows) to ensure that someone really is who they claim to be.

There is no silver bullet to security; it's a patchwork of small things that make a whole, so beware of tools or organizations that promise to solve your security problems. Security has to be a fundamental part of your product. The main exception to this, where you may want to bring in specialized outside help, is penetration testing. Finding vulnerabilities using external analysis is an important and learned skill, and a good penetration tester should work with you to discover that.

CHAPTER 13

Deployment

Once you've built your new web site, you'll want to put it somewhere people can see it and use it. However, waiting until the build is complete to do this is often too late—the way a web site is deployed can add additional constraints on how you build it. For example, if you're building an app for horizontal scale, then you can't store sessions in memory. If you're handling files that are being uploaded from users, then the size of your hard drive can make a huge difference.

At the heart of the DevOps movement is the idea that developers no longer "throw something over the wall" to operations staff. In most organizations, this straw man was never fully accurate—there was always some sort of relationship between dev and ops, but DevOps is about bringing the two disciplines together to help ops teams provision better environments for the software to run in, and for developers to help understand the constraints of the environment they're deploying to.

Another important concept to keep in mind is continuous delivery. Continuous delivery demands that teams release builds into production frequently and early in order to minimize waste and "shelf time," and expands on the idea of continuous integration, which was discussed in an earlier chapter. Indeed, mature teams will release their earliest "hello world" first commits into production to prove their build and deployment pipelines work before moving on to product development. These teams can often stand up brand new environments from scratch within minutes to minimize any overheads and prove their automation systems.

Twelve Factor Apps

Heroku, an early "platform-as-a-service" (PaaS) provider, codified a set of principles to simplify the process of running an application on a common platform. These "12 factors" are constraints placed on an app to give a consistent feel to the deployment and operation of an app, and to avoid common issues that can make running an app in production hard. The 12 factors have been criticized as being very Heroku-centric, but

295

© Chris Northwood 2018
C. Northwood, *The Full Stack Developer*, https://doi.org/10.1007/978-1-4842-4152-3_13

regardless of your deployment platform, they are relatively common, and you should consider each factor to see if it is appropriate for your application.

One Codebase Tracked in Version Control, with Many Deploys

When adhering to this factor, each service you deploy will have its own version control repository, which is where the code is deployed from. Regardless of which environment you deploy to, the code should come from the same place (and also the same branch). If your app requires multiple codebases to be copied to a server, then you should instead consider treating each codebase as a separate service or deal with them together, and if your app has different branches in different environments, it will be similar to having different repos. On the other hand, if you deploy the same repo several times for several services, then you should consider breaking out common functionality into shared libraries that you push into a dependency system, designating exactly one repository per service.

There is a popular technique that breaks this rule, called the "mono-repo." In a mono-repo, all services and libraries in an organization come from the same repository. This is often used to avoid having many versions of a shared library at once, as changing some shared code will cause all other parts of the application to pick up those changes, allowing for large adjustments across multiple codebases at once to be configured. There are other advantages to a monorepo, including simplifying repository configuration management, and this highlights that the 12 factors are not always gospel, but rather practices to consider carefully.

Explicitly Declare and Isolate Dependencies

A service should be explicit about the dependencies it has and isolate those from any system dependencies. Languages such as JavaScript using tools like NPM are good at this, as they will install all dependencies locally into a folder called `node_modules` by default, which is separate from any system dependencies. For a dependency to get there, it must be specified in a `package.json` file.

Being explicit reduces the number of manual steps required to deploy your application, minimizing the risk of missteps, as most automated tools will ensure that your dependencies are installed alongside an app. Isolation means that you can have greater control over explicit versions than a system-level library can give you, thus avoiding any issues if a system-level library is also used by another tool and different versions are needed. Isolation gives another advantage when it comes to deployment, in that your app and its dependencies can be moved around as one unit (for example, as a single `.tar.gz` archive), making it easier to deploy.

Many languages have their own dependency systems that can provide both, such as Ruby's Bundler, Python's virtualenv, and other languages provide it commonly by default, such as a "fat JAR" in Java, which includes all the dependencies.

Sometimes it is useful to partially break this rule. For example, some programs, such as ImageMagick or curl, can be very complicated to package as a dependency, and it might make sense to instead use a system-installed version of it. If you do want to depend on a system-level dependency like this, you should still be explicit in specifying it. A common deployment pattern is to package your application alongside its isolated dependencies using a system packaging tool, which allows you to specify system-level dependencies in this way (this is discussed further later).

Store Configuration in the Environment

In following this factor, your application should read any necessary configuration values from environment variables, and not from a file on disk. The config for your app is anything that might feasibly change between deploys, or that you might want to change on short notice without having to change the code. Configuration of how you might use any frameworks or libraries in your app (for example, setting up routes in Express) is not the same as your application's config, and it's okay to hardcode that. The types of things you might want to have in your config include usernames, passwords, and hostnames of database servers, any other "secret," or any per-environment variables, such as the address of the site (a developer environment will probably run at a different URL to your live site).

This rule is probably one of the most commonly broken. Although environment variables are a very common way to set config, often ops tools are set up instead to deal with config files, so your app can load config from a file in a well-known location. It is relatively easy to change, though. SystemD is becoming a common tool for running services at the system level, and is the default method of running service programs on many Linux distributions. It is relatively straightforward to set SystemD to load environment variables for a service from a config file, and other tools such as dotenv can be used to simulate this in other languages directly.

Another common way this rule is broken is by storing the config as settings files within your repo, and then having a single environment variable or switch that defines which environment you're running in, and therefore which config file should be loaded. Although config values that indicate whether or not you're running in a development mode are okay, this kind of high-level file is not, as it can make it very challenging to change the config on the fly without either editing the setting on the deployed instance or having to re-deploy the entire codebase. Not having your config checked into version control can also improve security, by not leaking any database passwords or API keys to anyone who has access to your codebase. The downside of this is that you now need an external config management system to manage this config, and ideally to have that version controlled to be able to roll back any config changes that might break things, as well as enabling auditing of any changes. Some teams do this by having a "config" repository that is more locked down than the main application repository, but this coordination of multiple repositories falls foul of the first factor.

Treat Backing Services as Attached Resources

A backing service is anything that your app communicates with over the network, such as a database or another API. Treating them as attached resources means you should assume that they're some other service that's distinct from your application and minimize any assumptions about where that service runs. Perhaps it's a database running on the same VM in a dev environment, but in production it runs in a third party–hosted environment. Maybe during testing it gets replaced with a broken variant to simulate failures. The important thing is that your app shouldn't care, and it should perform all communications over the network using the value determined in your config. Similarly, if you need to talk to two different APIs, each API should be configurable independently. Even if they are installed and running on the same hostname, they may be separated in future configurations.

Build, Release, Run

The process of deploying your application should have three distinct phases:

1. *Build.* Convert your source code into something that can actually run. This could involve installing any dependencies, or converting any front-end SASS into the final CSS.

2. *Release.* This phase gives us a distinct version number and ID for the build. It is common for configuration to be added here as well, so changing the configuration involves re-releasing the build (but not rebuilding it).

3. *Run.* Put a release (build + config) in an environment (perhaps on physical servers, on cloud virtual machines, or in a container) so that it actually starts and does whatever it needs to do.

Completing these as three separate stages will simplify how you can reason about your running software. Ideally, each build corresponds to a tag in version control (or at least a commit ID), so you know exactly which version of your source is running at any one time, whereas if the lines get blurred and you have changed code directly in production (in the run phase), it's then harder to see exactly what's going on. It also makes releases and rollbacks easier, because to make a change you just need to place a new release into an environment, and to roll the release back, you take the previous release bundle.

Blurring the stages causes other problems. For example, if you install dependencies in your run stage, and then a third-party server containing your dependency is down or a dependency has changed, and you need to restart your service on a new server because the old one has crashed, you won't be able to. Similarly, some frameworks allow you to build your source files on the fly, such as translating SCSS to CSS. This can create additional overheads, slowing down your application, and is more appropriate for a development environment. Prebuilding all of your assets up front allows for fast startup or restart times.

The only situation where you want to blur these lines is when running a dev environment locally, when you want to be able to make changes extremely quickly. Rebuilding your app, potentially only parts of it, while it is running in a dev environment allows you to quickly respond to changes. There is no reason to create a new release under these circumstances, as doing so adds no value and you would end up with a lot of releases very quickly. The lowest level at which a release should be created is in version control.

Execute the App as One (or More) Stateless Processes

This factor has several implications. First, your app should be started by invoking an executable that continues running (perhaps creating related worker processes when appropriate). Also, the app should not store any state locally, but always in an attached backing store. This might mean that any session data is stored in a database or caching layer like Memcached, or that any files go into a shared store like S3 rather than locally on disk. Having a file locally in memory or on disk while it is being processed is okay, but subsequent requests or other workers should not assume it is in memory.

This breaks down when it comes to PHP apps, and others that come from an old style of working known as CGI. In this style of working, your app consists of a series of scripts on disk that are executed in response to a request from a user, and then terminate. Other mechanisms such as mod_php or FastCGI speed this up by applying efficiencies, but it is essentially the same underlying principle. There's nothing fundamentally wrong with breaking this factor in this case as long as you take into account the different deployment style of these apps, but you should ensure that your scripts are stateless. This is actually easier in some ways, as you cannot persist things in memory with this approach, but you should ensure that any technique you do use (such as sessions or storing files) uses an attached backing store, rather than, for example, writing to disk.

Of course, if your app is itself a database, this rule cannot be followed.

This rule is the single most important one in terms of allowing you to scale. If you don't have anything stored in memory or locally, it will be easy to move your app to another server, or run it on many different servers behind a load balancer to provide a greater capacity. It also means you can restart your app, either during a deploy or to change a config value, in a way that minimizes impact on your users.

Export Services by Port Binding

This means that communication into your app should be over the network, and not locally with files or other mechanisms (such as UNIX sockets). This applies not only to your service, but to any services it depends on. Doing this allows you to split your application between multiple machines. Even if your initial deployment is doing something simple, like connecting to a database on the same machine, if you do so over a port you can move that database to a different machine as your app requires it.

This is another place where PHP and other CGI apps fall down. Instead of exposing their interfaces over a network, they expose themselves as files and let another tool (such as Apache) expose those over the network. The reason to use ports is to simplify your deployment to your app, rather than your app plus an additional server needed to run it. This also applies to Java "WAR" apps that run in an application server such as Tomcat, as opposed to standalone JARs that start their own network server.

Scale Out via the Process Model

This is similar to the stateless model approach. By having your app run as an individual executable process, you can scale by starting many processes (perhaps on other CPU cores in the same machine, or on other machines). By breaking down your wider application to a process type per service type (perhaps a queue worker separate from your web front end), each type of workload within your application can also be scaled independently.

Maximize Robustness with Fast Startup and Graceful Shutdown

Traditionally, the startup and shutdown types of an app were not considered important places to optimize, as these events occurred rarely. A twelve-factor app might be expected to do this more frequently, either as a result of scaling up or down, or to respond to issues such as another VM failing and needing to spin up a new one to replace it. It also enables you to deploy more frequently, in addition to benefitting your dev workflow.

By spending time on optimizing your startup time (so it takes no longer than a few seconds), you can make an individual process "disposable," meaning it needs less care. If it starts misbehaving, it can simply by killed and replaced with a fresh instance.

Graceful shutdown means that when a process is asked to stop, then it should take a moment to finish any requests in progress (but not start any new ones) and close any database connections so it leaves no trace of itself, but also that when a deployment or config change happens, it minimizes the chance of any users noticing if they happened to be connected at that point of time. If your app takes a long time to process a request (perhaps it's using web sockets or is a queue worker), then it should tell the client to either reconnect or place the request back on the queue for another process to pick it up.

Keep Development, Staging, and Production as Close as Possible

Minimizing the gap between all environments enables you to pre-empt environment-specific issues and increase your confidence in a deploy (and therefore do them more frequently with less of an overhead).

This might mean a large number of relatively small changes—for example, using the same database in all environments; some frameworks use a SQLite one in dev, but a hosted one for other environments. This can speed up initial setup, but can lead to subtle bugs due to different database implementations that waste more time in the long run. Instead, investing in automation to set up a dev environment that represents production (using VMs or containers) can minimize these issues. This is discussed in much more detail in the following section.

The original definition of the 12-factor app included three areas where it is important to keep environments as close as possible: time, personnel, and tools. Minimizing the time gap means reducing the time it takes between making a change and seeing it in production. For example, if you have a show-stopping bug that crops up in production, if the time since your last deploy is short, then the state of the dev environment should not have changed too much, and you should be able to reproduce and effectively fix that bug. This concept by itself is now known as "continuous delivery." Minimizing the difference in personnel—between the people developing your app and the people running it—means that any knowledge these individuals have about those two activities is shared as much as possible. This has grown into the DevOps movement. The final gap to minimize is that of tooling. Using different tools, or even different versions or configurations of the same tools, in different environments lowers the confidence that something that has worked in a previous environment will work in the next, as it has not had a chance to prove itself. Of course, some differences are allowed—for example, a staging environment might run on slower instances for cost-saving purposes—but that difference should be flagged and controlled.

Treat Logs as Event Streams

Logs should be thought of as a time-oriented set of events that occur in your application. Logs are typically written to a log file on disk, but sometimes an external tool might want to aggregate logs from multiple servers, or collect them together centrally. Applications that try to take too much control over the logs can make this more difficult, so instead you should simply treat all log events as one thing, and write them to a single place. Quite often this place is just stdout, which can help in development as they show in the console, but also gives the power to tools like SystemD to log them centrally, or in other interesting ways.

It can be useful to output logs in a structured format, such as JSON, but logs should be readable by humans (for example, on a developer's machine) as well as parsed by these external tools, so use caution. Logs should be timestamped and give enough information by themselves to be of use in diagnosing an issue or giving information on an error.

Run Admin and Management Tasks as One-Off Processes

It is important to get the code right for any admin or management tasks, even if it only runs once. As such, the code to run these tasks should be committed to your repository and stored alongside the code for the rest of your apps. This gives you confidence that when you need to run that task, you are running the right version of the task script in the right environment, since you are starting that process in the "run" phase of the app above. Other approaches (for example, having scripts that you run directly in a shell, or connecting to a database from a developer machine rather than the same environment as the code that is running) are open to error for the same reasons you've mitigated those issues in the other factors.

Developer Machines

For teams that aren't quite there yet, and want to be, setting up dev environments is often the first step toward a DevOps world. It used to be common for developers to install dev environments on their actual machines, using tools like MAMP, but this can cause problems. If a developer has to run their code on Windows or OSX, then the code often has to be cross-platform, or running from different install paths, or have unidentified dependencies that happen to be installed on that machine.

Fortunately, the rise of virtualization has changed this. Developers can now install a virtual machine with the same OS as their code, which eliminates a whole class of issues immediately. VM management tools like Vagrant have taken that a step further, allowing for automated and repeatable configuration between development environments, which means that each developer can now set up exactly the same environment too, which can massively improve efficiency. I've worked on teams where getting a working environment was considered a "rite of passage," and getting an instance of the product running in less than a day was considered a grand achievement! This is, frankly, unacceptable.

Vagrant is a fairly simple concept at its core—it creates virtual machines on your local machine from base images (e.g., a fresh, unconfigured Ubuntu or CentOS install, though for larger enterprises, this can be some other standard image), and then runs a script (or series of scripts) to provision it. It should be possible to configure a "Vagrantfile" that allows any new developer on your team to simply run `vagrant up` and have a fully running dev environment by the time the command has completed.

Beyond virtual machines is the concept of containerization, with Docker being a popular container management tool. Containers reduce the overheads of virtual machines by sharing some system resources such as the kernel, but otherwise are a similar principle to Vagrant, where a set of scripts is used to build it. Containers can get very complicated quite quickly if you have many moving parts, such as a database server. In a virtual machine, it is common to simply install these dependencies on the same virtual machine that is running your dev server, but with containers, a container per task is common, so a database container must also be running and then "orchestrated" so that your app container can access it. Container orchestration can be helpful in managing complex production environments, but this is beyond the scope of this book.

Production Environments

One question I hear from teams who are new to Vagrant is, "Can I now do run `vagrant up` into production?" but this is a misunderstanding of the role of Vagrant. Vagrant is very good at automating the process of local VM creation and running the scripts to provision that virtual machine, but lacks any fine-grained control of how that virtual machine is provisioned, deployed, or otherwise managed.

In an ideal world, it would be possible to use the same deployment scripts that you use to provision your local virtual machine as it is when it's deployed into a production environment, but there are often subtle differences between these environments that mean the exact same scripts aren't always suitable.

For example, in your local virtual machine, you may use shared folders to make the code available between your desktop and your virtual machine, enable features like hot-reloading, and run in a debug mode. For a deployed instance, you will probably not want to do any of these things, and your environment will probably be deploying your code either from a built package or a Git tag. However, there will probably be parts of your deployment process that you can reuse, and indeed you should! Appropriately used, containers can make this simpler, as you can run the exact same build of a container locally and in production.

Furthermore, you will often want more control over your infrastructure than Vagrant or containers alone can give you—for example, when setting up firewalls or SSH keys, and, for more complex deployments, things like auto-scaling groups, load balancers, and backups. However, the same rules still apply—you can use APIs to automate creating and provisioning these environments, and make them repeatable.

Most teams have multiple environments—their local developer environment (running on their machine); often several pre-production environments such as QA, UAT, or staging; and their production (user-facing) environment. In terms of how your app is deployed, once your code has left a developer's machine, these should all be considered to be production environments. No environment should be seen as a special case, so you can avoid any issues that only appear in production; you have a high degree of confidence that it works. It also proves that your automation works. Of course, there will be some differences (different URLs, different machine sizes, or different firewall rules), and expressing these differences can be achieved by configuration values.

Similar to the way you can configure your application in various environments to behave differently, you can configure your infrastructure to do the same. Most infrastructure tools support the concept of "parameters" for your definitions. When using these parameters in your definition for things like "instance type" or "number of machines," then you simply need to run the same code with a different configuration file—exactly the same as your app. As these templates and parameters are defined in code using automation tools, they can be versioned and managed exactly like any other code. It's often worth actually versioning this code in the same repository and alongside your application code, which eases the deployment and roll back of infrastructure changes and code together, rather than having to figure out any dependencies between your infrastructure and your application logic and deploy them individually.

Moving Code into Production

On a DevOps team, every aspect of the way your application runs becomes the responsibility of the team. Sometimes infrastructure teams can help, but on a purely DevOps team, the final responsibility always lives with the development team. In some organizations, especially large ones, this is not always the case, but is often an acceptable compromise. Each of the following sections will look at the layers of the stack of a running web app, as shown in Figure 13-1.

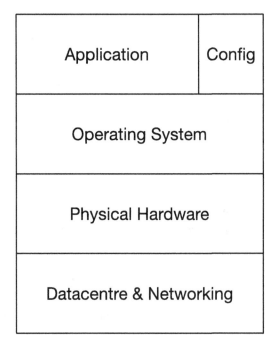

Figure 13-1. *The layers of abstraction in a deployed web app*

Let's assume for a moment that you are working at a traditional IT organization, and your ops team is responsible for providing a configured server or VM on which you will deploy your app. The simplest way to do this might be to SSH in, use Git to check out your software onto the box, change a config file, etc. You may need to run `gulp` or `npm` `install` too, in order to get all of your dependencies on the box or build your assets. As you move to DevOps, it can be easy to automate this with a shell script or a job in your deployment pipeline to SSH in and run this, but this could present challenges. What happens if the versions of Node installed are subtly different, or some other minor configuration difference means that the static assets that get built are slightly different than the ones on the other environments? What happens if Composer, or Ruby Gems, or NPM is down when you try to install? This could delay a crucial bug fix being deployed.

One of the factors of the 12-factor application discussed above is that the build, deploy, and run phases of your application should be distinct. By applying this principle, you can simplify complex deployment processes by taking the build to another phase. As a developer, you should be deploying a package, rather than checking your app out from source control. For Java developers, deploying a JAR seems natural, but for other languages this is not necessarily the case.

It can be very powerful to bundle and deploy your application using the same type of packages as your OS: Debs on Ubuntu/Debian or RPMs on Red Hat/CentOS, etc. If you take this approach, you can manage your application just like any other package that gets installed. This can seem daunting to beginners, though; many OS package builders have developed over time to be very powerful, but complex, tools. Tools like fpm, which can be used to quickly build packages of certain types, are useful, but it is also worth coming to grips with how to build packages using native tools as well.

It can be just as valid to simply package your app in to .tar.gz files that are downloaded and unpacked onto the box you wish to deploy your apps to, but one advantage of using an RPM or deb is that you can specify dependencies and run post-install scripts. For example, you could include a systemd unit file in your RPM and then run systemctl enable my-application, which will cause your service to auto-start on boot and be managed by OS as part of the normal boot process. A common alternative is to use a tool like forever that manages long-running processes, but this tool does need to be linked to your boot process somehow, and keeping it simple by using the same tools the OS uses makes sense.

Specifying dependencies is very important too, and a 12-factor app should do this explicitly. RPMs and debs allow you to specify any dependencies as part of the package, and when installing the package, the installer will automatically bring in anything else it needs. It is important to separate these kinds of OS-level dependencies from any application-level dependencies. For example, in a Java application, the .jar will include any dependencies, and for languages like PHP, NodeJS, or Ruby, you can install the required dependencies in a folder alongside the code (e.g., a vendor folder for PHP with Composer, or node_modules for Node.JS), which you can bundle up as part of your package, and use the native tools for your language to manage those, rather than try and deal with them as OS-level dependencies. OS-level dependencies include things like the language runtimes themselves, so depending on `nodejs` (sometimes a specific version of it) in your RPM is good, in addition to any other libraries (like ImageMagick or `libxml`) that are normally installed using an OS-level package manager. You could also, in your package, include config files for Nginx or Apache, and then depend on them too, if you're using those as a reverse proxy.

If executed correctly, all you should need to install your application onto a box is use your package manager to install it onto a fresh image. This is very straightforward, and very easy to automate. As you're just installing code, rather than doing any building as part of the install process, it is likely that installing that RPM onto a different box (in a different environment) will work. These packages are usually built by a CI server upon successful passing of all tests, and then published into a package repository, ready for deployment.

If you are using containers, then the same principles apply. The main difference is in the tools you would use, and often instead of producing a package for your application, you instead create the container directly, and then treat that as your package.

Configuring Your Box

Although you can simplify deployment by building your application in a way that it can be easily installed, that isn't the only thing you need to worry about. Installing a package means our code is installed, but doesn't mean it is configured. There are also often other components that may need to be set up and configured, such as database servers.

It is common for there to be differences in configuration between environments, but these differences should be minimized. For example, enabling a higher level of logging on a test environment might be okay, but installing different versions of a database on your production environment to your QA environment is not. By standardizing environments and your approach to configuring them, you minimize any risk that could be caused by your production environment being different than your pre-release environments.

Fortunately, there are many tools here that can help. The simplest tool might be a shell script, which you run on an unconfigured box to set everything up the way you want, but there are much more powerful tools that can also be useful. Tools like Puppet, Chef, and Ansible work by defining what the state of a system should be, and then the tools run on that system to ensure that system is brought into that state. Rather than a set of instructions, you describe what you want the configuration of the system to be, and the tools then figure out the difference between the current state and the new one, and make changes to bring it up to date.

Often the first thing to configure will be the application itself. The principles of the 12-factor app encourage configuring your application by environment variables. Others prefer to provide a config.ini or JSON file containing the configuration settings. It is often the job of your automation tool to create these files, as the exact contents may depend on the machine and environment it is being deployed to. Regardless of how you choose to get the configuration into your app, you should inject the config values into your application, rather than hard-code them in. It is common to ship config files as part of your app, or to introduce code that performs based on the environment you are in, but it is preferable to instead keep the configuration separate from your app.

You may need some to configure some general tools that work alongside your application, but that relate to your infrastructure rather than specifically to your application. These may include things like log management (sending logs to a central aggregator) or a metrics collector for monitoring (see the In Production chapter for more details), and this type of configuration tool should also provision them.

Lower-level OS configuration matters here too. This includes things like firewall rules or configuring users who are allowed to SSH into a machine, and the common automation tools should make it easy for you to set these up too.

All of these things can and should be automated, and once you have automated them, you will have a high degree of confidence in your deploys, including the ability to spin up new environments for testing, as well as simplifying your deployment process, because you can just re-run the scripts for each environment to make a deployment.

SSH BASTIONS

An aside on SSH: it is generally considered good practice to hide individual machines from the open Internet. This can be done for the web by placing web servers behind a firewall or in a firewalled subnet that only allows connections from a load balancer or gateway on ports 80 and 443, but that means you can't SSH into a box directly. There is a school of thought that says you should never SSH into a box, and your monitoring should be good enough to allow you to remotely diagnose issues, but for many, being able to SSH in remains a powerful diagnostic tool.

To get around these restrictions, you can use an SSH bastion (or jumpbox/jumphost). An SSH bastion is a specially secured machine that is only used for accepting incoming SSH connections. This machine should also be trusted in the firewall for SSH, so developers can first SSH into this machine, and then use it to SSH into an individual server as needed.

Infrastructure

In organizations that have not fully embraced the DevOps movement, infrastructure is traditionally configured by sysadmins, and then made available to developers to deploy their code. The "production" environment is often locked down further where the sysadmins also deploy the code.

As explained above, we can set up an individual server (or perhaps a fleet of servers) using automation tools, but with the advent of cloud computing, we can also automate the infrastructure that runs these servers. Historically, this may have involved installing physical servers and making physical network changes, but with virtualization and cloud technologies, all of these tasks are now hidden behind an API.

Infrastructure in this case can consist of computing resources in the form of virtual machines and network infrastructure (such as firewall rules), but also covers a number of components that may have previously been called "appliances" when deployed in one's own data center. An appliance is typically a box you install and configure, as opposed to having to install software on existing machines. Most cloud providers will offer some common functionality, such as databases and load balancers, as appliances, sometimes providing a hosted version of software to avoid managing it yourself.

In the context of the cloud, infrastructure refers to the additional components that allow your application code to serve your users. At one end of the spectrum, this might be virtual machines (or even bare metal servers) where the hardware and host are managed by the cloud provider, but at the other end of the spectrum, so-called serverless options, where your code is executed as a function call rather than a long-running process, still require configuration of your serverless host. Although this may be enough to run an application, you will often want to deploy more components outside of your application, or set up firewalls and other security rules that sit around your compute ability and correspond to these appliances.

One of the more common pieces of infrastructure is a load balancer. By placing a load balancer in front of your application, you can either have multiple instances of your application running to spread the load and provide resilience, or to minimize downtime by spinning up a new version of your application in parallel to an existing instance and then just having the load balancer switch over which version it's sending traffic to. Other bits of infrastructure, like nameservers for DNS hosting, are commonly needed too.

There are many other components of infrastructure that can be deployed. Services like AWS and GCP also allow you to provide API keys for their services as infrastructure, with appropriate permissions set on them, as well as configuration for their own monitoring tools to support your applications. These providers may also offer other APIs for features like single sign-on or machine learning tools, in addition to more generic utilities like load balancers. The most common types of these include forms of storage, such as object storage (for storing files) and databases, from relational databases to NoSQL or key-value stores. Other useful tools that are available as infrastructure components include message queues and caches, although you sometimes might choose to deploy these yourself on top of the compute layer rather than use a vendor-specific tool to avoid lock-in, or if the tool doesn't quite meet your use case.

The final piece of infrastructure to consider is that of a content delivery network (CDN). CDNs are essentially a, HTTP caching layer that caches data closer to your users to minimize response time. A CDN is just a distribution mechanism. They do not by themselves allow you to actually serve any content. To use a CDN, you must configure an "origin" for it, which is where the content that the CDN serves comes from. The origin could be a simple object store for serving static files, or it could be the application itself. In either case, then cache headers in the HTTP response are used by the CDN to cache it, meaning future visits will not need to go all the way to the origin, but are instead served from the "edge" of the CDN where it is cached.

Those who practice DevOps are typically responsible for provisioning their own infrastructure, and there are two main approaches to doing this. The first has been called "platform-as-a-service" and the second "infrastructure-as-a-service."

Although these terms are often associated with third-party companies like Heroku and Amazon Web Services, there is a concept known as "private cloud," which at first might seem like an oxymoron, but can allow organizations to continue managing their own servers and physical infrastructure. A private cloud often simply provides APIs and tools on in-house infrastructure that offers similar functionality to what is available from third-party suppliers, but the main constraint is that these in-house tools sometimes seem immature in comparison, and lack some of the flexibility that external providers can bring.

PaaS is more like the traditional organizational model of having sysops run the servers and the developers perform deployments to them, although additional infrastructure components such as CDNs may or may not be a default part of this platform. An early pioneer here was Heroku. Infrastructure-as-a-service gives you the same control a traditional sysadmin or network engineer may have, except you don't actually have to go to a data center to rack servers or maintain the physical infrastructure. You simply define what resources you want, and a configuration around them, and they are made available to you.

PaaS is often simpler than infrastructure-as-a-service, but in exchange for that simplicity comes a lack of flexibility, so some constraints exist, such as a lack of persistence or being limited to one OS. In PaaS, you still have to do some definition of your infrastructure, but this is generally at a very abstract level—perhaps simply a number and type of servers. Infrastructure-as-a-service (IaaS) offers a high level of control, at the cost of exposing the underlying complexity to you, which can be daunting for newcomers. It is common for organizations that use IaaS providers to provide tooling and a set of defaults around the service based on that organization's preferences to make it feel more like a platform, rather than just raw resources. This "opinionated defaults" approach allows teams who need it to reach into the complexity and alter things, but for teams who are following the common practices of that organization, it can speed up the process and lower the barrier to entry by simplifying the setup. This latter approach can be very powerful and provide the best of both worlds.

In both cases, APIs and tools are available to manage how that deployment is set up, but manual alternatives are available too. For an effective DevOps team, automation must be in use, so using those tools and APIs to manage deployments is important. For example, Amazon Web Services provides CloudFormation, where a JSON template is used to list each Amazon resource you want, and any inter-dependencies/references between them (for example, you could define a database and a web server, and then set up a firewall rule to allow each other to access one just by referring to the other resource, rather than needing to know their IP address, and other information, which may only be available after the resource has been created, and may change between environments). Many other providers do not offer this kind of templating language, but rather APIs that allow you to manipulate resources directly. Fortunately, a tool called Terraform provides a CloudFormation-like experience, where you define the state you wish to have, but then wraps around the APIs of other providers to provision the needed resources, and maintains the infrastructure state itself.

At times, you will need to specify different aspects of your infrastructure, and most tools support some idea of parameterization, where you can specify some values of your infrastructure definition as a type of configuration. For example, you might decide to use cheaper/less powerful machines on a testing environment than in production, but want all other infrastructure to be defined in the same way. In such a scenario, you would use the same template for infrastructure on prod and test but use parameters to specify what spec of machine should be used.

Another reason to use parameterization is as part of your deployment process. For example, if you are deploying virtual machines, then the output of your build process is likely to be a virtual machine in a registry (on Amazon, this is an AMI) with an ID. Usually your infrastructure definition will contain the ID of the virtual machine to boot, so to deploy your app, you can change the parameter with the virtual machine ID that gets booted to your new one, and likewise if you need to roll back.

When it comes to developing apps, having a local environment, often on your dev machine, is an effective way to work, as we discussed earlier in this chapter. However, the flip side is that you may not be running on the same infrastructure as the production environment, but instead on something that mimics it. For example, your local code might not be served via a CDN, or your application might not sit behind a load balancer. These are reasonable trade-offs to make, but you should be aware of them. For more complicated apps—for example "big data," or machine learning types—then it might make life simpler to run some of your infrastructure locally, with other parts running on environments that are provisioned in the same way as the production infrastructure for your app.

A desire for local development environments may result in developing code that's relatively portable between infrastructures, which can be important to avoid vendor lock-in. It is common for your infrastructure provider nowadays to be a third party, but there is an important trade-off between leaning too heavily on their infrastructure-which can leave you open to the risk of the third party discontinuing a service you use or changing the pricing in a way that is unsustainable for you-or to ignore convenience to avoid lock-in, but then create a poorer version of that system.

Immutable Infrastructure

Immutable infrastructure means that once you've deployed your app, the infrastructure and the code and configuration that runs on it never changes. If you need to make a change, instead of trying to tweak a running part of the service, you instead delete the bit that's changed and replace it with a new version with the updated configuration. This helps you avoid "fragile" infrastructure by fully describing the state of the infrastructure in code, rather than as a result of changes made over time. It also makes it straightforward to set up other environments that are identical, from the same infrastructure definition, to allow for testing.

This is sometimes referred to as the "phoenix deployment" pattern, as you regularly burn down your environments and then launch them again from scratch. By doing this frequently, you ensure that your app remains deployable from scratch, instead of accidentally building on top of something that was specified previously but then removed and has remained available because it wasn't cleaned up. It is surprisingly easy to introduce bugs such that a program can no longer be installed cleanly, but only works because of something left over from a previous deploy (perhaps a log directory).

You may do this regularly in a test environment, but it is useful in a production context too. A pattern known as "blue-green" deployment means that you have two production environments, although only one at a time is actually serving production traffic. To use immutable infrastructure here, you tear down the environment that is not in use and then build it up from scratch. This can be combined with a "canary" rollout strategy, where you can then gradually point some traffic at this new environment to confirm it is working, and then switch over all traffic eventually. If the deployment fails, you can then switch traffic back to be served from the previous environment.

A 12-factor app, especially when it comes to the "stateless" factor, makes introducing immutable infrastructure straightforward. You can easily apply this pattern by having any state stored explicitly in attached services and not in your app. Even when your service is a database itself, it must still persist its data somewhere—ultimately, a disk. You can then treat this disk as an attached service and designate the rest of your infrastructure around your database as immutable.

Continuous Delivery & Continuous Deployment

Continuous delivery and continuous deployment are two distinct techniques that are often confused with one another. Continuous delivery is a set of engineering principles that aims to reduce the time an organization takes to make a change to software. Continuous deployment is a technique where every change is automatically deployed from development into live.

Continuous delivery is covered in the Planning chapter, but as a reminder, at the core of continuous delivery is the concept of a pipeline, through which a feature or change travels from inception to delivery. Each stage of the pipeline features automation of rote tasks to minimize the risk and cost of an item going through the pipeline. Towards the end of the pipeline, it's common to want to deploy your code to live, and this is where continuous deployment and continuous delivery overlap. Sometimes you may want to have a manual gate in your pipeline—for example, you may have human sanity checks or usability tests before a final release—but many teams choose to automate the whole process, and this is where continuous deployment comes in.

Continuous deployment can seem risky, and takes significant discipline to fully realize, but having the technical capability to do so, even if you do not fully use it, is powerful and can help implement continuous delivery even if there is a manual check. Continuous deployment comes from fully automating a deployment, and manifests itself in a team having a single command to deploy the latest version of your application to an environment. This single command can be triggered by a developer or, more often, by some sort of hosted tool, such as a traditional CI server like Jenkins, or by a newer generation of CD servers like GoCD, which have workflows built around the pipeline metaphor instead of individual jobs, as CI servers tend to be.

There are other techniques you can use with continuous delivery, especially when using continuous deployment, to help manage this process. When building a feature, you may make multiple commits to the codebase that contribute to a working feature, but you may not want to reveal that feature immediately. For teams that do not apply pure continuous integration, this often means working on a feature branch until that feature is completed, and then merging it in. Continuous integration is predicated on the idea that merging is risky, and therefore advocates continually committing ("integrating") to a single branch, at least daily, that all releases are then made from. Continuous delivery is predicated on the idea that releases are risky, so releasing often means you are forced to mitigate that risk in your process. For teams that practice continuous integration but not continuous delivery, often a release is only done after a feature is built and tested, so it is not prematurely released to an audience. This introduces a new risk: if there is a quick bug fix that needs to be made, or a higher priority change comes along, then a release with only that fix in it becomes hard to make, as the master branch will also contain the work-in-progress feature. You can work around this by branching and abandoning continuous integration temporarily, but that reintroduces the risks of merging that continuous integration aims to avoid.

Feature flags (or toggles) are a code-level mechanism to enable both continuous integration and continuous delivery. The simplest implementation of a feature flag is an `if` statement around some code that disables it based on an external config value. For example, if you're building a new part of a web site, you may have a config file in your developer environment that sets a config value, and then use that config value when defining the routes for your application and exposing links to those new pages—for example, in a navigation bar. Exactly how a feature is enabled/disabled depends on how it is implemented, and there are more complicated ways to manage feature flags than just configuration files, but this is the core idea behind it. The feature flag should turn your code into dead code when it is disabled to minimize the impact of any bugs you may have introduced and reduce the QA overhead of regression checking when a flag is off.

Feature flags are useful too, if you are upgrading or replacing an existing feature. The simplest way to implement a feature flag is using an if/else to choose between two code paths, an existing one, or the new one.

Using feature flags can result in more complicated code due to the period of overlap of an old version of a feature and a new version, and requires discipline to clean up after completing a new feature. However, feature flags can allow you to better control the rollout of a new feature if needed, perhaps enabling it only for a subset of users or on a subset of servers to verify that the feature works in the production environment before rolling it out fully. Rolling back a feature with a feature flag, if issues are identified, does not mean actually having to revert code or deploy an older version of your application, but instead changing a config value, which still gives you the freedom to make other changes to your application unrelated to that feature. It can also feed into usability tests at scale, where the same mechanism that allows you to flag a feature could be used to serve different variants to your users to collect data for A/B testing.

Summary

The DevOps movement is an important part of modern software development, as it empowers a full stack development team to manage their software in production, minimizing communication overheads and, potentially, delivering changes faster. In order to achieve this, software has to be built that minimizes the friction of supporting it in a production environment.

One method used to do this is applying Heroku's "12 factors," which are concerns about how an application runs that allow it to be managed through multiple environments and easy to support.

The first step on many DevOps journeys is to automate the creation and management of local environments. Virtual machines are commonly used to do this, as they allow you to spin up an environment that's close to the production environment, as well as give some degree of isolation between that and your running system. Once this is done, automating the process of moving code to a production or pre-production environment follows. Instead of deploying code from source on a server by hand, a single package should be built, and that package deployed onto the server. For all of these environments, tools can be used to deploy not only that package, but the configuration for it separately—this means you can quickly change the configuration of a running service without having to rebuild and redeploy the code.

As more and more teams move to cloud computing, they gain a self-service capability to manage the underlying infrastructure. This infrastructure can be defined using templates and managed alongside your code in version control, a technique known as infrastructure-as-code. More advanced techniques, including immutable infrastructure, can also be applied to your deployments, which can minimize their risk by replacing your infrastructure with the new version as it changes, rather than trying to upgrade it in place.

With this automation, more regular deployments can be made, each one with a smaller change. This deployment even involve work-in-progress code, which can be either inaccessible to the running app or enabled and disabled using config values known as feature flags.

Being able to make smaller, more regular deployments is a key factor in differentiating full stack teams in digital organizations from those in more traditional environments. This allows a much faster pace of change and minimizes the time it takes for changes to be made.

CHAPTER 14

In Production

In a digital organization, stakeholders put a lot of trust into their full stack team's ability to make the right decisions, and into the approach they take to developing software. However, as Spider-Man's Uncle Ben said, with great power, comes great responsibility. When a team has control over how it builds software, what gets built, and when it deploys, the team should also take responsibility for how that software runs in production. The term "DevOps," a contraction of "developers-in-operations," embodies this new skill set and mindset.

A full stack team will have an embedded QA (the result of a movement referred to as "developers-in-test"), but when this happens, it's not just about increasing the level of test automation in a product, but also about ensuring the whole team is responsible for the quality of the output. DevOps is sometimes contextualized as "DevOps team" or "DevOp," but this often refers to a traditional operations team that is using modern automation techniques, rather than one where developers and operations are embedded together in a shared team. At best, such teams are simply mimicking the process of DevOps by using new automation tools, confusing cause and effect. Teams that embed the DevOps culture may use automation, but that's the result of the culture that has emerged. The most important part of the DevOps culture is that the team as a whole is responsible for how the product behaves in production. One common way this manifests itself is in a "build-it-and-run-it" team, where that team is the first line of support for any issues that occur in production. Some teams, especially those with a large user base, may have an external support team that handles the front line, with checklists and run books to help diagnose common issues, but those documents are developed by the team, which has a close relationship with front-line support.

IT in a traditional organization, especially those where teams are built around technical functions, can develop a silo mentality. All too often, teams operate with a "works on my machine" mentality, rather than accepting joint responsibility for the good of the organization and its users. At its very core, DevOps aims to break down those

© Chris Northwood 2018
C. Northwood, *The Full Stack Developer*, https://doi.org/10.1007/978-1-4842-4152-3_14

barriers, with more reliable software and a short time to fix issues when they do occur, being the aim. When a team I was working on adopted DevOps, having to carry around the "batphone" (an on-call mobile phone that could be used as a first point of contact for issues) drove home how real these new responsibilities were. No one wants a 3 a.m. phone call because their product has fallen over.

Fire Drills

The people who best know how a product can break are the people who built it. Fire drills are an effective way to explore these scenarios and identify work needed to harden your software.

For a team new to DevOps, a fire drill might just be a theoretical exercise. It starts by asking questions such as "what would happen if our database became corrupted?" The team identifies any potential problems, and suggests solutions to these. For all of the identified scenarios, the team can check the following:

- How would we know this situation is happening? Do we have sufficient monitoring around the application to identify this as a situation, and how would it manifest itself?

- Do we know what the impact will be? Is there any temporary mitigation we could put in place?

- Do we know how to recover from this situation?

- How likely is this situation to occur?

By answering these questions, the team can identify work that might be needed; perhaps additional logging or alarms need to be implemented, or a checklist added to the application's run book. Mitigating against these scenarios can be captured as work and added to the backlog like any other work. User stories such as "As an on-call developer, I want the system to fail over to a database replica when the primary becomes unavailable, so that I can minimize downtime during an incident," or "As a member of the support team, I want to see hostnames in error logs when a connection fails, so that I can quickly identify whether a single back-end server has failed" are perfectly acceptable, and phrasing them in that way helps product owners prioritize the work. No one wants an outage! However, identifying likeliness can also help with this. If your application is deployed to a cloud provider across multiple regions, it is possible to have a multi-region failure (so you may want to also use a second provider to host an instance of your application to mitigate this risk), but the likelihood of such an occurrence might be so low that it is not worth the investment to make the improvement.

Once a team feels confident they have a product that is resilient, they can start turning these fire drills into more practical exercises. Identifying flaws in a recovery plan in a controlled environment is much better than discovering them in a real incident.

For example, in a test environment, a team may decide to corrupt a database, or take a key server offline, and check that the system handles the failure as expected, or any manual recovery steps (such as restoring a backup) work as intended. This only works, of course, when there is parity between these environments and the production environment. Particularly brave teams often choose to run these fire drills in their production environment, especially when there should be no impact on the user. Even the best-intentioned team will have differences between environments—such as the volume of data, or the load on a system—which can change the impact of an incident.

Every team member should take part in fire drills, and they should happen regularly. This can include non-technical team members, such as the product owner, to help build a whole team mindset about operating the service. Sometimes it's obvious that a change or new feature to a system can impact how a system responds to an incident, or introduce a new way a system could fail, and those can be identified and dealt with early—but sometimes it's less obvious. Identifying and rehearsing ways of handling the most common or likely failures will significantly improve your time to respond.

There is a growing set of tools that can automate the process of running a fire drill by deliberately injecting failures into a system on a continuous basis. This can result in a high level of resilience, forcing you to build in automated recovery for certain types of failure (and reducing your support workload). Netflix's Simian Army is the most famous example of this, and includes the Chaos Monkey, which randomly kills single servers, but there are other tools (such as introducing latency to network connections) too. If your team feels comfortable running these tools in production, then you should be proud that you have a high degree of confidence in the resilience of your product.

Run Books

Run books for an application become a kind of bible while an incident is occurring. In a high-pressure situation like an outage, the last thing you want to be doing is trying to remember where on disk a log file is stored, the URL for a status page, or the details of any important upstream systems the application depends on.

The other thing a run book should include is checklists. When an alarm goes off in flight, an airline pilot will have a series of checklists to run through to help diagnose what could be wrong with the plane and how to correct it. The last thing they want to do is crash because they forgot to check the flaps were in the right position, which is a simple task that is easy to overlook in an emergency.

Fortunately, when an incident occurs in your application, it's unlikely to be a life-or-death scenario, but there will almost certainly be real pressure to resolve it, which may induce panic in the severest cases. Having a checklist that was written by you and your team when you had a cooler mind will allow you to negate some of that panic, and get the incident dealt with quicker.

What should a good checklist do? It should give you a clear set of actions to take in response to an alert. An alert could be an error report from a user, or one generated by your monitoring system. Take, for example, the following two checklists:

ZENOSS HAS GENERATED A LOWDISKSPACE ALARM FOR THE MYSQL SERVER

Impact: None yet, may escalate into an outage for the e-commerce catalogue

1. Log in to MySQL server

2. Delete all records from the session table that were last updated over seven days ago

---

USER HAS REPORTED THEY HAVE NOT RECEIVED THE DAILY MARKETING REPORT E-MAIL

Impact: Internal users may not be able to track performance of time-sensitive A/B tests

1. Ask user to give their e-mail address, and to check their spam folder.

2. If the message is not in to the spam folder, log in to the report system at `https://reports.marketing.example.com/admin/` and select "Edit Report Recipients," and ensure that their e-mail address is in the list of recipients. If it is not there, re-add it.

3. Once the user is in the recipients list, select the user and the "Manual Resend" action on the screen to trigger the re-send. Ensure the user has received the report.

4. If the user believes they should previously have been a member, then select "Audit Log" on the admin screen and check for any actions that would have removed them, and follow up with the responsible user.

5. If the user was on the recipients list, then select "Report Generation Status" and ensure that the report run time field is showing a time at approximately 6 a.m. that morning. If the report has not run, escalate the incident, as it will affect all users, and follow the "Daily Marketing Report Not Generated" checklist.

6. If the report was generated, then log in to the SMTP gateway with SSH at smtp-gw.platform.example.com and run: grep <email address> /var/log/mail/outgoing.log. Check for any errors or deferments in the log. If there are deferments, then force the message to be processed by running "process-mail -mid <messageid>" with the message ID from the log file. If there are errors, escalate to the corporate e-mail team.

7. If the message does not appear in the outgoing log, then check the mail reporting application log by accessing the logging portal using the credentials in the team password store. Apply the "marketing report error" filter, then check for any appropriate error messages.

The second checklist may seem overly verbose, but if you're unfortunate enough to be a new developer on a team doing an after-hours on-call rotation when an incident occurs, you'll be grateful for the detail.

Being explicit can also help avoid mistakes. For example, on the first checklist, it might be easy to accidentally access the test database to make the change, and then wonder why the issue has not been resolved. If this is a system that has been stable for a number of years with little need for maintenance, then it's easy to forget exactly which MySQL server it runs on, or what the credentials are—is it my personal developer login that will give me access, or some global one? How exactly do I access the database—is there phpMyAdmin, or can I connect using a desktop tool, or do I need to SSH in and run the command line? The second line is also potentially dangerous; all it takes is for someone to write a SQL statement with a less-than swapped for a greater-than, and all recent sessions have been lost. Better to have a simple script that can be used, or better yet, a scheduled maintenance task to avoid the situation ever occurring. The first checklist is also incomplete: what happens if it's not due to a temporary table getting full that the server is out of disk space?

Write checklists assuming that its reader knows nothing about your product, or your organization. This is especially true when you're not first-line support for your application. It can also be helpful to link to previous incidents (which may be recorded in a ticketing system), as comments on those tickets can help diagnose complex issues.

The final elements a run book should include is a clear path of communication. For high-severity incidents, communicating the impact is key. For example, in an outage where the checklist has not resolved the incident, contacting the technical lead for that team can provide additional insight into how to proceed. In another case, if an outage has impacted a critical business function, such as the ability to sign up for the web site, then the marketing or customer support team might need to know, so they can handle any complaints coming via e-mail, or suspend a major marketing campaign that is expected to drive sign-ups until the incident is resolved.

Many an incident has been delayed simply because no one knows who is responsible for a service that is causing an outage, or they can't get in touch with the right people to help resolve it, so it's important to keep this list up to date. People join, move around in, and leave organizations constantly. You might want to consider simply including roles, and linking to a global address book, or some other solution that works best in your organization.

If your product only needs support during business hours, then having a team e-mail address or similar might be enough, but for after-hours support, you may need to get in touch with a particular person who is the designated support contact, or the person an automated monitoring system escalates to, for a particular period of time. To accomplish this, an on-call system can be used, where team members take turns providing out-of-hours support. For this system, a rota is drawn up and published, and the person who is on call ensures they are available outside of those published hours. Often, this rota with contact information is linked to or inserted in the run book, and when someone else needs to escalate to you, they can consult that book, or a monitoring system can programmatically query it to know who to page. Other approaches include having a physical phone that is passed like a baton with a set phone number, or simply updating the contact details in the runbook and monitoring system at every hand-over.

For complex issues, there may need to be an escalation plan in place to bring in other team members, or members of the wider organization, if a situation is particularly complex and critical and cannot be resolved solo. This should also be put in place, but the decision to escalate left to the person on call, rather than to third parties. Some automated on-call systems do allow automatic escalation if an incident is not acknowledged, too. This can mean that the team is always on call, but these escalations should be infrequent.

THE HUMAN FACTOR OF ON-CALL ROTAS

Many organizations introduce an on-call rota as part of moving to a DevOps culture, but this should be done with caution, as it can change the nature of the work and severely impact work-life balance for a team. At the very least, people who are on call should be able to influence any shift patterns they are given. Being on call for too long can lead to burn-out, and spending all night fire-fighting a live incident and still being expected to turn up for a nine-to-five working day is usually not feasible. Many jurisdictions have rules around working hours and minimum break requirements that must be taken into account when planning a rota. When introducing an on-call system, you might also need to consider how the compensation for a team member might change, as they are expected to take on additional work, and what flexibility may be needed to support their work-life balance.

Monitoring

Every product with users will be monitored by default, but if the best way to know if your system is down is because your customers are tweeting about it, you have a problem. Implementing effective monitoring will allow you to know about problems before your customers do, and get them resolved quicker. Even better is monitoring that can alert you to a problem before it turns into a full-blown outage (for example, increasing response times or low disk space).

Monitoring can give us two types of data: qualitative and quantitative. Qualitative data is easy for humans to read an interpret, but harder for computers. Quantitative refers to numbers: counts of requests, CPU load, etc. This is the data computers are great at processing. In terms of monitoring, we generally talk about logs (qualitative) and metrics (quantitative). Sometimes logs can be very structured, such as HTTP access logs, and these are often transformed into metrics, but often they're much less structured, such as tracebacks or other log messages. During an incident, both types of data are important. Metrics can tell you something is wrong and give you a start as to where to look, and logs can give you further context and a high level of detail.

Monitoring is incomplete without alarms or alerts. Capturing a lot of data can be useful for post-mortems or other analysis, but for the purpose of monitoring your system in production, you need the data to tell you something on the spot. These alarms are typically set against the metrics that your monitoring system captures, leaving the log files available to give you greater insight into your system.

Alerts are often triggered by rules that set thresholds against the metrics, and often contain a severity. For example, you might specify a rule such as "Raise an alarm for 'LowDiskSpace' with level warning when the free disk space is less than 5GB," in addition to different severities against different thresholds. Often, these alerts can be configured to clear automatically when the rule no longer applies, and many alert systems employ the concept of "flapping," which occurs when an alert is raised and then cleared several times in rapid succession. Systems often have different notification rules for these alarms—for example, a warning message might simply send an e-mail to be dealt with during office hours, but a higher severity might cause a text message or automated phone call to be sent. Figure 14-1 depicts an example of how an application can be monitored.

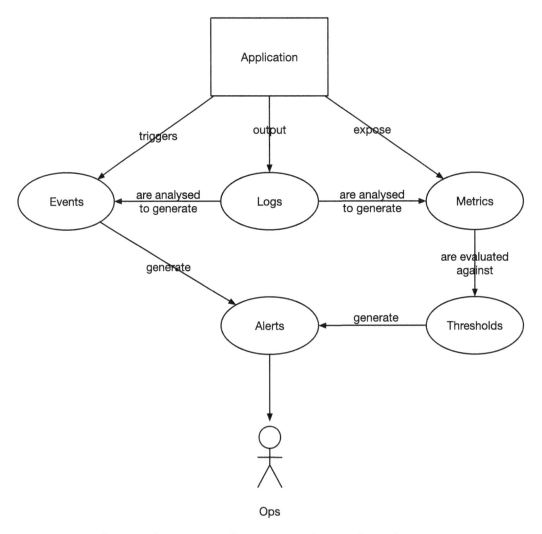

Figure 14-1. *Showing how an application can be monitored*

When setting alerts, it's important to consider any cases where absence of data can indicate a problem. Setting a threshold to say "more than five errors per minute" makes sense, but a threshold such as "serving less than 10 good requests per second" can be helpful in diagnosing network or load balancer issues that are stopping requests from hitting your server.

Sometimes alerts can be triggered directly as the result of an event. For example, if a circuit breaker is triggered (see the Designing Systems chapter for more on circuit breakers), you may want to flag an alert directly, rather than going through a metric.

Metrics come in various shapes and sizes too. Something like CPU usage or disk space is an absolute value that can be sampled, and thresholds set against directly. Others are simply counters. Counters are incremented when certain events occur (such as number of requests or errors served). These counters require processing to be made useful for thresholds to be set against them, usually into a per-second or per-minute rate, or even measuring the rate of change. Sets of data can be even more advanced in the form of response times that can be processed, such as averaging, to give a more meaningful metric.

There are lots of tools available to help you monitor your systems, from hosted and managed systems like Datadog or New Relic to self-hosted systems like Nagios, Sensu, or Grafana. Some try to do everything, but others separate monitoring and alerting. Some try to give you many metrics out of the box, but there will always be domain-specific metrics you will want to expose directly, so when building your code, it's important to consider how you might want to hook into monitoring and metrics around key functions. This might include communications with dependencies (number of responses made to a back-end system, errors received, response times, cache hits and misses), or other business rules, such as average size of a response.

It can be tempting to set the metrics of your monitoring system, business KPIs and analytics to track the same thing, but actually these concerns are all different. The first relates to monitoring the health of your system from a technical perspective, and the others are about tracking how well your application is meeting its business goals and user behavior. The same solution might not satisfy all three different needs.

A final note about logging. Separating out your logs based on concerns will make life a lot easier for you when an incident occurs. Trying to find an error in the middle of a busy access log is hard, so you should try to keep a log of activities that happen on your system (such as an access log) separate from any audit logging or error logging. In an incident, the error log will be your first port of call, so ensuring only relevant information remains in that will make your life a lot easier. The error message that you log should contain enough information to help you debug an issue. If a request has failed, then make sure you log enough information about the request (such as the URL it was trying to hit), as well as the reason for the error so you can attempt to reproduce the error condition, and to understand how that error condition can propagate through your code. If the same error could occur at multiple points in your codebase, make sure you include a way of tracking it back to the exact line of code where the log message actually got written, to help you verify that the branch of code you expect to be executing is doing so. Logging tracebacks from exceptions (taking care not to expose these to end users) can be invaluable. The last thing you want to do is have to make a deploy of your code during an incident in order to add enough logging to diagnose a problem. However, be careful with what you log. Adding in log messages around login or password validation can lead to accidentally logging people's passwords and creating a security breach. This is especially true when enabling raw logs—for example, for database connections or web connections, where the body of the request is kept.

There are many logging frameworks available for most languages. At the very least, you want one that will allow you to add timestamps to messages, as well as make it clear in a plain log file where a multi-line log message ends and the next one starts. There are also good tools for reading logs, including some that can aggregate the same (or similar) messages together and provide a count, which can help you sift through busy ones. However, having a plain text log file on disk in the middle of a crisis can provide quick access to logs that these more complex tools can cause issues with.

If your application is deployed on multiple servers, or you're using the immutable infrastructure pattern, you will also want to consider a particular way of aggregating logs: sending them off your box to a central service that allows you to see the state of your whole application (including figuring out if an issue is limited to one server). In the case of immutable infrastructure, aggregating is necessary to maintain your application's logs so you can diagnose them at a later date. Otherwise, they are lost when an instance is deployed or reloaded.

Responding to Incidents

An incident always happens as the result of a change—a change in code, configuration, or underlying database, or a request by a malicious user. This change can be very subtle. It could be a particular combination of long-standing requests that exposes a bug that was never tested, or even just the onward flow of time. The change may not be made by the development team, but there is always a root cause for an incident, although it may not be possible to diagnose the very root cause (for example, a failing hard disc). When it comes to an incident, your job is not only to resolve it and recover any loss in service, but also to understand what change caused the incident to keep it from happening again (a root-cause analysis).

Incidents ideally start with a team being notified when a system has failed. If you are being notified by a third-party, such as a dependency, or by your users, this highlights a gap in your monitoring to be resolved in future. The first point of call should be the run book to find if there are steps to resolve it, or if there are any known issues or previous occurrences that way indicate which actions should can be applied.

When following steps, you should make a note of what you have done, perhaps in a logged chat system or on a ticketing system. This will allow you to look back at what you've tried, and if you need to escalate, to quickly hand over that information. It also allows some stakeholders to monitor progress, and at the end of the incident, for you to look back at what you did and use that to drive any future improvements.

Of course, the actual actions that are taken are context dependent, but using pre-prepared tools—such as your run book and any debugging tools you may have identified as needed in your fire drills—should hopefully allow you to address the incident in the short term, and then identify a root cause and any deficiencies in your system to be addressed.

Summary

In many organizations, full stack teams are empowered to build and run their own systems. Running a system requires a different skill set than building it, and this was often reflected in organizations' structures, with separate operations teams and development teams. When development teams run their own systems, then they must apply those operations skills themselves, leading to a way of working known as DevOps (developers-in-operations).

When building a system, you should consider how you will detect and diagnose any operational issues. The most common ways to do this are to emit useful logs and metrics that can be collected and searched, and to use monitoring tools that run checks against the system to catch common failures. When a check fails, then an alert is sent to the team, or a nominated on-call developer, which causes them to start investigating the fault. Alerts can also be triggered when metrics breach particular thresholds—for example, if an error count spikes.

To ensure that an incident can be resolved quickly, rehearsals known as fire drills can be run that simulate failure in a controlled way to instill confidence in resolving issues. These procedures to resolve common issues, or pointers about how to debug or what a particular alert means, should be recorded in a run book for that particular application.

With these in place, a team can confidently run their services and take incidents in stride.

CHAPTER 15

Constant Learning

One area where the modern full stack developer working in a digital organization will differ from a traditional enterprise is that the products they are working on will constantly evolve in response to the real world at a rapid pace, rather than simply in response to requirements being pushed upon them by the organization. It is no longer enough to build something to meet some acceptance criteria and then push it out into the world; you and your team will have to check that any change you've made is actually having the impact you want it to have.

Getting into a position to do this can be hard unless your team is truly working as a core part of your organization. Any new feature you build or change you make also requires you to understand *why* that change is being made—is it to increase sign-ups or sales, or to satisfy some other business need? Once you understand this underlying motivation, then shipping a feature is no longer enough, if that feature cannot satisfy this underlying cause.

Collecting Analytics

Many organizations are now relying on data to make informed decisions about strategies, but before the data can be interrogated, it must be collected and held centrally. The buzz term "big data" is sometimes used to talk about this, but this usually means collecting large amounts of unstructured data and analyzing it for insights. For many organizations, getting a handle on individual bits of data can be very powerful. These could be simple numbers, like value of sales, and can be recorded by standard business processes and then aggregated and displayed to stakeholders.

Another type of analytics is derived from data on how a user interacts with your web site: the path they took to a particular webpage, how long they spent on it when they got there, whether there were any errors made while completing a form, etc. The Web is very powerful in allowing you to collect this data, but there have been many

© Chris Northwood 2018
C. Northwood, *The Full Stack Developer*, https://doi.org/10.1007/978-1-4842-4152-3_15

abuses of it (for example, Uber's "God View,") that have led many to be wary of analytics and tracking scripts. In many countries, privacy law no longer allows you the ability to collect this data unless the user opts in, and when using analytics, it can be tempting to simply collect everything and then decide how to use it later. This approach may seem technically simpler and give you much more flexibility, but will often fall foul of these laws, as the data then becomes "personally identifying" and may contain very sensitive information. This means you must protect and manage this data in a much more careful way. To avoid this, you must consider what data you want to collect in advance.

Ultimately, the way you want to collect most data is by aggregating it together into counters, such as "how many people clicked this button?" Having a single counter may be useful, but often you will want to ask questions like "how many people clicked this button yesterday?", "how many people clicked this button on a mobile phone?", or "how many people clicked this button and then ended up buying something?". Implementing a simple counter isn't enough, so you often have to think about "segmentation." In this case, a high-level metric is a bucket that contains a number of other metrics that allows you to slice it into other meaningful pieces. For example, instead of incrementing a counter, you add a record to a bucket that contains a number of key/value pairs. Let's say you have a bucket called "`product_button_clicked.`" Then, whenever someone clicks that button, you might add an entry like:

```
product=12345;
browser=Safari;
device=Windows_PC;
time=2017-12-19T09:00:17Z
location=ManchesterUK
```

You must be careful not to collect information that can ultimately lead back to the user, as this becomes personally identifiable, but these labels allow you to segment the total count of items in the bucket in different ways to ask interesting questions. Most analytics toolkits will collect some of these things for you (especially time, location, and browser info), and others require you to add the segments yourself. However, this doesn't help answer the final question, which is often something like, "how many people clicked that button and then went on to buy something?".

To achieve this, most analytics software will also add a "session ID" to the bucket, which then allows you to see which actions happened in the same session. This can be dangerous, as correlating actions across a single session can allow you to identify an individual user, hence losing the anonymization achieved by placing actions into buckets. Many people accept this as a risk and store all activities, but others only store the session data for a period of time until after the last bit of activity in that session, and then look at the session data to generate answers to those questions before discarding it. A final approach is to set a flag such as `"clicked_button=true"` in a session and then store that as an additional segment later on in appropriate actions, which avoids capturing any session data at all.

The final thing to consider is exactly what interaction data to collect. Simple things like "opened a page" and "clicked a button" (or had some other sort of interaction) are useful and happen in response to direct user actions. Others may happen more implicitly (such as recording time spent on a page, whether the user reached the end of an article, or if the page was left open with no interactions for a long period of time). To determine what's useful, it's important to talk to your stakeholders and any user experience practitioners on your team to find out what they need.

The same mechanisms used for collecting analytics can be used beyond this use case—for example, to develop personalization and recommendation systems—but those use cases are not covered here, and have their own set of ethical and legal implications. You should always make it clear to your users what information you're collecting and why—otherwise, they may assume the worst.

Experiments

In addition to reflecting on the performance of your site using analytics, it's also possible to experiment directly with your users by giving them different versions of the same page and seeing how they respond. Experimenting on people is can be morally fraught, but it happens constantly, so how does one do so ethically? The core question is to ask whether or not either variant could result in harm to a user. For example, testing the size and placement of a button probably will not, but applying a "dark pattern" to entice a user into spending more, or A/B testing pricing structures where some users may end up paying more than others based on which segment they are placed into, can cause harm and should be avoided. Other scenarios are less clear cut, and informed consent can be useful, perhaps by allowing a user to opt in to a "beta trial" and making it clear that they will be participating in experiments, but then leaving most users out of it.

Experiments can be useful when you're trialing new site features and you are unsure how to achieve a specific goal. An A/B test is a fairly simple experiment: you start by giving 90% of your users the existing version of a page (the "control"), and then 5% a variant "A", which might have a new feature, and 5% variant "B", which could have a different design or workflow for that feature. You run the experiment for a period of time and add appropriate analytics (remembering to segment whether or not the user is in the control, A, or B group) and then compare the results to see which of variant A or B is better (or if the new feature is actually worthless or helps less than it not being there at all, by comparing it to the control).

With A/B testing, you can only test one change at a time, which can be slow. Multivariate testing has grown out of it which allows you to run several A/B tests in parallel, but the analysis of the results is more complex in order to separate any effects one test may have on another.

Analyzing Results

It is not enough to simply frame your updates in terms of the underlying change you hope to make, but you must also have a way of measuring that change in a meaningful way. Although often misused, key performance indicators (KPIs) can be a useful way to measure these. KPIs fall down when they measure things that are easy to measure but are not actually what the underlying goal is. For example, a KPI might be number of visitors to a page, as this is easy to measure, but if many of those visitors simply leave a page without completing a meaningful action, then by making page views a KPI, this can make a team focus on getting people to a page, but forget about what they do once they are actually there, which is the thing that actually matters.

As always, the right KPIs are context dependent, and can require some deep thinking to make sure you get it right. In some cases, KPIs can be hard to directly measure quantitatively, but some qualitative measures can be applied instead.

Quantitative measures are often desirable though, as they are easy to collect and seem easy to understand. A headline number can be easy to understand, but a simple number can have many depths that can lead to naive, but wrong, interpretations. The process of deriving a figure can be complex, and it's important to understand those trade-offs.

BAYES THEOREM

Bayes theorem is a fundamental theory in probability, and you may have come across it before. Expressed as an equation, it reads as $P(A|B) = \dfrac{P(B|A)\,P(A)}{P(B)}$. It expresses the probability of event A occurring if some other event B is true (the "conditional probability"), based on the probability of the inverse and the probabilities of each of those events occurring independently of each other. It highlights how some headline figures can give misleading results.

If a test for cancer is 99% accurate, and that this cancer occurs in 0.1% of the population, then through Bayes theorem, if this test detects you have cancer, it means you only have a 9% chance of actually having the cancer. This can seem counter intuitive due to the 99% accuracy, but because the cancer is relatively rare, this rareness cancels out the accuracy to give you the "conditional probability" of 9%.

This book isn't the place to go into statistics theory, and if you're lucky, you'll have access to people who have a good understanding of analytics and data (sometimes called data scientists), or good tools, to help you understand them. An important concept to understand is called the confidence interval, which expresses the percentage confidence that a value is within a specified range. The important thing to remember is not to trust a headline figure. For example, in an A/B test, if result A is 52% conversion and result B is 48% conversion, then actually the two results could be the same, or result B could actually be better performing, depending on the margin of error, which causes the confidence intervals to overlap. The more data you have, the smaller your margin of error becomes, but if, say, the margin of error was ±3%, then the result for A is (with 99% certainty) between 45-51%, and for B, it's between 49-55%. So there's a chance A could be 51% and B could be 49%.

When looking at analytics, although this numeric data can help give you an idea of high-level trends, if will not often tell you why those trends are occurring. For that, you need to use qualitative data. This qualitative data comes through understanding your customers, rather than just watching aggregated metrics. User testing of designs is one way of achieving that (you can user test a built design), as well as having panels and focus groups that allow you to ask questions directly. Another alternative is to capture analytics for every possible metric and store them in a way where you can look at all of the analytics of an individual session and dive into each session individually, but done in bulk this violates the privacy of an individual user, and is a level of observation that a user should explicitly consent to (this is why user testing is a good place to do it).

Hypothesis-Driven Development

Hypothesis-driven development has been proposed as an alternative way of expressing work to be done in user stories, by phrasing it in a way familiar to a high-school science student. Unlike user stories, which express a change from the perspective of a user, hypotheses go one level deeper and express a change in terms of a question. Barry O'Reilly proposed the following form:

- We believe *<this change>*

- Will result in *<some outcome>*

- And we will have confidence to proceed when *<a measurable impact>*

For example, for a marketing landing page:

- We believe that adding a mailing list sign-up to a product landing page

- Will result in an increased number of mailing list signups

- And we will have confidence to proceed when the number of mailing list signups in a week is 15% higher than the typical signup amount after seven days

This means that your feature does not finish once it ships, but instead you must revisit it seven days afterwards to ensure that it has had the desired impact, and then either roll back the change, revisit the design, or hypothesize a new change to test to have the same advantage.

One challenge with hypothesis-driven design is identifying the meaningful change that you want to impose, rather than simply naming something that might be easy to measure. For example, placing some content behind a sign-in might increase your sign-in metric, but is that actually the ultimate measure you care about, or is it something more core to the fundamentals of your organization?

Summary

The work of a full stack development team is not done once a feature is delivered. Rather, you should be monitoring the feature to make sure it does what you expected, as well as constantly learning from how your site interacts with users to identify improvements that can be applied to continuously improve your product.

Collecting analytics, and taking care to be conscientious about how you do so, can provide invaluable insight into how your product is really used by your end users, and how that use may change over time. When you are less sure about a change, you can also run experiments on the running site to see how different variants behave in practice. Care must be taken when analyzing this data to not fall into statistical traps that falsely draw conclusions.

Hypothesis-driven development is a way of formalizing this approach to review, by stating changes in terms of hypotheses to be tested, highlighting that the work isn't done until this hypothesis is tested.

CHAPTER 16

Epilogue

When I first started out in software development, I didn't know what I didn't know. I thought all I had to do was to grow my knowledge and experience in the programming languages I was using to be the best coder I can be. Throughout my career, I have learned that what we do as software developers isn't write code, but rather develop software to solve people's problems. I think this is what differentiates what I have termed the modern, full stack team from a traditional programming team, and our role within that as developers.

A week in the life of a full stack development team might not see you use every skill and technique mentioned in this book, but it's likely that you'll have some level of contact with it all. Your week may start with a planning meeting, which is the foundation of the development work you do. Starting with a proper understanding of the task at hand, and the process for discovering that, will make you a stronger developer in terms of devising solutions. Similarly, taking a moment to think through high-level solutions at a design stage rather than ploughing straight into code can minimize wasted work that started in the wrong direction. Being able to communicate these with your team and wider organization helps the development team become an important and equal part of the rest of the business—another hallmark of a digital organization, not just a team that performs rote tasks.

As you build a system, you will find different skills and approaches are needed for different parts of it. These can be thought of as layers, from the data storage needs of your application; to the APIs that allow you to access and manipulate that data and communicate between systems; to the front end, where your system interacts with your users. Each level of this stack uses different technologies, but familiarity with each is what gives you flexibility and effectiveness as a full stack developer. You need not be an expert in all of them, and knowing your limitations and how to research to find more answers is another core skill you will need. If there is one technology that it is worth focusing on, it's JavaScript, and the whistlestop tour of the language given in chapter 8 should give you the basics to know what's out there, and the concepts of applying JavaScript at different levels of the stack that will allow you to research further.

339

© Chris Northwood 2018
C. Northwood, *The Full Stack Developer*, https://doi.org/10.1007/978-1-4842-4152-3_16

Chapter 12 covered another important part of a modern software system, and that is security. Despite security being a very deep and nuanced topic, there are a number of high-level rules and basics that you can apply to prevent the most dangerous and most common mistakes. Security is best applied in depth, and building it into your system as you go along, rather than adding it later, is the best way to achieve this.

It's important to always remember the humans in your system, as those are the people who will ultimately use it, and whose lives it will influence. This means not only the user experience design, but the front-end implementation of your system, and making that implementation work for the range of humans that exist using accessibility techniques.

At the end of the build process is the other key differentiator between a full stack team in a digital organization and a traditional one: DevOps. DevOps is a culture of developers taking responsibility for their products and services as they run and users interact with them, and again broadens the skill set needed to be a full stack developer. Again, knowing the fundamentals is often enough of a starting point to be able to be effective. However, running your service is more than just a technical endeavor, and you should be able to measure how well your application performs at solving the original problem it set out to solve, and that continual learning process should feed back into your development process.

A running theme throughout this book has been one of the most important traits of successful people: empathy. Empathy for your users, empathy for your colleagues, and also empathy for the past. I have given details of the history of why the Web has grown into what it is today, and as imperfect as it is, it is the Web we will have to live with. We must also have empathy for society, and this is best expressed through behaving in an ethical manner. Ethics is not easy, but is one of the most important challenges facing the software development discipline as it grows and plays an increasing role in society. We should strive to make the world a better place, and leave a positive mark on it. It's never wrong to stop and ask yourself if you're doing the right thing.

Remember that, as a full stack developer, you are uniquely poised to solve whole problems, not just parts of them, and you can only do that if you have the big picture. This book covers a broad set of skills, and you must continue to grow by applying them in practice, and then continue to develop your individual skills as you gain professional experience. So go on. Be brave, ask questions, set a good example, and become a great full stack developer. I hope I've given you a strong foundation to start from.

Index

A

A/B testing, 55–56, 334
Accessibility, 209
    avoiding common mistakes
        alt attributes, use of, 223
        buttons *vs.* anchors, 223
        color contrast, 224
        multiple h1s, 222
        hover and focus
          styling, 221
        icon fonts, 223
        order of headings, 222
        skip link, 222
    development, 210
    testing for, 219–221
    type, 210
    web site, 210
        See also Assistive technologies (AT)
Affordance, 50
Agile movement, 12
AJAX technique, 227–228
Analytics
    big data, 331
    collecting, 331–333
    experiments, 333–334
    result analysis, 334–335
APIs, 339
    discovering, 244–245
    event-based, 243–244
    responsibilities, 229, 231

    securing, 240, 242
    using, 245–247, 249
        See also REST API
App store distribution mechanism, 5
ARIA technology, 211, 213
Assistive technologies (AT), 209
    ARIA, 211, 213
    semantic HTML, 212
Astral plane, 177
Asynchronicity, 160–161, 163
Asynchronous module definitions
    (AMDs), 164, 172
Atomic Design, 62
Autoprefixer, 119

B

Backends for frontends concept, 229
Bayes theorem, 335
Behavior-driven development (BDD)
    functional requirements documents, 148
    natural language, 149
    three amigos technique, 149–151
    waterfall projects, 149
Big data, 331
Billion laughs, 239
Blacklisting, 273
Blue-green deployment, 314
Bower, 205
Bugs, 40–41
Business as usual (BAU) development, 21

X, Y, Z

Printed in the United States
By Bookmasters